THE MORALITY OF EVERYDAY LIFE

THE MORALITY OF EVERYDAY LIFE

Rediscovering an Ancient
Alternative to the Liberal Tradition

Thomas Fleming

University of Missouri Press
Columbia and London

Library of Congress Cataloging-in-Publication Data

Fleming, Thomas, 1945–
    The morality of everyday life : rediscovering an ancient alternative
to the liberal tradition / Thomas Fleming.
        p.   cm.
Includes bibliographical references and index.
    ISBN 0-8262-1509-2 (alk. paper)
    1. Ethics.   I. Title.
BJ1031.F576   2004
170—dc22   2003023962

♾™   This paper meets the requirements of the
American National Standard for Permanence of Paper
for Printed Library Materials, Z39.48, 1984.

Designer: Jennifer Cropp
Typesetter: Phoenix Type, Inc.
Printer and binder: Thomson-Shore, Inc.
Typefaces: Minion and Bodoni

TO GAIL

CONTENTS

THE MORALITY OF EVERYDAY LIFE

INTRODUCTION

Prisoners of Dilemmas

The practice of the world goes farther in teaching us the degrees of our duty, than the subtlest philosophy, which was ever yet invented.

—David Hume, *A Treatise of Human Nature*

Il n'y a rien de meilleur que le pain cuit des devoirs quotidiens. (There is nothing better than the baked bread of everyday duty.)

—Charles Péguy

"To be, or not to be: that is the question," or at least one of the questions. Shakespeare's muddleheaded Danish prince was trying to make up his mind what to do about a serious domestic problem. Hamlet had several options: He could kill his uncle Claudius, who had murdered the young man's father and married his mother, or he might, out of respect for his mother, simply carry on as if nothing had happened, or, if he could not endure the sight of his uncle, he could go into exile; he could even, as his famous soliloquy suggests, kill himself. Who would endure the injuries and insults of everyday life, he asked, "when he himself might his quietus make with a bare bodkin?"

I have never faced such a dilemma; few of us have. But supposing we were Hamlet's loyal friend, how would we advise him? The advice would probably depend on the moral and religious traditions in which we

1

were brought up. His friend Horatio, who studied with Hamlet in Wittenberg, has become (let us imagine) a quietistic Anabaptist—a sort of Quaker or Amish man. He would tell him that violence is never the answer and suggest either exile or some form of civil disobedience against the illegitimate government.

Rosencrantz and Guildenstern, who are also students of political philosophy, have been studying (let us further suppose) the English tradition, then in its infancy. Rosencrantz, a sort of socialist or collectivist liberal (with a utilitarian bent), asks Hamlet to take into consideration the welfare of all Denmark, which might be plunged into a ruinous civil war that would end up oppressing the poorest classes. He tells Hamlet to make his choice on the basis of "the greatest good for the greatest number," and that it would be selfish of him to consider either the honor of his family or his feelings for his father. Going further, he even suggests that Hamlet, as an educated member of the elite class, should apply as his sole moral criterion the principle that the best policy is that which has the best effect on those who are least well-off.

Guildenstern, on the other hand, has studied with the predecessors of John Locke and Ayn Rand, and, as a budding anarcho-individualist liberal, asks the prince to consider what is in it for himself, deriding all superstitious attachments to father and mother: "Kill Claudius and seize the throne, by all means (if that is what you want), but not out of any misguided desire for revenge for a dead father or resentment against an unchaste mother."

Hamlet is too old-fashioned to pay attention to any of his progressive friends. Although, as a medieval Catholic, he is not supposed to seek revenge, that is exactly what is on his mind. It is interesting to note that Dante, who puts traitors like Claudius in the lowest part of hell, says little or nothing about revenge killings. (Dante, in fact, uses *vendetta* to mean justice.) Vengeance played a central role in Germanic systems of justice, and although the Normans attempted to eradicate dueling and vengeance from England, the spirit never entirely died out, and vengeance was the most popular theme of Elizabethan tragedy. What is Hamlet's alternative? To ask his uncle the king to do the right thing? In the absence of a legitimate authority, his vengeance upon Claudius would be only rough justice, especially since it has been commanded by the ghost of his father, the last real king of Denmark. In fact, one of Hamlet's primary concerns is theological: His father, who died without benefit of confession or the rites of the Church, is a soul in pain, and Hamlet believes that if he kills Claudius at his prayers, he may send him straight to Heaven—not much of a revenge.[1] For a similar reason, he is afraid to do away with himself: Although he may want to "die, to sleep," he is worried about the nature of that unending sleep:

> To sleep: perchance to dream: ay, there's the rub;
> For in that sleep of death what dreams may come
> When we have shuffled off this mortal coil,
> Must give us pause.

Each of Hamlet's friends would have reasons for regarding him as foolish and immoral, but Hamlet might easily reply to them: "You believe in your traditions, on no better evidence than I have for believing in mine, 1,500 years of the Church's moral teachings, which have been anticipated both by Hebrew prophets and pagan philosophers. At least my moral sense comes (so I believe) as a divine revelation from God and his Church, while you do not even pretend to believe that. Our way of life in Denmark and Europe rests upon my moral tradition, but if any of yours were adopted, it would be the end of Denmark and all of Christendom in less than five hundred years."

Modern men and women, living five hundred years later, may not have to face (at least, not often) Hamlet's dilemma, but we have problems enough. Suppose you are a school nurse who hears that the father of a student is smoking marijuana on the weekends. You believe it is your duty to call the police, but you feel uneasy, knowing that, despite his drug use, he is an otherwise responsible parent.

Or perhaps you are a law-abiding citizen who wonders about the limits of his civic duty. You go to bed early, because you have to leave for work by 6 a.m. Several times a month, however, you are awakened by your neighbors, who come home late and get into a screaming match. On at least two occasions, the husband has slapped his wife. Should you (a) rush in to defend the wife, (b) call the police, or (c) leave well enough alone for now but tell your neighbors, some time in the future, that they are disturbing your rest? You are inclined to choose (c), because

---

1. Shakespeare may well have come from a Catholic recusant family, which would partly explain his curious acceptance of Purgatory. See Eric Sams, *The Real Shakespeare: Retrieving the Early Years.*

the wife is far from noncombative and has never complained or shown any signs of abuse. Nonetheless, you have heard that it is everyone's duty to protect battered wives.

You have received a large legacy from a maiden aunt, and although you are tempted to quit your job and move to Provence to grow grapes, your social conscience tells you to devote 10 percent of your windfall to the welfare of others. But you are torn between helping a poor but deserving nephew go to college and writing a check to the Red Cross to help the Albanian refugees from Kosovo.

Broadening our scope still further, imagine that another ethnic civil war has broken out in Eastern Europe, this time between Ruthenians and Carpathians, whose conflict stems from a religious quarrel between the Catholic and Orthodox churches. Incidents of violence and repression, committed by both sides, go back several centuries, though, in the past two years, the Ruthenian government has been cracking down on the Carpathian minority, which has mounted a terrorist campaign in an effort to gain independence. As a NATO official collecting evidence, you are in a position to make a decision, even though you do not know either of the languages or enough of the history of either people to form an intelligent opinion, and even though you will never have to suffer the consequences of a mistake. Do you advise NATO to (a) threaten a bombing campaign against the Ruthenian capital if they do not desist from oppressing Carpathians (knowing that this is tantamount to giving the Carpathians an independence that they may or may not deserve) or to (b) sit tight and let the squabbling locals settle their own problems?

Supposing that this is one of the rare instances where NATO governments do not have a stake in the outcome, most members of the "international community" would fall back on the language of international human rights: All people everywhere have a right to use their own language, form their own communities, and practice their own religion, and the Ruthenian government may not be permitted to deprive its citizens of these and other fundamental rights, even if it correctly perceives that its traditions and customs, which had been systematically violated in earlier centuries when the Carpathians controlled the country, would be jeopardized in any area where the Carpathians returned to power. History is bunk, says the international community, and all that matters are individuals and their rights. Religion, in particular, can only be exercised as a personal choice, not as an ethnic tradition that might infringe the rights of other religions.

Despite the usual rhetoric about the "world's great religions," however, different traditions of faith often entail important moral and political distinctions. Some traditions require human sacrifice, while Christianity has always maintained a respect for innocent life. When an abortion clinic opens in a predominantly Italian Catholic section of Gotham, members of the "right-to-life" movement debate what they can do to stop the killing. One young mother is in a quandary, not knowing if she should take time away from her children, whom she is homeschooling, to attend the demonstrations. Her priest has said in his sermon that no one was doing enough in the cause of life, but she wonders if teaching her children does not make a stronger statement than attending a protest.

She also wonders how far she can go during the demonstrations. Should she keep the statutory distance between herself and the clinic, or should she risk arrest by following the pregnant women up to the door? Should she go further and join Operation Rescue's raids, in which property is invaded and equipment destroyed? Is it wrong, even, to blow up an abortion clinic? After all, she reasons, the employees are accessories to murder.

In discussion with her friends and allies, the talk is all of the human rights of the unborn, but the young mother has learned from her Calabrian grandmother that it is often better to mind your own business and do whatever good you can in the sphere of life in which you find yourself. Should she sacrifice a concrete good—namely, her children's welfare—for the sake of the hypothetical good of a stranger's child? If the answer is yes, then where should she draw the line? Why confine her protests to Gotham, when the children of London and Paris and Jakarta are also dying?

In conversation with her priest, she raises the more general question of whether or not she has a duty to go out of her way to help strangers. Of course, she says, she has religious reasons for wanting to protest abortions, just as she does for believing that it is in the public interest to inform on a drug user. "I certainly have the right to call the police," she says, "but I also have the right to get drunk in the privacy of my own home." Exercising that right may not necessarily be a good idea, and even if it were—even if her personal code were *nunc est bibendum*

("I think I'll just sit here and drink")—she does not have to act on this or any other bright idea.

Her priest tells her that she is being morally irresponsible and that she is trying to justify her cowardice by appealing to feelings. Her grandmother was dispensing only the peasant wisdom of proverbs and folktales, while the right to life is part of natural law, which is derived (like the Pythagorean theorem) from right reason and applied universally to all cases, regardless of special circumstances or location. But the priest has never taken the trouble to read St. Thomas Aquinas, much less to study the real tradition of natural law, which teaches that there are specific duties attached to each sphere of life (such as motherhood or citizenship) and that a mother's first duty is to her children.

There are rarely obvious or simple answers to moral dilemmas, and the little scenarios that I have sketched out illustrate the difficulties we face in making up our minds about where our responsibilities lie. In each of them (including *Hamlet*), people are forced to decide when it is right to take responsibility for the lives of strangers. The most common answer, which pro-life activists use to defend their protests and rescue missions, is that we all have a duty, when confronted by an emergency, to save a life or prevent injury. This duty, they argue, supersedes any routine obligation, such as the obligation to obey local and national laws that protect property or international laws that guarantee the sovereign independence of nations.

The example usually given is that of a neighbor drowning in a bathtub. Surely, one has the right—the obligation—to break into the neighbor's house to save his life. Perhaps, but real-life dilemmas are rarely that simple. In the first place, a neighbor is not a complete stranger, and one can safely assume that he wants to be rescued, that he would gladly give permission to enter. In the scenarios I have sketched out above, we can probably take it for granted that neither the pot-smoker nor the wife-slapper wants to be arrested. In many cases, even the abused wife may not want her husband to face the shame and possible monetary loss that would result from prosecution. She could, after all, divorce him or bring charges herself.

Even if we believe that the abortionist and his patient are cold-blooded murderers who deserve execution, it may not be our responsibility to stop them, especially since our actions may have very unpleasant consequences for the husbands and children who depend upon a wife and mother's support and affection. And how is it possible for private citizens to discharge their responsibility to save the lives of people whom they might never meet in the ordinary course of life? Not relatives, friends, and neighbors—people over whom they might have some influence—but total strangers, who may live on the other side of the globe?

Liberal Consensus

There is a strange convergence in the style of reasoning employed by international philanthropists, liberal "do-gooders," and right-to-life activists. Our obligation to do right, they tell us, does not come out of the peculiar circumstances of being a mother or a Christian or a Jew, but from a philosophical or theological commitment to a global responsibility as determined by a rational individual who considers the matter objectively and keeps his attention not on things as they are and have been, but on how they ought to be in an ideal world. Universality, rationality, individualism, objectivity, and abstract idealism: these, in fact, are the hallmarks of the modern (that is, since the seventeenth century) ethical tradition, which, for the sake of convenience, I am calling liberalism. Although *liberalism* in recent decades usually signifies the milder forms of state socialism, and *conservatism* is used to refer to the ideology of individualism and free markets, these ideologies, far from being opposed, derive from the same tradition. The ideology of individualism and free markets went by the name of liberalism in the nineteenth century. Despite obvious differences, the philosophical underpinnings of the two positions are virtually the same. Ludwig von Mises, for example, an outstanding representative of free-market classical liberalism, is as insistent upon rationalism as John Rawls and hardly ever departs from a style of analysis in which only individuals and states are actors. The liberal perspective is farsighted in both senses of the term. Liberals, in freeing themselves from the shackles of particular circumstances and traditions, attempt to take the long view of human life and its possibilities; however, in keeping their eyes fixed upon the perfect sun setting beneath an ever-receding horizon, they are apt to ignore the little things that may be just under their noses. Such moral and political idealism can produce brilliant utopian theories, such as Plato's *Republic* and More's *Utopia,* but it can often lead to an indifference toward everyday life. Although Americans are not the first or only Europeans to yearn for an ideal social order, they may be the first to have been so naive as to think they could build Utopia out of the ordinary building materials used to construct a shopping mall or suburban development. Good old American know-how and the Yankee can-do attitude seem inevitably to produce a sterile idealism that is abstract without being noble, banal without having the charm of provincialism.

Idealists have appeared in many nations, but America has excelled in producing idealists unable to distinguish between the City of God and the City of Man. In Anthony Powell's novel *Temporary Kings,* an English classical scholar tries to explain the character of a young American literary critic whose behavior strikes her colleagues at a conference as somewhat eccentric: "Of course he remains essentially American in believing all questions have answers, that there is an ideal life against which everyday life can be measured—but measured only in everyday terms, so that the ideal life would be another sort of everyday life."

The United States, despite a certain provincial conservatism in the American reaction to political and cultural avant-garde, has quite rightly been regarded as the laboratory for every sort of liberal experiment. America is the first universal nation (to use Ben Wattenberg's phrase), cut loose from all the local patriotisms and blood-and-soil nationalism that made "old Europe" a charnel house. Americans who are satisfied with the results of 150 years of social experimentation may not need to cast about for an alternative point of view; those who are troubled by rootlessness and anomie, the grotesque frequency of homicide and suicide, the collapse of marriage, and the celebration of ugliness and perversity for their own sake may have to look outside the liberal tradition (and the leftisms and so-called conservatisms spawned by liberalism) for a sounder and more practical approach to the moral dilemmas offered by everyday human life.

Liberalism has been correctly described as "the political theory of modernity."[2] Some postmodern intellectuals have criticized the liberal consensus from Descartes to John Rawls as nothing more than an artifact of the modern West. Alasdair MacIntyre, H. G. Gadamer, radical feminists, some communitarian leftists, deconstructionists, and neo-Freudians, have all been troubled by the smug uniformity of the liberal

2. John Gray, *Liberalism,* 90.

tradition. But few of them have been prepared to abandon the tradition, much less to seek alternatives in the premodern traditions of, for example, classical antiquity and Judaism, partly because those traditions have themselves been misrepresented as forerunners of modern rationalism. Even the most severe critics of liberalism, such as MacIntyre, seem content to point out the shortcomings of liberalism; they have been reluctant, for the most part, to take the final step of recommending some form of premodern ethics as a positive alternative.

Human societies are, it goes without saying, diverse in morals no less than in manners. However, on certain points—such as the need for a social order, the importance of the family as an institution for rearing children, and the significance of kinship and friendship—there is a convergence not only among the civilizations of the ancient world but also with the enduring peasant morality that lies just beneath the surface of modern life. In fact, Aristotle and St. Thomas (to say nothing of Moses and St. Paul) are far closer in spirit and outlook to the common sense of ordinary people than they are to the thought of most modern philosophers. As the liberal tradition has unfolded, it has made increasingly impossible demands upon men and women who, confronted with the choice between moral heroism and amorality, have no choice but to become amoral. However, the ancient traditions—pagan, Judaic, and Christian—provide a realistic alternative that bears remarkable affinities with non-Western (that is, Chinese, African, Native American) traditions. The distinction is not purely ancient versus modern. Stoics and Epicureans (and even Plato) furnished many weapons to modern liberals, while Hume and Nietzsche (among others) were highly critical of central planks in the liberal platform.

If anything separates these other traditions from modern rationalism, it is their emphasis on what Jefferson deplored as "the wretched depravity of particular duties." Where Descartes or Locke looked at the everyday world and saw nothing but a few universal rules reducible to a mathematical formula, Aristotle and the writers of the Old Testament discerned an intricate network of peculiar obligations arising from specific circumstances and experiences. Where modern philosophers (from Kant to Kohlberg) regard a mother's self-sacrificing love for her children as beneath the level of morality, folk wisdom tells us it is nearly the highest morality, taking precedence over the duties of citizenship or the claims of humanity.

In the modern theories, moral conflicts can almost always be resolved into a choice between right and wrong, between human rights and oppression. The older tradition was more complex. A soldier might owe loyalty to his commanders and nation but also have conflicting duties to his family and his church. He might be forced to choose between obeying orders or obeying his religious conscience, between staying with his unit or returning home to save his family from distress. In the premodern era, such conflicts were taken seriously by Aristotle and Cicero and by rabbinical commentators on the Torah.[3]

Hard Cases

Since the Middle Ages, the case-by-case analysis of such dilemmas has been called casuistry, a sophisticated tradition of ethical discussion whose practitioners have included Aristotle, Cicero, and St. Thomas, as well as such prominent Protestant theologians as Jeremy Taylor and Richard Baxter. A genuine casuistry is based on two principles: first, that there are general and universally applicable moral laws governing human conduct; second, that these laws may not be applied simplistically and uniformly to the great variety of human circumstances and situations. Most older moralists denounced lying and stealing as evil, and even the loosest of casuists would agree. There are occasions, however, when stealing might be justified—for example, when a poor man must provide food for his starving children. A severe casuist like Baxter would ask hard questions: Has the poor man tried begging? Has he tried to get work, or is he stealing because he is lazy? Even if he must steal, he remains under an obligation to pay back his victim at the earliest opportunity. The mere fact that a theft is a means to a good end does not make it less immoral.

Catholic casuistry had its classical moment in the eighteenth century, when rigorist Jansenists contended against what they regarded as the moral laxity of the Jesuits. The compromise position, often referred to as probabilism, was elaborated by St. Alphonsus Maria de Liguori (1696–

3. Jacob Neusner compares Aristotle's concrete method with the exegetical techniques of Talmudic writers (*Rabbinic Political Theory: Religion and Politics in the Mishnah*, 1–6, 180–200).

1787), whose *Theologia Moralis* was regarded for nearly two centuries as the standard manual on casuistry. The primary purpose of such manuals was not the instruction of laymen but the education of confessors, who had to face a variety of complex moral dilemmas. St. Alphonsus, who had initially been attracted to the harshness and severity of the Jansenists, eventually learned that ordinary human beings could not live up to so austere a standard. Rejecting absolutism as both impractical and, in this human world, impossible, he argued from the basis of probability, always making allowances for human frailty. The result of his method is a mature and humane approach to moral problems that has never been equaled.

By the beginning of the eighteenth century, Protestant Europe and North America had embraced the universal moral abstractions of Locke and Leibniz, which eliminated, so it was thought, the need for analyzing particular relationships and particular cases. During the same century, however, English novelists, such as Samuel Richardson, Henry Fielding, and Fanny Burney, were treating the moral complexities of everyday life with the respect they deserve. Small wonder that ordinary people preferred to take their moral instruction from *Pamela* or *Evelina* rather than from Locke's political and psychological treatises on government.

Different casuists, whether philosophers or novelists, will come to different conclusions, because ethics is not (as St. Alphonsus acknowledged) an abstract science; it is more like the art of tuning a piano or tacking a sailing ship against the wind. The rules are as fixed as the points of the compass or the overtone series, but applying them to the imperfections of human life is a messy and sometimes dangerous business.

Many counselors and advice columnists would concede as much, at least in principle, but, since the time of Descartes, philosophers have been acting more and more as if a moral algebra or an ethical calculus could be devised from a few simple axioms, and, as a corollary, they have tended to reduce the complexities of human life to abstract formulas that override such everyday facts of life as kinship and friendship.

Rigorously applying their schematic principles to the rough-and-tumble of everyday life, modern philosophers—and their disciples who manage the affairs of nations—reach conclusions whose puritanical austerity is an invitation to evasion and amorality. Rich foods are condemned wholesale on the grounds of health; the minor vices are either hemmed in with taxes and restrictions or proscribed outright; the consumption of animal flesh is vilified either as cannibalism or as an immoral luxury that deprives people living ten thousand miles away of their daily allowance of cereal grains. Sex is alternately banned and elevated into an absolute necessity or human right.

Rigorism is a perennial temptation for the moralist. The ancient Pharisees insisted on following every jot and tittle of Judaic custom; Plato's logic led him to imagine a state in which property and wives were held in common; seventeenth- and eighteenth-century Jansenists tried to plant their cold and austere moral absolutism in the lush soil of the Mediterranean world, banishing all that was not perfectly good to the realm of evil; contemporary ethicists, arguing that there is a moral obligation to equalize conditions between rich and poor individuals, and even between rich and poor nations, condemn the favoritism we show our friends and countrymen as so much selfishness and greed.

To each of these absurd conclusions, the best response is often not to deny what may be quite reasonable (if incomplete) assumptions about social or religious obligation but to invoke the equally valid counterprinciples that force an imperfect compromise. "The Sabbath was made for man, not man for the Sabbath," was Jesus' answer to the Pharisees who criticized Him for gathering food on a day dedicated to the Lord, and, from the beginning, Christian ethics and moral theology have been inherently casuistic in taking full account of the spiritual condition and intention of the sinner as well as of the circumstances in which the sin was committed. The rigorism of Montanists, Donatists, and Calvinists is an aberration.

Mark Twain turned against the Sunday School rigorism of his youth and mercilessly mocked a Victorian moral code that forced people into moral dilemmas. His Huckleberry Finn had received just enough of this instruction to believe he had the duty to betray Jim, the runaway slave who had befriended him, and turn him in to the authorities. The law, after all, makes no exception for friendship. Huck is asked to assist in a search for runaway slaves, and, after dishonestly promising to help, he returns to the raft "feeling bad and low, because I knowed very well I had done wrong."

Huck is all too aware of his inadequate moral training, but the thought occurs to him that he would be just as unhappy if he gave Jim up: "Well, then, says I, what's the use you learning to do right, when it's troublesome to do right and ain't no trouble to do wrong, and the wages is just the same? I was stuck. I couldn't answer that. So I reckoned I wouldn't bother no more about it, but after this always do whichever come handiest at the time." The pharisaism of Victorian morality has its inevitable result: a total rejection of all moral principle.

The fault, however, does not lie with Christianity per se, which is far from being a killjoy religion. On the contrary, the Christian doctrine of the Incarnation should teach Christians that God thought well enough of this part of His Creation that He sent His own Son, in human form, to redeem it, and the mainstream of Christian moral teaching has almost always taken account of ordinary obligations and of human frailty. That earlier and more complex Christian ethic had been seriously eroded by the early twentieth century. By then, the Catholic Church was already falling under the spell of a rigid neo-Thomism that was as abstract as any German school of philosophy, and Protestants had either adopted the liberal philosophy of John Locke and Adam Smith wholesale or else retreated into the austere rigorism of a puritanical Calvinism that not only eliminated the pleasures of everyday life but also set the moral bar so high that virtually no one could jump over it—at least not without kicking everyone he loved in the face. While a Northern Puritan might have argued with Huck's Southern Puritan Sunday-school teacher, saying that it was Huck's duty to sacrifice his own life to free a slave, neither Puritan would have thought that Huck's affection for Jim had any bearing on the question.

The full flowering of Christian ethics was expressed in Aristotelian language. In answer to Plato's vision of a perfect justice, Aristotle repeatedly reminds us of our humanity and the folly of any effort to rise above our nature. Justice cannot be reduced to simple universals, because different kinds of virtue are required of different people. One cannot be just to one's children, for example, because they are so much a part of oneself. "A father's or a master's justice are not the same as that of the citizens" (Arist. *Ethica Nicomachea* 1134b).[4] The casuists, in their subtle fashion, went even further, distinguishing the peculiar moral problems of specific professions. St. Alphonsus, for example, dedicated an entire book, *The True Spouse of Jesus Christ,* to the special problems encountered by nuns. The same act, argues Aristotle, may be regarded as just or unjust according to the character of the actor and the state of

---

4. Unless otherwise indicated, all translations are my own.

his mind. If a man sleeps with another man's wife out of passion, his crime is different from an adultery committed out of envy, revenge, or mere covetousness, and he is not morally guilty of adultery if he was not aware that the woman is married.

According to Aristotle, laws are, by their nature, universal statements that cannot comprehend every contingency. For human beings, at least, fairness and reasonableness *(epieikeia)* are better adapted to the needs of justice than the kind of dogmatic absolutism that leads to error (*Eth. Nic.* 1137b), and, while Aristotle seems to be discussing actual legislation, his strictures apply with equal force to the moral laws proposed by philosophers.

Contemporary ethics is in even greater need of a casuistry that would restore some sense of reality to the discussions of philosophers. Following one line of argument that takes individual merit as the starting point, some libertarian philosophers conclude that fairness or justice is based on the principle of *cuique suum,* of letting each man get his just deserts, no matter what the consequences to family, friends, and society. Other philosophers, beginning with the principle of equality, have insisted upon wealth-transfer as a necessary means for equalizing opportunity. Both lines of argument lead to an absurd conclusion—either to an insistence upon sacrificing all personal interests for the sake of the common good or to complete moral indifference to other people.

Religious conservatives are not the only people to have felt uneasy with the dichotomy between the principle of merit and the principle of equality and with any plan that weakens family integrity by transferring wealth from parent A to the child of parent B. This conflict of moral priorities is described by liberal philosopher James Fishkin as a "trilemma"—that is, a situation in which only two out of three positions can be congruent. It is possible to imagine various social systems in which two of these three concerns—merit, equality, family integrity—are maximized, but not all three. The best we can hope for, concludes Fishkin, is a messy compromise that includes some attention to all three concerns.[5]

Casuistry, far from being the kind of moral arithmetic or algebra imagined by Descartes and Locke, is more like ecology in refusing to divorce

5. James Fishkin, *Justice, Equal Opportunity, and the Family,* 5–10, 44–105.

organisms from their interactions both with each other and with their environment. Perhaps it is time to make a tentative approach to a kind of moral ecology, to find a way through the twisted and interlocking territories that compose the labyrinth of human life by using the evidence of history, literature, and science as so many clues in a treasure hunt.

Although casuistry fell into disgrace at the end of the seventeenth century, our need for such an approach has never gone away. In fact, ordinary people have not turned to moral philosophers for enlightenment but to novelists, essayists, and advice columnists. At the very time that fiction came to be taken seriously as something more than light entertainment, casuistry was being extinguished by moral rationalism, and, as noted, ever since the eighteenth century, people have referred to great novels as the framework for moral discussion: Richardson's *Pamela,* Austen's *Emma,* Thackeray's *Vanity Fair,* Scott's *The Heart of Midlothian,* Twain's *Huckleberry Finn.* In the twentieth century, they turned to philosophical novelists, such as François Mauriac and Walker Percy, or to writers of detective fiction, such as Dashiell Hammett and Raymond Chandler, or, increasingly, to films. Robert Coles, in interviewing adolescents, discovered that they well understood the moral questions posed by films like John Ford's *The Man Who Shot Liberty Valance.*

Even the most popular fiction may have lessons to teach, as G. K. Chesterton argued in defense of "penny dreadfuls." There is nothing inherently wrong with escapist fiction, if the world into which we escape is filled with heroism and honor. For some children growing up in troubled families, a good story may be more than escape: it can be a contact with a better world. This was the case of the young Dean Koontz, who grew up to write his own escapist fantasies. In Koontz's thriller *The Voice of the Night,* a troubled boy takes refuge in science fiction, and when he begins to tell his mother terrifying tales, she can only assume that his mind has been poisoned by cheap fiction. Ironically, it is precisely his favorite fantasy books that have prepared the boy to understand life in modern California.

Storytelling is the most ancient and perhaps the best way that human beings have found to make coherent sense out of their experience. This is one of the reasons why the text of this book is studded with allusions to myths, plays, novels, and films. If moral and social questions are not reducible to logical abstractions—which is my central point—then it is essential for us to learn moral reasoning by considering the nuances and textures of human life. Intellectual historians and philosophers may find this approach unsatisfying, and they may be even further repelled by the various digressions into history and law. However, the interweaving of Greek myths and recent news stories is part of a deliberate plan to lead readers out of the algebraic simplicities of schoolroom morals and into the complex labyrinth of moral reality. Plato relied on dialogue for a process of intellectual clarification; St. Thomas used the elaborate scholastic apparatus of questions and responses to chart a sort of zigzag course to the truth; and I have followed Samuel Johnson in adapting the form of the informal essay as a means of tacking my way not, God knows, to certitude, but toward something like common sense and traditional wisdom.

Ordinary people seem to need a nontechnical casuistry that accords the real problems of everyday life the serious attention they deserve, an attention that is often (though certainly not always) denied them by academic philosophy. Even if readers end up rejecting these arguments as eccentric or irrelevant to modern life, I hope they will return to the mainstream of liberalism with a clearer knowledge of what the older tradition represents. One cannot rationally hold an opinion without considering the alternative. Plato was probably wrong: The unexamined life may well be worth living, so long as it is lived in accordance with traditions that are consistent with human nature and encourage the fulfillment of human needs. But it is precisely those traditions that have been destroyed by rationalist ethics. When a tradition of thought leads to moral dissolution, social chaos, and music and poetry that speak only to professionals, it may be time to wonder how people lived and thrived before they were called upon to be citizens of the world, dedicated to absolute standards of right and wrong.

To certain kinds of liberals and leftists, those who defy their conclusions and refuse to join the revolution are outside the moral sphere. To a certain kind of Christian, this world is the devil's playground, whose only value is in the opportunity it provides for rising above a material existence which, if not entirely evil, contains little that is good. For the moral absolutist, everyday life, with its play of light and color, is but the surface of a sea in whose depths is staged a conflict between absolute good and unspeakable evil. It is the task of the moral hero to penetrate through the surface and to know all.

"All visible objects, man, are but as pasteboard masks. But in each event—in the living act, the undoubted deed—there, some unknown but still reasoning thing puts forth the mouldings of its features from behind the unreasoning mask. If a man will strike, strike through the mask! How can the prisoner reach outside except by thrusting through the wall? To me, the white whale is that wall shoved near to me. Sometimes I think there's nought beyond. But 'tis enough. He tasks me; he heaps me; I see in him outrageous strength, with an inscrutable malice sinewing it. That inscrutable thing is chiefly what I hate."

Melville's Captain Ahab may not be a Christian, but, in his obsession with a natural creature he finds evil, we hear the accents of his Puritan forebears, who thought the New World was the property of the devil (served by Indians and Catholics) before they came to redeem the continent. To these absolutists and their spiritual and political descendants, humility and restraint are no virtues. "Talk not to me of blasphemy," Ahab retorts to Starbuck, who accuses him of taking "vengeance on a dumb brute . . . that simply smote thee from blind instinct." Ahab says he would "strike the sun if it insulted me."

Ahab cannot be free of his obsession until the whale "spouts black blood and rolls fin out." As Melville realized (and as Barry Goldwater's speechwriter did not), extremism in the defense of liberty—or even of virtue itself—is, in fact, a vice. Ahab destroys his ship, himself, and all of his crew except the man who lives to tell the tale. Whether the white whale being pursued was communism or capitalism, inequality or social injustice, Jews or Christians, the absolutists of recent centuries have inflicted more suffering on innocent people than all the Alexanders, Atillas, and Genghis Khans of previous ages. Better by far the ancient wisdom of "nothing in excess" and "know thyself"—that is, know that man is man and not a god to lash the sea or strike the sun.

HELL AND OTHER PEOPLE

"If everybody minded their own business," the Duchess said in a hoarse growl, "the world would go round a deal faster than it does."

—Lewis Carroll, *Alice's Adventures in Wonderland*

Minding other people's business is a full-time pursuit. So much to do, so little time, say the reformers who devote themselves to taking care of other people's children or curing other people's bigotry. No surprise in this, conservatives will say. Leftists since the days of Robespierre have made it a principle to sacrifice private life to public good, to see in every social problem an opportunity to build up government at the expense of society. But what do the same conservatives say about the declared enemies of the left? Of conservative Christians who wear themselves out trying to prevent nonbelieving women from aborting their unborn children, or of the libertarians who say they are indifferent to the fate of other people but who lie awake at night worrying about what small-minded bigots in Cincinnati may be doing to suppress the rights of pornographers?

There is something strange in the spectacle of so much conservative do-gooding. The one essential insight of free-market economics is that human beings are more efficient at providing for their own needs than any set of *other* people could possibly be, no matter how enlightened. In pursuing their own self-interest, the argument runs, greedy and even vicious individuals confer benefits upon the whole of society, and the world, as a result, tends to "go round a deal faster." Two thousand years before Adam Smith wrote *The Wealth of Nations*, Aristotle noticed that privately owned property was taken better care of than property that was owned in common. "The tragedy of the commons," so well known to modern environmentalists, was summed up by Macaulay in a famous aphorism: "The business of everybody is the business of nobody."

Neither Aristotle nor Macaulay would have denied that each of us owes something to some other people; they were not, after all, anarchists or even libertarians. What would have puzzled both of them is the notion—defying common sense—that each of us owes something to everybody else. Aristotle believed what most ordinary people believe—that we should be dutiful children, cooperative neighbors, and loyal citizens. However, since the eighteenth century, moral philosophers have been telling us to identify ourselves and our duty with all of our society (or with humanity itself) and its needs, since "duty is that mode of action on the part of the individual which constitutes the best possible application of his capacity to the general benefit."[1]

In the twentieth century, this reasoning led to the conclusion that the citizens of a just state had to commit themselves to the goal of economic equality.[2] This and similar assumptions are so ingrained today that we take it for granted that Dickens's miserly Ebenezer Scrooge is the epitome of moral irresponsibility. At the beginning of *A Christmas Carol,* when Scrooge is asked by two philanthropic gentlemen for a charitable contribution, he replies that they should put him down for nothing. "You wish to be anonymous?" they persist, and he replies: "I wish to be left alone." Scrooge is informed that many of the poor would rather die than go to the workhouses and prisons supported by his taxes. When Scrooge professes that he doesn't know what the poor might wish and the gentlemen inform him that he *might* know it, he replies: "It's not my business.... It's enough for a man to understand his own business, and not to interfere with other people's. Mine occupies me constantly. Good afternoon, gentlemen!"

1. William Godwin, *Enquiry concerning Political Justice,* 190.
2. See John Rawls, *A Theory of Justice,* 150.

It is not for the London poor alone that Scrooge is asked to care. When he praises his late partner, Marley, as a good man for business, Marley's ghost admonishes him: "Mankind was my business." At this point, Scrooge would be justified in throwing up his hands in despair. "Oh, well," he might say, "I could raise Bob Cratchit's wages and do something for nephew Fred; I could even subscribe to all the local charities and leave the rest of my fortune to a foundling hospital. But mankind? No, sir, my entire fortune would do nothing for all mankind; it would be like pouring a pitcherful of water on the desert."

As a sharp businessman, Marley should understand the problem of economic scarcity at least as well as do the Church fathers. "Since one cannot help everyone," remarked Augustine, "one has to be concerned with those who by reason of place, time, or circumstances, are by some chance more tightly bound to you."[3] A Christian saint, if he had the power to do everyone good, would be obliged to exercise it, but such powers belong to the divine and not to the human. People make a very basic mistake when they assume that, even in principle, we have an obligation to act in such a way that "everybody" (however defined) is better off. Most valuable resources are limited, and, in disposing of food and water, property and time, we must choose between one action and another, one person and another. If the greatest good to the greatest number were the goal, then I might be justified (as some utilitarians have argued) in killing one man to save the lives of millions, in accordance with the military maxim "the sacrifice of few to save many."

But many ordinary people seem to know, by common sense or intuition, that murder is murder and that it is never right to violate a "thou shalt not" command in order to carry out a virtuous or charitable impulse. It cannot be right to rob Peter to pay Paul, even if Peter is rich and Paul is poor. "The fact that benevolence is a virtue," observes Philippa Foot, "and a virtue which dictates attachment to the good of others, does not, then, give morality a universal end or goal."[4]

Before his conversion to the religion of philanthropy, Scrooge is not an unscrupulous cynic but a utilitarian liberal who believes that kindness and charity are worse than humbug; kindness to the poor, after all,

---

3. Augustine, *De Doctrina Christiana*, book 1, chap. 28.
4. Philippa Foot, "Morality, Action, and Outcome," 32.

only increases the surplus population. Acting on the principles of moral individualism and the greater good, he rejects charity as a destructive impulse. If he was a scoundrel who manipulates pension funds instead of an honest man of business, his conversion to the religion of philanthropy would be an easier matter; indeed, it is good business to write a check once a year to the United Way or give a series of lectures, as Michael Milken has done, on the ethics of business. Scrooge could continue to mistreat his employees and relatives, while at the same time acquiring a reputation for philanthropy. This is exactly what the modern Scrooges do; they treat their customers as suckers and their employees as enemies, while giving lavish pittances to charitable causes designed to assist strangers. The Enron executives who hoodwinked investors and persuaded employees to keep their pension funds invested in the failing company were also, up to the very end of the drama, lauded for their generosity.

Selfish Greeks

What, exactly, do we owe to strangers? In the United States, it is increasingly common to hear that taxpayers are morally obliged to provide for the needs of illegal aliens. But in some of the village cultures from which the aliens come, the stranger has few rights, and, whatever their national laws say about such things, villagers may think they can rob or kill the stranger with impunity. However, contempt for strangers is not confined to village cultures. Before the twentieth century, the concept of a universal obligation that comprehended strangers as well as friends and neighbors was embraced by only a handful of visionaries, and a good part of the whole duty of man consisted of minding one's business.

In that land of "once upon a time," the duties of ordinary people were restricted to the tiny sphere of everyday life. It was enough for us to take care of our own, to be as fair as we knew how in all our dealings, and to be loyal to our country and to the gods. No one, perhaps, does a better job of summing up the common wisdom than the amateur philosopher Plutarch, whose works have been remarkably popular since the Renaissance. The object of teaching moral philosophy to children, he reminded his readers, is to enable them to learn basic responsibilities:

what is good and what is base, what is just and what unjust, what generally is to be chosen and what avoided; how one ought to deal with the
gods, with his parents, with his elders, with the laws, with strangers, with
rulers, with friends, with women, with children, with servants; that one
must revere the gods, honor one's parents, respect one's elders, obey the
laws, give way to rulers, love one's friends, exercise restraint toward women,
be affectionate with children, and not mistreat slaves. (Plut. *Moralia* 7d–e)

Plutarch's platitudes appealed to the common sense of the ancient
world, but his biographies and essays were widely read even in frontier
America. The emphasis on particular responsibilities—as opposed to
"duty" in the abstract—is not exclusive to Plutarch: it is as commonplace as proverbs and Mother Goose rhymes. "Charity begins at home,"
"The shoemaker should stick to his last," and "There's no place like
home" are the expressions of parochial sentiment, as is all the folk wisdom on the defects of other nations summed up in phrases like *French
leave* and *French pox, Dutch courage* and *Dutch treat*—or, to give the
French and the Dutch equal time, *perfidious Albion* and "Only Yankees
and fools predict the weather." "Be slow when strangers haste to give" is
an American proverb that expresses a universal suspicion of outsiders,
as is "What ain't your duty ain't your business."

Cicero, in a work that Dr. Johnson said should be read every year,
said that doing one's particular duty is the difference between virtue
and vice: "For there is no part of life—neither in our public nor private
affairs, neither at home nor in the marketplace, neither if you conduct
some business with yourself nor if you make an arrangement with another person—that can be without duty; all honest living consists in
cultivating duty, all baseness in neglecting it" (Cic. *De Officiis* 1.2). This
Roman view of duty, comprehensive as it is, imposes no unusual burden of obligation; in fact, it is only a higher expression of the common
opinion of ancient pagans—that there are specific duties, arising out of
one's station in life, owed to neighbors, relatives, friends, and political
allies. Greeks and Romans, Jews and Assyrians all made the obvious
distinctions between neighbors and strangers, kin and non-kin, compatriots and aliens, noble and baseborn, and—most sweeping—between
friends and enemies.

Ancient literatures are filled with examples of extreme cruelty practiced against outsiders by otherwise moral people. The Greeks at Troy
were said to have killed the child of Hector to prevent him from

growing up to seek revenge, and, while later Greek poets probed the moral dimensions of this act, few kin-based societies would absolutely condemn the decision. Prohibitions on theft and killing applied to friends and compatriots within a society and not, necessarily, to strangers. Piracy and brigandage were honorable occupations in early Greece, and it was not rude to ask the wandering Odysseus if he was a pirate.

In Athens, resident aliens did have legal status, but an alien "could not hold any public office in Athens, nor be a juror. . . . He was also not allowed to own land or houses . . . nor (after 451/50) to marry an Athenian woman."[5] He was, however, liable to taxation and military service. It was Pericles, the democratic philosopher-king, who restricted citizenship to the offspring of two citizen parents, and the various welfare provisions of Athens were jealously confined to citizens. A later philosopher, Aristotle, warned his fellow Greeks against the perils of a large commonwealth in which aliens can usurp the privileges of citizens.

Greek poetry and proverbs make it clear that universal benevolence was not the Greek ideal. As a famous line of Archilochus puts it, "I know one thing, but it's important: to punish terribly the one who has done me wrong." This attitude was prevalent enough that one of the speakers in the *Republic* interprets the phrase "giving every man his due" as "[owing] good to friends and evil to enemies" (Plato *Respublica* 332a).[6] In Athens, if a citizen wanted to recover stolen goods or have a criminal arrested, he gathered up his friends and did the job himself.[7]

A Greek was not supposed to go to law against family members and friends, if he could avoid it,[8] and in Athens homicide remained a family affair, as it was for ancient Jews. It was up to the victim's family members to prosecute his murderer. Justice in most parts of the ancient world depended on the efforts of a man's family and friends, especially in the legalistic Roman republic. The reactionary Greek poet Theognis

5. Douglas M. MacDowell, *The Law in Classical Athens*, 75–76.

6. See K. J. Dover, *Greek Popular Morality in the Time of Plato and Aristotle*, 180–81.

7. Virginia Hunter, *Policing Athens: Social Control in the Attic Lawsuits, 420–320 B.C.*, 143–51.

8. Hence the apologies at the beginning of so many speeches, such as Lysias 32 where one family member is suing another. A Greek was, however, supposed to seek revenge from enemies.

prayed for powerful friends to avenge him: "Thus would I seem to be a god among men."

Aristocrats are frequently tempted to regard themselves as members of a different race, or even species, from the lower orders. India's caste system may be the most famous example, but in early Rome patricians were forbidden to marry plebeians, on religious grounds: The patricians had divine blood that ought not to be contaminated. Similarly, the poems of Theognis made a sharp distinction between the social classes and advocated a eugenics program to prevent noblemen from taking wives who were rich but baseborn; this almost racialist arrogance of class was just as pronounced among Italian, French, and English aristocracies.[9]

Early Greek morality is not universal but particular: "It may be said in broad terms . . . that an Athenian felt his first duty was to his parents . . . , his second to his kinsmen, and his third to his friends and benefactors; after that, in descending order, to his fellow-citizens, to citizens of other Greek states, to barbaroi, and to slaves."[10] Even within Athens, a citizen felt only limited obligation to his fellow Athenians.

Consider a situation that is frequently presented to advice columnists. You have just found out that a married neighbor is having an affair with another man's wife. Assuming that you think adultery is immoral and destructive, what should you do? Telling the injured spouses might be a good deed, but, on the other hand, you just might make trouble for yourself. The conflict, then, is between the duty to tell and a prudent desire to stay out of trouble.

The ancient Greeks viewed the matter from the opposite perspective. In the early fourth century, an Athenian citizen named Euphiletus was tried for murder after he killed his wife's lover in her bedroom. The woman who informed on the couple had prefaced her revelation with a disclaimer: "Euphiletus, don't think I am accosting you because I am a busybody. In fact, the man who is wronging you and your wife happens to be my personal enemy" (Lysias 1.16). In other words, minding your own business is the positive virtue; interfering has to be justified.

According to Pericles (in Thucydides 2.20), it was an Athenian peculiarity to consider the man who stayed apart from public affairs not as a

---

9. Much of the class antagonism of medieval Italian cities was between the Germanic aristocracy and the Roman-Italian middle classes.

10. Dover, *Greek Popular Morality,* 273.

non-busybody *(apragmon)* but as a good-for-nothing, and this theme was a commonplace of Athenian politics.[11] The Athenians' sense of public duty grew out of the Greek thirst for distinction, the need to win honor in the public activities of war and politics. However, a private citizen in Athens, even if he were politically ambitious, was usually very reluctant to meddle in the private affairs of another citizen and his household. Elsewhere, Pericles uses *apragmon* in its conventional sense of "minding one's own business" (Thuc. 2.63), arguing that the Athenians must defend the empire to preserve their peace. It has been argued, albeit unconvincingly, that Athenian *apragmosyne* was "un-Greek."[12] On the contrary, it was the excessive public demands made by the Athenian democracy that is unusual.[13]

This is not to say that Athenians and other Greeks were not prone to stick their noses into their neighbors' affairs. In Mediterranean village communities, it is virtually impossible to keep anything a secret, and Greeks took a frequently malicious interest in all that went on in their neighborhoods. Plutarch devotes one of his most charming essays ("On Busybodiness") to this vice of *polypragmosyne,* and his advice—knock before entering a house to avoid surprising people, don't peer into doorways as you pass by, don't tittle-tattle about your neighbors—is as instructive as it is amusing. Plutarch assumes that the man who meddles in the affairs of others is motivated not by benevolence but by *Schadenfreude* (the Greek word is *epichairekakia*) and praises the lawgiver of Thurii, who made it a crime for a citizen to return from a trip and ask if there was any news (*Mor.* 518–19).

Plato was mad enough to think that a city was better off when the words *mine* and *thine* were rarely heard, and the Stoics told their followers to be citizens of the world, but such idealism was regarded as, at best, an eccentricity. The most systematic of ancient philosophers, Aristotle, made all the routine distinctions and regarded at least some foreign races as fit for slavery. Just behavior was not, for Aristotle, a universal and undifferentiated category, because different people must display different kinds of justice, as husbands to wives, citizens to citi-

---

11. David Cohen, *Law, Sexuality, and Society: The Enforcement of Morals in Classical Athens,* 80.

12. L. B. Carter, *The Quiet Athenian.*

13. S. C. Humphreys, *The Family, Women, and Death: Comparative Studies,* 1–32.

zens, and so on. Rather than a theory of duty, of course, Aristotle's is a theory of justice. (However, much of what he has to say on this topic would be covered in English by words like *duty* and *obligation*.) For example, Aristotle regards justice from one perspective as a state of character that disposes us to act justly and wish for justice (*Eth. Nic.* 1129a). That which is just is therefore the right thing to do, but it is also conformity with the law. Justice is also sometimes said to be another's good—that is, virtue in relation to others. It is therefore difficult to speak of duty toward children, since they are part of oneself.

Selfish Christians

It was not until the Stoics that Greeks were to take seriously the notion that all men were brothers or that each of us should live as if he were a "citizen of the world." The Stoics' talk of human brotherhood seems to echo in St. Paul's declaration that "there is neither Jew nor Greek, there is neither bond nor free, there is neither male nor female: for ye are all one in Christ Jesus." But modern commentators have overstated and distorted Paul's message. The first Christians were practicing Jews living under a law that emphasized God's exclusive contract with His chosen people and the inferiority of all other nations. Even the Torah, in forbidding usury, exempted loans made to foreigners (Deut. 23:20), and among the worst punishments proclaimed against disobedient Israel was that the alien would rise above the Jew (Deut. 28:43). Greeks and Romans, narrow-minded as they were, professed to be shocked by Jewish parochialism and its double standard, which they took as evidence that Jews (and, later on, Christians) were misanthropists. Jewish suspicion of aliens extended even to the Samaritans, who deviated not much more from the standard Judaism of the day than one sect of modern Protestantism does from another.

This is the context for Jesus' parable of the Good Samaritan (Luke 10:25–37). An expert in Jewish law asks Jesus what he must do to gain eternal life, and he is told to keep the great commandments: "Thou shalt love the Lord thy God with all thy heart, and with all thy soul, and with all thy mind; and thy neighbor as thyself." When the quibbler persists in asking who his neighbor is, Jesus tells the story of a man who is beaten, robbed, and stripped of his clothing. A priest and a Levite pass by without stopping, "but a certain Samaritan, as he journeyed, came where he was; and when he saw him, he had compassion on him."

Jesus was tweaking his Jewish followers by distinguishing between those who are outwardly ministers of God—that is, the priest and the Levite—and those who actually do his will, and he makes a similar distinction between practicing Jews and the heretical but merciful Samaritan. The point is sharpened by the next story, which puts the problem of faith and works in a different light. While Martha attempts to show her greater zeal by performing menial services, her sister Mary sits and listens to the Master's words (Luke 10:38–42).

The external and physical distinctions of priestly rank or officious service, then, are of lesser virtue than the true faith that reveals itself both in acts of charity and in attentiveness to the Master. Jewish blood, circumcision, priestly status, outward conformity—all fall short of the true and inner faith. Directly confronted with human suffering, we are obligated to be merciful, and even Samaritans are believers capable of being "neighbors" in the extended sense in which Christians were to apply the term.

Jesus did not, however, preach the abolition of all distinctions, ethnic, religious, and social. Asked by a Phoenician woman to heal her child, He responds with asperity: "I was sent only to the lost sheep of Israel.... It is not right to take the children's bread and toss it to their dogs" (Matt. 15:24–26). While Jesus soon relents, anticipating the extension of His ministry to the Gentiles, He also displays His feelings as a Jew who has no intention of overturning the Law.

In considering Christ's message of universal love, it is important to bear in mind that He was almost always addressing Himself to particular questions raised by the parochial Jews of His time. His admonitions have to be read as an extension of the prophetic tradition that attempted to correct the ancient tendency (as prominent among Greeks as among Jews) to exclude "the other" from the human species.

Bad Samaritans

How far are we obliged to go in doing our duty, either as natural men or as Christians? Consider the case of what may be called Bad Samaritans—people who fail to render assistance to those who might be drowning, starving, or under attack from muggers or rapists. The situations are so variable and complex that it is difficult to formulate a rule. It is easy for a passerby to throw a rope to a drowning man, but other cases are less simple. Should a mother or father of small children attempt to rescue a person drowning in a dangerous river, when in all likelihood the only result of the intervention will be the death of the parent? Should you endanger your life to save someone from his own imprudence? The situation cannot be that uncommon. Suppose you are a black man drinking in a club in a black part of town, and a group of white college boys enter, noisily demanding drinks. Is it really your duty to interpose your own person between the boys and the trouble they are looking for? Preventing injustice is obviously the right thing to do, but not if it means suicide. Partly because of the difficulties involved in determining what is a reasonable risk, Anglo-American law has traditionally attached few penalties to the failure to help.

The classic statement on this subject was made by Macaulay. Jailers or nurses whose dereliction of duty causes the death of their charges are guilty of murder, concedes Macaulay, but "it will hardly be maintained that a man should be punished as a murderer because he omitted to relieve a beggar, even though there might be the clearest proof that the death of the beggar was the effect of the omission." Macaulay goes on to enunciate the general rule that "the penal law must content itself with keeping men from doing positive harm, and must leave to public opinion, and to teachers of morality and religion, the office of furnishing men with motives for doing positive good."[14]

No other conclusion is possible on the classical liberal understanding of liberty as an essentially negative right *not* to be murdered and *not* to be robbed, and, in *On Liberty,* J. S. Mill is skeptical of most attempts to impose a more positive obligation not to allow harm to be done. However, with the left turn taken by British liberalism in the late nineteenth century, the notion of liberty as a positive right not to go hungry or lack education became the dominant note of liberal ethics. On this understanding, it is reasonable to argue that just as the state cannot let a man go hungry simply because he is lazy, or without schooling because his parents are poor, so too we citizens or subjects cannot stand idly by and allow Macaulay's beggar to starve to death.

14. Macaulay, "Notes on the Indian Penal Code by the Indian Law Commissioners," note M, 315–23 (see also 314).

There is a growing literature on the ethical and legal aspects of Bad Samaritanism, and the arguments, however subtle and complex, generally amount to no more than either the old liberal or new liberal understanding of liberty. Beginning with the assumption that individuals are the only genuinely moral actors, the question is then posed in the abstract: Do we have natural or inherent duties to every so-and-so in such-and-such a situation? If we are egoists, like Ayn Rand and certain other individualists, then our only duty is to ourselves, because society as such does not exist, or because, as Mandeville argued in *The Fable of the Bees*, the greatest good is arrived at only by the realization of all the selfish interests in society.

On the other hand, the doctrine of selfishness, it is argued by left-liberals, is a dead end that does not enable people within societies to resolve conflicts. Besides, modern ethics is based on the principle that one cannot privilege either oneself or one's group, and "there is no general difference between oneself and others, to which each person can appeal.... Therefore, Ethical Egoism is unacceptably arbitrary."[15]

An egoist might respond, probably at the top of his lungs, that he rejected both the Golden Rule and the Categorical Imperative. An individual's only duty, he would say, is to himself, and just as he would reject charitable assistance of any kind as degrading, he would refuse to give it. His ultimate justification is not the greater good that derives from a commitment to individualism but the greater good that derives from the mere fact of being an individual whose only rational strategy is to make the most of his life. If socialists and other collectivists think acts of charity are part of a full life, they are free to perform them, but the individualist is bound by no such obligation.

Both positions are logical, once their counterintuitive premises (that is, that moral obligations are universal and that human beings can be individualists) are accepted. But if we consider the case of a nursing mother who will not spare a drop of the milk that belongs to her and her baby to save the life of another if it means the slightest possible risk to her own child, the futility of both arguments becomes apparent. From the egoist position, the mother—unless she has made a voluntary and rational contract—has the right to save the milk for herself or sell it to a stranger. However, it is obvious that she has the milk only insofar as

15. James Rachels, *The Elements of Moral Philosophy*, 93–95.

she is a mother. Many mothers have a hard time distinguishing their children's interests from their own, and even if they can, the children often take precedence. These are facts of life that cannot be explained away by one or another theory of "false consciousness."

From a universalist perspective, one might argue that it would be better for the mother to preserve the life of Jonas Salk, who is on the point of discovering the polio vaccine that will save thousands of children's lives. From the utilitarian perspective, she might choose to save Howard Hughes, on the condition that he sign over to her so many millions of dollars, some of which will be used to benefit her child and the rest to benefit either herself or her country, the human race, or an endangered species of rat—the choice will depend upon the ethical flavor of the week for which she has a craving.

Viewed from the perspective of actual nursing mothers, both selfish individualism and altruism must appear like so many discarded nursery toys—children's carpentry tools or chemistry sets, fine to play with but not to bring into the shop or factory. To this extent, the followers of Ayn Rand are correct: As individuals, we have no obligation to other individuals. The pretense that we do rests upon premises that we may choose to accept or reject.

But the egoists are equally deluded: Only a creature created in a laboratory, in isolation from all other creatures, could be properly regarded as purely an individual, and even he would owe some special obligation (if only revenge) to his creator.

Even on its own ground, the case against Bad Samaritanism is flawed. Ordinarily, we think we *have* to help a stranger only when it is part of our professional responsibility (as policemen, nurses, priests) or when we have, by our own actions, put him at risk. We are not obliged to feed all the children in the world, only those we have produced or adopted or agreed to provide for. Unless we are physicians, we do not have to devote ourselves to keeping all accident victims alive, only those whose accidents we have somehow caused.[16]

If for no other reason than limits on our time and money, we are compelled to help only some people some of the time. When liberal ethicists came to this realization, they began designing lifeboat scenarios

16. See Eric Mack, "Bad Samaritanism and the Causation of Harm."

in which we are asked to decide whom to rescue, our spouse or a great humanitarian? The liberal can argue one way or the other, choosing to emphasize the contract with one's wife or the greater utility derived from saving the humanitarian.

For nonliberals—that is, nearly everyone in the history of the human race—there is simply no dilemma. Family relations take precedence over any claim from any stranger no matter how good or holy, and Christians are under no less obligation than nonbelievers. "If anyone does not take care of his own," says Paul (1 Tim. 5:8), "and especially of his own household, he has denied the faith and is worse than an unbeliever."

Individualism turns out to be a weak foundation for the notion that we each have a positive duty to help other people. Why not, then, transfer responsibility to the state: "The duty to give emergency assistance is grounded... in the state's duty to protect the general welfare and in the reasonableness of the burdens imposed on citizens who are 'deputized' to provide easily rendered assistance."[17] As moral deputies of the state, we do not have to worry about what we think as individuals. All we have to do is obey orders, and while the deputy's star might be made a bit lighter if we stipulate that reasonableness and ease can be elements in our decision to provide help, there is no theoretical justification for limiting the state's right to deputize citizens, once the principle of a generalized *in loco parentis* responsibility or moral conscription is granted.

If individuals do not have such a responsibility, however, where would the state get it from? And if the state wishes to deputize us, when does its authority override our own refusal? It may be possible to find answers to these and other questions, even to arrange a workable compromise between the general principle of universal obligation and the exigencies of everyday life, but are such equivocations really necessary? The very notion of citizens acting as the state's moral deputies implies both a deification of the state and a denial of individual responsibility that would erode the foundations of morality. But as silly as such an extreme conclusion appears on the surface, it is an entirely logical deduction once we accept the premise that it is ultimately the state's responsibility to provide for the welfare of its citizens.

17. Alison McIntyre, "Guilty Bystanders? On the Legitimacy of Duty to Rescue Statutes," 160.

Charity at Home

Welfare states are, in fact, beginning to pass laws requiring their citizens to play Good Samaritan, and some countries with a Catholic substratum to their legal codes already impose more strenuous requirements than are found in most countries whose legal system goes back to English common law. But there is a difference. In Christian theology, helping other people is a duty we owe to God, not to the state. Confronted with a human being in distress, the Christian—whatever the law may state—is obliged to do what he can, when he can, so long as he is not, by his interference, breaching other equally serious principles, such as his prior obligation to his family and to others who may depend upon him for support and protection.

In cases of mere charitable assistance, the individual, Christian or not, has to recognize (with Augustine) that his resources are limited and that his existing obligations take precedence. We may not starve our family to feed a stranger, and we may not always be justified in doing good to the wrong people. In his discussion of *caritas,* St. Thomas makes it clear that charity is owed first to those who are closest to God and second to those who are closest to us by nature. He even goes so far as to say that we are bound to love those connected to us more than we love those who are better, and, in the next article, he proves that family connections trump other friendships, because they "pertain to substance."[18]

If we give up the notion that all human beings are equivalent individuals whose transcendent identity is found in the state, we must, as Christians, Jews, or pagans, recognize that our duties to others are severely circumscribed both by our means and by our rooted obligations. If a Christian is tempted into practicing heroic charity, he must, above all, not be misled into doing evil that good may come of it—that is, breaking a good law in order to prevent another good law from being violated.

A Christian may, for example, think seditious or pornographic materials are dangerous both to the community and to those who possess them. He is not, however, obliged to break into a neighbor's house in order to seize the offending documents, or even justified in doing so. Similarly, we are not justified in telling truths for the sole purpose of

18. St. Thomas Aquinas, *Summa Theologiae,* 2.2, 26.7.

injuring another man's reputation or in stealing his car to prevent him from carrying out an adulterous assignation.

We have seen how an Athenian had to justify herself for informing on an adulterer, but what if the sin is a more serious crime? One of the differences, it is said, between Europe and the United States is the American willingness to collaborate with the police. But at what point does good citizenship degenerate into mere meddling? In combating the use of drugs, state and federal agencies rely heavily upon informants and frequently issue appeals to the general public for information. Schoolchildren are even asked to denounce their parents, "for their own good," if they suspect them of illegal drug use.

Suppose a repairman notices a suspicious plant in a customer's home. All too frequently, he will call the police, sometimes expecting a reward. When this happened in 1994 in Belvidere, Illinois, drug-enforcement officers arrived at the home of a forty-nine-year-old widow, kicked her door in, maced her dogs, and ransacked the place only to discover a plastic bamboo plant. The repairman's employers issued a statement saying they were sorry the officers overreacted. But they would have done better to discharge the busybody repairman, who, as it turned out, had been criticized by the customer for failing to fix the air-conditioning properly.[19]

Similar tips have led to arrests of innocent persons and even to shootings. But, even supposing the information to be accurate, does a visitor have the right or duty to spy upon strangers and use his information to harm them? When it is merely a case of administrative and regulatory law—regarding such things as pet licenses, car registration, leaf-burning, Sabbath-breaking, and substance abuse—that has been violated, the sane person's answer should be, "It's none of my business," and I am not sure that I would turn in a more serious but nonviolent offender who posed no danger to the community. Rapists, armed robbers, and murderers would fall into a different category, although one might think twice before informing against a man who had killed in self-defense or justifiable anger.

When in doubt, which is probably most of the time, we should refrain from minding other people's business, especially since the consequences of such *polypragmosyne* can rarely be foreseen, either in personal life or

19. *Rockford Register Star,* November 21, 1994.

in international affairs. All too many campaigns to end Third World poverty have resulted in more harm than good, and most of the wars, police actions, and armed interventions of this century, ostensibly conducted with the highest motives—"keeping the world safe for democracy" or "protecting human rights"—have been hard to justify in the event. If democracy American-style is so precious, American leaders might work to improve the domestic article before presuming to export it, at bayonet-point, to Africa, the Caribbean, and the Balkans.

If every person did a good job of taking care of his own business, if families and neighborhoods did the same, and if governments devoted less energy to other nations and more to their own, then there might not be much need for Good Samaritanism, apart from emergencies. Since it is precisely the overactive Good Samaritan that is responsible for so much of the world's miseries, whether he is the puritan snooping into his neighbor's affairs or the puritanical government that bombs civilians in order to punish a despot, the relevant rule remains the Golden Rule: Mind your own business, or someone else might decide to mind yours. As Hank Williams put it: "If you mind your business, then you won't be mindin' mine."

Some Christian busybodies have apparently not read their own scriptures. The apostles, time after time, enjoined loyalty and obedience from wives to husbands, children to parents, slaves to masters, subjects to empire. John the Baptist was content with telling the Jews to share their food and clothing with the destitute, the tax collectors to collect no more than was due, and the soldiers not to extort money. Similarly, Jesus told a rich young man that to gain eternal life he had only to honor his father and mother and obey the commandments. It was only when pressed that He added, "If thou wilt be perfect, go and sell that thou hast, and give to the poor, and thou shalt have treasure in heaven: and come and follow me" (Matt. 19:21). He did not say that the Roman state had a right to confiscate the young man's wealth in order to alleviate famine in Gaul.

The rich, Jesus concluded—and among the rich He might have included over half the population of the United States today—have as much chance of entering the Kingdom of Heaven as a camel has of going through the eye of a needle. The heroic task of giving their goods away to the poor was apparently too much even for the disciples, who wondered, "Who then can be saved?" The obvious answer is, in human terms, no one, because "with men this is impossible; but with God all things are possible" (Matt. 19:24–26).

Even the Son of God distinguished between the ordinary goodness of day-to-day moral life and the supererogatory works that characterize a saint. Throughout most of the two Christian millennia, theologians and philosophers continued to make these distinctions, and Christian princes, with the blessings of their Church, carried out crusades against pagans and heretics and waged wars against even Christian enemies. Only in recent centuries has Christianity been identified as the philosophy of timidity and nonjudgmental benevolence that Nietzsche quite properly derided.

The Moral Duel: Voltaire versus Johnson

Without going deeply into intellectual history, one can see that the universal benevolence of contemporary Christianity derives not from the Bible directly but from the attempts of Enlightenment philosophers to purify scripture of its more "barbaric" elements and to universalize its teachings. To cite only one example, the deist Thomas Jefferson prepared his own edition of the Bible, which was expurgated of all Jewish particularities and theological interpretations. As he explained in a letter to John Adams, Jesus' purpose had been the reformation of the "wretched depravity" of peculiar duties, and it was Jefferson's intention, "in extracting the pure principles which he taught," to "strip off the artificial vestments in which they have been muffled by priests, who have travestied them into various forms."[20] In one way or another, the moral doctrines of Voltaire, Kant, and the New England transcendentalists all derive directly or indirectly from the sort of bowdlerization that Jefferson undertook. It was during the same period—the eighteenth century—that Stoic conceptions of universal brotherhood, international law, and world government reemerged.

In its earliest phase, deism had been an optimistic philosophy that sought to justify the moral order of the universe with systematic methods that paralleled those of Newtonian science. Leibniz's *Theodicy* was an elegant demonstration that the world was only as evil as it had to be,

20. Thomas Jefferson to John Adams, October 12, 1813.

and Pope's *Essay on Man* gave a convincing literary shape to the argument. Theologians still grappled with the problem of evil, but most deists, including Voltaire—the most prominent deist of all—thought the problem had been explained.

François Marie Arouet had every reason to be complacent. Brought up in a comfortable middle-class family, he went to the best school in Paris, where he fell in with a circle of young aristocrats who were to befriend him throughout his life. Well-read but far from erudite, Voltaire (as he renamed himself) climbed to the highest pinnacle of French literary and intellectual life, although few of the productions on which his fame rested—his poems and tragedies—can be read today without impatience. Wildly successful and honored throughout Europe, Voltaire remained unsatisfied. His irreverence brought him into frequent collision with censors, and more than once he had to flee Paris to avoid imprisonment. Possessed of a forgiving conscience, he was also quarrelsome and did not shrink from libeling friends and benefactors, once he felt himself provoked. He could almost in the same instant deny his authorship of a libelous pamphlet and give instructions for its distribution. As Voltaire grew older and more embittered by the misfortunes he had brought on himself, he began to doubt the wisdom of providence and the justice of the universe. Finally, in 1755, the Lisbon earthquake gave the spoiled sophist the occasion he needed.

The earthquake struck Lisbon on All Souls' Day and, while leveling large parts of the city, had killed tens of thousands of people. Voltaire devoted two major works to explaining the disaster's significance: a philosophic poem and the short novel *Candide,* written to refute the cliché that this is "the best of all possible worlds." His response to the earthquake was only the beginning of a new phase in his career. In the years to come, Voltaire became a champion of lost causes and a spokesman for what we would now call international human rights.

Although the life of Voltaire represents the high-water mark of the Age of Reason, the same period was also dominated by the literature of sensibility (for example, Henry Mackenzie's *The Man of Feeling*), in which hypersensitive heroes and heroines are constantly meeting beggars and victims of oppression with whom they immediately sympathize and endeavor to assist, usually to the accompaniment of copious tears.[21]

21. See Janet Todd, *Sensibility: An Introduction.*

This cultivation of sensibility, even for charitable purposes, had a more unpleasant side—namely, a fondness for the grotesque and an attraction to terror. Gloomy desolation, natural disasters, and monstrous acts of gratuitous evil helped to form the taste of the readers of the moralist Richardson, the skeptical Voltaire, and the incomparable Sade. The pornography of suffering, so prevalent in modern journalism, has its origins in such eighteenth-century writers. The moral consequence was a profound shift from an ethics based on duty to one based on feelings and noble motives.

> [E]thical theory, in its search for the true inwardness of the good life, dropped out the indispensable element of obligation, the moral judgment... it came to put all its trust in feelings, assuming that human nature is one and whole and good.... [T]he man of feeling surely had a noble ancestry, a noble upbringing, and like Shelley, he was sure that he acted always from the highest motives. And yet, as he abandoned himself to what he thought was his complete humanity... he became susceptible to all those spiritual diseases which come under the category of *mal du siècle*, and that is how he came to crave and enjoy the morbid.[22]

This strange mixture of skeptical rationalism and uncritical philanthropy has characterized the European intellectual class since the end of the eighteenth century. In the case of Voltaire, the impact of his conversion to humanitarian sensibility was immediate. It is not too much to describe his "Poem on the Disaster of Lisbon" as the symbolic kickoff of international humanitarianism. One of Voltaire's sympathetic biographers singles out the philosophe's response to the earthquake as one "derived from a simple, humane impulse of pity. His poem found a response in both the minds and hearts of his generation.... In short, men were stirred not so much by the disaster itself as by the event seen through the sensibility of a great man."[23]

According to his admirers, this natural disaster awakened the philosopher from his dogmatic optimism and turned him from a world-weary cynic into a champion of social justice. But there is an odd resemblance among most of Voltaire's causes: In nearly every case, the victims had been oppressed by the Catholic Church, and it is difficult to tell whether it is his humanity speaking when Voltaire defends a

---

22. Louis I. Bredvold, *The Natural History of Sensibility,* 100–101.
23. Theodore Besterman, *Voltaire,* 369.

Huguenot family accused of murdering their son on the grounds that he was converting to Catholicism, or only his hatred of priests. Throughout *Candide,* priests and monks are treated as the source of evil. Dr. Pangloss, for example, contracts syphilis from a maid who got it from a Franciscan friar, although the more remote source was a Jesuit who got it in direct line from a member of Columbus's crew—an early example of the anti-Catholic/anti-European version of modern history that is now standard.

In Voltaire's first written response to the Lisbon earthquake—a letter to Tronchin the banker on November 24, 1755—his "simple, humane impulse of pity" is overshadowed by his cynical wit and anticlerical fanaticism: "One would be rather embarrassed to figure out how the laws of motion bring about such terrifying disasters in the best of all possible worlds, a hundred thousand ants, our neighbors, wiped out all at once in the anthill." It is not pity that reduces suffering men and women to ants in a hill. With the advantage of perspective, the philosopher can reduce suffering humanity to insects—or worse, to ammunition in his war against the Church. Voltaire was consoled with the reflection that "at least the reverend fathers, the inquisitors, will have been wiped out like the others. That ought to teach men not to persecute men."

Since Voltaire regarded himself as a victim of clerical censorship, it was no small personal satisfaction to imagine the suffering and death of his enemies. Voltaire was, in fact, the very model of the modern sentimentalist. A chronic liar who flattered the very people he was libeling, faithless in love and friendship, he forfeited the esteem of Frederick the Great when he speculated on the devalued Saxon currency after learning that Frederick—who had forbidden speculation—was going to redeem it. Proclaiming the loftiest standards of human justice and defying the Creator himself, Voltaire would cheat a benefactor out of the price of a load of firewood. Even Rousseau was appalled by the hypocrisy Voltaire displayed over the earthquake: Here was a man of inordinate wealth and fame complaining against the unfairness of the universe!

When the English Christian Samuel Johnson first heard of the earthquake, he doubted the reported magnitude (in contrast with Voltaire, who almost exulted in the "hundred thousand" dead).[24] In Johnson's

---

24. James Boswell, *Boswell's Life of Johnson,* 3:136. Mrs. Piozzi recalled: "I once asked him if he believed the story of the destruction of Lisbon by an earthquake

novel *History of Rasselas, Prince of Abyssinia,* the hero responds to his sister's tirade against natural disasters by censuring all such exaggerations:

> "Examples of national calamities, and scenes of extensive misery, which are found in books rather than in the world, and which, as they are horrid, are ordained to be rare. Let us not imagine evils which we do not feel, nor injure life by misrepresentations. I cannot bear that querulous eloquence which threatens every city with a siege like that of Jerusalem.... On necessary and inevitable evils, which overwhelm kingdoms at once, all disputation is vain: when they happen they must be endured."

Prince Rasselas goes on to explain that despite the horrors of civil war and revolution, the work of the world must go on. By one of history's more appealing ironies, Dr. Johnson was writing *Rasselas* at the same time Voltaire was finishing *Candide*. What a study in contrast! Unlike the mocking deist, Johnson was seriously troubled by the problem of evil. Reviewing an English philosopher who had recapitulated Pope's and Leibniz's argument for the best of all possible worlds, Johnson insisted upon the difficulty of the mystery. Suffering and pain are real, Johnson declared, and he would not tolerate any attempt to trivialize them. Although Dr. Johnson has generally been regarded as a pessimist, his gloomy view of life was partly the result of his own early poverty and his constant ill health. He had seen life from the bottom up and watched his friend Richard Savage die of want and neglect. In place of the early Voltaire's glib optimism or his later facile pessimism, Johnson offered the mystery of a universe that was filled with joy as well as suffering. Instead of canting upon the theme of social injustice, Johnson advised patience and fortitude. He was no Stoic, because the Stoic philosophy tended to minimize the reality of pain.[25]

As much as anyone of his time, Johnson was a man of virtuous character and performed acts of kindness even when his philosophy could

---

when it first happened: 'Oh! not for six months,' said he, 'at least. I *did* think that story too dreadful to be credited, and can hardly yet persuade myself that it was true to the full extent we all of us have heard.'" (Hesther Lynch Piozzi, *Anecdotes of the Late Samuel Johnson, LL.D.,* 92). Johnson probably authored a tract on the Lisbon earthquake. Later in life, hearing of a quake in Staffordshire, he predicted, "It will be much exaggerated" (Boswell, *Life of Johnson,* 3:130, cf. 1:309).

25. See, for example, "Of a Free Enquiry into the Nature and Origin of Evil," Johnson's review of Soame Jennings's defense of the best of all possible worlds.

not justify them. Almost a liberal in his economic philosophy, he thought a rich man might do more good by buying luxuries whose manufacture gave employment to thousands of families than by distributing charity, but he disposed of a large part of his own income in giving food and shelter—in his own home—to a set of quarrelsome dependents whom he did not turn out "because if I did not assist them, no one else would."

Over and over throughout his life, Johnson evinced a concern for the poor. A high Tory in politics—at times a Jacobite—he suspected the Whigs of opposing the crown for selfish reasons. Intellectually, at least, he was an ancestor of the nineteenth-century Tories who railed against the exploitation of the lower classes. Johnson thought the lives of ordinary, decent people were worth "a judicious and faithful narrative," because "there is scant any possibility of good or ill, but is common in human life." A reader contemplating Johnson's life might learn the opposite lesson from what is taught by the biographies of Voltaire and Marx. Kind to the poor, faithful to his wife, loyal to his king and country, constant in the exercise of his religion, Samuel Johnson saw his duty neither as a bloodless universal law nor as a bloody call to arms to lift mankind above the merely human.

To the growing demand that we should love all mankind, Johnson answered that "to love all equally is impossible" unless we are to suppress our own natures. When his friend Boswell spoke obsessively of the Corsican struggle for independence, Johnson brought him up sharply: "Mind your own affairs and leave the Corsicans to theirs."

It was Johnson's nature, as well as his duty, to be kind to fellow-suffering members of the human race, and courted as he was in later life by the great, he was content to pass much of his time in the company of old and humble friends, whom he never failed to assist when they fell on hard times.

> He enjoyed and accepted the blessings which his fame had brought him. . . . But poverty, illness and misfortune were to him bedrock facts of life. . . . His goodness of heart needs no further demonstration than the bare facts of his life provide. The sheer number of the people he helped and the variety of ways in which he helped them easily entitle him to be called one of the most benevolent men who ever lived. From the young men for whom he tried to get jobs, and the needy writers for whom he wrote prefaces and dedications to the fever-ridden prostitute he found slumped in a doorway in the early hours of one morning, and slung

across his shoulders, and carried home and nursed back to health, Johnson gave his resources of time, of energy, of money, with no sparing
hand.[26]

John Wain, who made this sketch of Dr. Johnson's benevolence, concluded that his moral and political views should be employed as "a survival kit" for post-civilized man. He might have added that Johnson is
the ideal antidote to the poison of sentimental universalism that had
already infected Johnson's own world and swept across our own as the
moral equivalent of the Black Death.

26. John Wain, *Samuel Johnson: A Biography*, 267. Mrs. Thrale commented: "The
poor...he really loves them as nobody else does" (Piozzi, *Anecdotes*, 42).

CITIZENS OF THE WORLD

2

A steady patriot of the world alone,
The friend of every country but his own.

—George Canning, *New Morality*

People in the modern world lead a double life. As we go about our business from day to day, we devote most of our energies to the same tasks that absorbed our ancestors' attention. We work to provide the necessities of life; we eat and sleep, beget children, rear families; we visit friends, go fishing, and in time grow old; we conceive high hopes, flourish or go bankrupt—all within the narrow round of day-to-day life and in the confined circle of small towns, local neighborhoods, and restricted social groups. Our highest hopes are to outdo our classmates or win the admiration of a few thousand colleagues. No one, after all, can be entirely at home in a city the size of New York or even in Manhattan. In large cities, we inevitably search out the little corner that may come to seem as familiar as the village in which our ancestors lived and died.

But if we are still a tribal and domestic race in everyday life, we are all made aware of the other, larger universe that includes the entire human race. On Sunday, if we go to church, we are told that it is our duty to protest the nation's policies on abortion, to assist the victims of famine and civil war in Rwanda and Kosovo, or to shelter illegal immigrants from Central America within the sanctuary. If, on the other hand, we stay home to watch the weekly round of television interviews that serve as liturgies for the political church, we are urged to help solve the global environmental crisis or to support free-trade policies that benefit Chinese and Mexican workers, possibly at the expense of our next-door neighbors.

While international capitalists are convinced that the nation-state is dead, international socialists stigmatize every manifestation of patriotism, ethnic pride, and local attachment as racism. Many Christians, echoing the socialist rhetoric, deplore any form of provincial or patriotic loyalty that stops short of the Kingdom of God. When a philosopher (Alasdair MacIntyre) wonders, in the title of an essay, "Is patriotism a virtue?" the answer from all sides is a resounding no.

Premodern Particularism

It was not always so. Most peoples that are known to historians and anthropologists have regarded local and ethnic pride as a necessary virtue, and the absence of such attachments was taken as a sign of treason and irresponsibility. Even so-called primitive peoples, who lived in tribes that had developed no sense of nationality, much less a state, drew sharp distinctions between an "us," made up of family members, tribesmen, and fellow villagers, and a "them" made up of foreigners, strangers, or even just people from a nearby village. E. E. Evans-Pritchard's classic studies of the Nuer portray one case out of thousands; to his discomfiture, the British anthropologist slowly became aware that among such peoples there was no obligation to tell the truth to strangers.

The Nuer, who lived along the upper Nile, had no political authority beyond the tribal level, and if a member of one tribe robbed, killed, or harmed a member of another, the only recourse was war or mediation. Moral obligation, even on this basic level, did not extend beyond the tribe. This limited moral outlook was not a localized phenomenon found only in remote parts of the world. It persisted quite late in European peasant societies. Edward C. Banfield, after studying the moral basis of society in a southern Italian village, concluded: "The ideas of right and wrong which are the peasant's own ... relate mostly to the central theme of his existence: the family or procreation. Goodness and badness exist for him mainly in connection with two statuses, that of 'parent' and that of 'outsider-who-may-affect-the-family.'"[1] Crimes that did not affect the family were of little concern. Even neighbors and fellow villagers counted for little in such a scheme, although they counted for a great deal more than any foreigner. One villager complained that she had been swindled by a neighbor who sold her a defective sewing machine. This was not right, she argued: Her neighbor should have cheated some foreigner instead.

Village life in Calabria, as Banfield observed it, may be an extreme case for Europe, but not for most of the world for most of its history. The Cheyenne are not the only premodern people to call themselves "human" as a distinguishing characteristic, and foreign strangers could be killed with impunity in many tribal societies that viewed all social life as an extension of the family. Family and tribal loyalty has been the central fact of our moral life for as long as we have been human. As we have seen, even the highly civilized Athenians sharply distinguished between citizens and strangers. In international relations, the Athenians at the height of their power acted without restraint, condemning the people of Melos—who only wanted to preserve their independence and their traditional friendship with Sparta—to death (for adult males) and slavery (for women and children).

Thucydides appears to be critical of his city's severity, but such criticism had to be framed within a Greek moral and religious tradition, whose claims the sophisticated Athenians were prepared to defy. Otherwise, Greek morality had to be expressed as the responsibilities of kinship, friendship, and social class, all of which are summed up in the words spoken by Sarpedon in the *Iliad,* when he explains to his friend Glaucus that their high social position among the Lycians—a product of their noble birth and family traditions—requires them to set an example: "Glaucus, why have we received such high position and wealth, the seat of honor, and meats and cups of wine in Lycia, where everyone looks upon us as gods . . . ? Now we must stand, therefore, among the foremost Lycians, and abide the heat of battle" (Homer *Iliad* 12.310–28 ff.).

If the early Greeks had an international morality, it was bound up with the duties of hospitality *(xenia),* a personal relationship that cut

---

1. Edward C. Banfield, *The Moral Basis of a Backward Society,* 126.

across the usual boundaries of political and feudal obligation. Earlier in the *Iliad* (6.119–236), Glaucus encounters the Greek hero Diomedes, who asks him his lineage. When they realize that their grandfathers were guest-friends *(xenoi),* the two men agree to avoid each other in battle, since there are plenty of other Greeks and Trojans to kill. Even the incident that sparked the Trojan War involved a question of hospitality. The great sin of Paris in carrying Helen to Troy was not so much adultery as the violation of Menelaus's hospitality. The great god Zeus himself, as *Zeus Xenios,* had set the rules of hospitality and punished offenses against them.

In later Greek history, we meet with the strange institution of *proxenia,* in which a family of one city—for example, Athens—serves as host and informal ambassador for that of another, even in times of war. Such social mechanisms of hospitality were of vital importance in a world of independent towns and cities battling it out in a state of nature. But while the Greeks gradually arrived at a series of understandings and agreements that facilitated the conduct of affairs between cities, they were very slow in acknowledging obligations toward the non-Greeks they lumped together as *barbaroi.*

The Brotherhood of Man

Universalism was introduced by a Phoenician merchant named Zeno, who founded the philosophical school later known as Stoicism. Inspired by Alexander's dream of universal empire,[2] Zeno preached that "men should not live divided into different states and peoples, each under its own law, but in a world state, of which all men are to be citizens."

The Stoics developed such novel doctrines as the brotherhood of man, the equality of free men and slaves, and cosmopolitanism—that is, world citizenship. "Never say," wrote the ex-slave Epictetus, "when you answer the question what country do you belong to, that you are an Athenian or a Corinthian, but that you are a citizen of the world" (Arrian *Epicteti Dissertationes* 1.9). In their utopian moments, the Stoics advocated a community of shared property and wives, but even the founders of the sect insisted upon the fulfillment of primary obligations to family and country, and, in Roman hands, Stoicism became an unofficial doctrine

2. See Plutarch, *On the Fortunes of Alexander.*

of the empire—which claimed, after all, to be the world. The Stoic emperor, Marcus Antoninus, was more ambivalent. Dividing his nature into a social being and a rational being, he acknowledged that "in so far as he was Antoninus, his country was Rome, but as a man, his country was the world."

The idea of an international order or global state, which began to be popular during the Enlightenment and took on a sense of urgency in the twentieth century, is usually attributed to a desire for respite from the destruction and havoc wrought by European wars. The Duke of Sully, whose "Great Design" projected a federation of European states, lived through one of the most disastrous periods of French history—the civil war between Catholics and Protestants—and his and other schemes for a federal Europe were designed not to eliminate states but to reduce the horrors of war.

Certainly, in the period between the two world wars, the dread of war and a longing for peace made reasonable men hope for a more potent successor to the largely futile League of Nations. As World War II was breaking out in Europe, H. G. Wells concluded that the world could be saved only if a "new world order" were established on the basis of "the three ideas of socialism, law, and knowledge."[3] Wells's formula, though globalists might quibble over the precise words, is a reasonably accurate summation of the movement toward an enforceable international order, and its accuracy stems in part from the science-fiction writer's participation in the intellectual currents that were converging on the ideal of the global state.

The idea of an international law and an international legal order goes back to the Roman Empire. The world had seen empires before and has seen them since, but none of them could match the extent, the majesty, or the endurance of the Roman order, which began its march through the Italian peninsula before the sixth century B.C. and lasted in the West until the end of the fifth century A.D. (and in the East until less than fifty years before Columbus's discovery of America). Though the empire encouraged the use of two official languages (Latin and Greek) and permitted the use of differing cultural and legal traditions, Roman law, which was further codified and rationalized in the reigns of Theodosius and Justinian, was available to all citizens of the empire.

3. H. G. Wells, *The New World Order*, 111.

Odovacer deposed the last "little Augustus" in A.D. 476, but neither he nor his Ostrogothic successors (defeated by Justinian in the sixth century), nor even the Lombards, were able to retain control of Italy itself, much less the rest of the Western Empire. Political legitimacy, such as there was beyond the level of tribal and feudal allegiance, derived from the emperors in Constantinople until Christmas of 800, when Charlemagne was crowned emperor of the West. Charlemagne's often impotent successors—down to Emperor Francis I's resignation as Holy Roman emperor, under pressure from Napoleon—represented one aspect of universal order, and Roman law, which was revived in the later Middle Ages, became the basis for thinking about international law.

Even apart from the conversion of the Holy Roman Empire into Hapsburg Austria-Hungary, the Roman imperial dream was borrowed by Russian czars, French emperors, and Prussian kaisers, who adopted the language and ceremonies of their Roman and Holy Roman predecessors. The dream of international order, in other words, could also be made to serve the ends of a national state. The Duke of Sully might conceivably have called for a reinvigoration of the Holy Roman Empire, but that would have played into the hands of France's archrival, Austria.

The Universal Kingdom of God

The significance of Rome as eternal city and eternal idea was put to the test during the barbarian invasions. Augustine responded to the Visigoths' sack of Rome in 410 by writing *Civitas Dei* (the city—or rather, the commonwealth—of God). In the sixteenth book, Augustine pronounced that Rome, the commonwealth of man, was flawed from its inception because Romulus, the founder of the city, killed his brother Remus in a struggle for power (a decidedly Augustinian twist on the old story). But while Cain belonged to the commonwealth of man, the innocent Abel was a citizen of God's commonwealth, and the Christian Church, with its emphasis on love, was an earthly representation of the heavenly kingdom, where neither national borders nor wars of conquest had any real meaning.

Thus, although the universal empire remained a vibrant political dream, it had a serious competitor in the Catholic Church, which claimed universal jurisdiction over souls, direct political rule over much of Italy, and a limited political jurisdiction over the Catholic West. Although Catholic social theory has never been remotely Marxist, the Church's emphasis on love and brotherhood, especially when contrasted with capitalism, might easily be viewed by Wells as a socialist morality that aims at limiting and ameliorating man's natural competitiveness. In the early Church, Jesus' followers shared their possessions, and even in the highly competitive Christian societies of the eighteenth and nineteenth centuries, Christians were supposed to give alms to those who had failed to succeed.

Early Christian views on the place of nations were shaped by several influences. The Roman world, in which they grew up, was an international order within which (and outside of which) particular nations existed, sometimes as independent or quasi-independent states. The nation and quasi-state serving as a point of reference was the Jewish nation, part of which was ruled (under Roman supervision) by the Herods. Jewish aspirations for national independence were not sanctioned by Jesus, and they erupted into revolutionary violence, first under Nero—when they were decisively squelched by Roman general and soon-to-be emperor Vespasian and his son Titus, who sent many of the inhabitants of Judea into exile—and later under Hadrian. Christians viewed the Jewish disaster to some extent as a judgment on the Jews' repudiation of Christ. In reacting against Jewish nationalism, Christians put strong emphasis on the universal brotherhood of man.

They could not, however, break free from the teachings of the Jewish scriptures, which not only assigned a special role to one nation but seemed to view the world as divided, by divine decree, into separate peoples. Christians learned from the book of Genesis, for example, that although the descendants of Adam had spoken one language for many generations, the attempt to build the tower of Babel brought divine punishment:

> And they said, Go to, let us build a city, and a tower, whose top may reach to heaven; and let us make us a name, lest we be scattered abroad upon the face of the whole earth. . . . And the Lord said, Behold, the people is one, and they have all one language; and this they begin to do: and now nothing will be restrained from them, which they have imagined to do. Go to, let us go down, and there confound their language, that they may not understand one another's speech. (Gen. 11:4–7)

Henceforth, any project of constructing a global empire would be seen as a second rebellion against God. Although the punishment for Babel was canceled at Pentecost, when every man "out of every nation under heaven" heard the Galilean apostles "speak in his own language" (Acts 2:5–6), this was a spiritual and not a political unity. Augustine himself (in the preface to *Civitas Dei*) told his readers not to believe that the end of all earthly states was at hand but to put their hope in God.

A Christian's love for the universal Church was not inconsistent with his duty of obedience to a secular, even non-Christian, ruler (as Paul made clear in the famous thirteenth chapter of Romans). Although the pagan emperor Julian forbade Christians to serve in the army on the grounds that they could not shed blood, this was a slander. In fact, many Christians had faithfully served in the Roman army.[4]

In the Christian Middle Ages, Thomas Aquinas, following Aristotle, compared the power of the king with that of the father and took it for granted that kingdoms were part of the natural order ordained by God. Protestant churches were, for the most part, national institutions that enjoined obedience and respect for the nation and its rulers, and even the Catholic Church, which claimed universal jurisdiction, did not dispute the legitimacy of nations or nation-states. In the difficult years following the Italian kingdom's conquest of the Catholic Church's estates, when the Church forbade Catholics to take part in Italian politics, Pope Leo XIII declared (in his 1890 encyclical *Sapientiae christianae*) that a supernatural love for the Church and a natural affection for one's country were "twin affections sprung from the same everlasting principle."

There is hardly any need to speak of the great reformers who established national churches. Luther's strictures against disobedience and rebellion are well known, and the leaders of national churches in England, Scotland, and Sweden were hardly likely to deny the authority or significance of the nation-states to which they ministered and for whose rulers they regularly prayed. The Orthodox churches, which are both universal and national, have played an important part in the national

---

4. This is not to deny the fact that many Christians were opposed to even the lawful violence engaged in by the Roman army, as indicated by the story of St. Martin, the Pannonian soldier who abandoned a military career because of his faith.

liberation struggles of Greeks, Serbs, and Bulgars, and there is nothing in Orthodox social thought that would justify contempt for patriotic loyalty.

Although the Christian Church did not teach the abolition of nations or states, it did represent an international model of human cooperation. Before the Battle of Kosovo, the Orthodox Prince Lazar of Serbia was said to have chosen a heavenly kingdom, which spelled defeat and destruction for his people, but he was nonetheless revered as both a patriot and a saint. In the West, the idea gradually grew that, in abandoning Rome, the Emperor Constantine had donated his political authority to the pope, and although the Renaissance scholar Lorenzo Valla was able to debunk the documentary evidence for this "donation," the myth was, for many centuries, seen as reality. Christendom was a rich concept in the years before the Reformation: it meant a religion universally accepted in the West, the common customs of the European peoples, and an ecclesiastical authority that could punish even kings and emperors who broke its rules.

Universal Kingdom of Man

During the Renaissance, Christian universalism began to be converted by nonbelievers (such as Pico della Mirandola and Montaigne) into a secularized theory of human dignity and universal obligation that trivialized more local attachments. But, quite apart from the re-invention of Christian moral thought that took place in the eighteenth century, "enlightened" philosophers—even those who devoted themselves to serving the interests of France or Germany—were bound to swear allegiance to an international order based on universally recognized principles.

One major goal of the Enlightenment was to achieve a Newtonian revolution in morality and politics—that is, to discover the universal laws of morality and society. While moral and political philosophers were following up Descartes' hints about an abstract theory of morality, Leibniz called for a universal language of philosophical discourse that could express thoughts about anything with the abstraction and lack of ambiguity of mathematical symbols.[5] In his 1677 essay "Towards

---

5. For connections between Descartes, Leibniz, and Newton, see Stephen Toulmin, *Cosmopolis: The Hidden Agenda of Modernity*, 98–117.

a Universal Characteristic," Leibniz made it clear that his philosophical Esperanto was to be used to solve everyday problems. Just as the microscope and telescope increased the power of vision, the reduction of moral questions to a numerical basis would bring greater clarity.

To enforce such universal, rational, and objective principles, some form of international order would be required. In other words, if all true laws and moral principles are universal, then only world government can have the power to enforce them. In the beginning, however, the various projects for world peace did not aim at the elimination of nation-states, but only at establishing a federal union of nations.

The Abbé de Saint-Pierre, author of "Projet de Paix Perpetuelle," was a typical—perhaps stereotypical—Enlightenment intellectual with an unbounded faith in the goodness of human nature and the blessings of progress. His concern for *bienfaisance* (benevolence) led him to propose graduated taxation to benefit the French lower classes and, ultimately, to outline a plan for a world confederation that would eliminate war. Rousseau, who commented on and popularized Saint-Pierre's essay, concluded that it might take a revolution to bring about a European federation to end war.

Unfortunately, the revolution, when it came to France shortly after Rousseau's death, initiated one of the bloodiest periods of European history. The French Revolution was the seminal event of modern times, the period when Enlightenment theories of liberty and equality, natural rights and the social contract assumed a concrete form. All subsequent history in the West has been a series of attempts to extend (or resist) the principles of the revolution, and since World War II there has been no serious opposition to the ideology of 1789.[6]

The leaders of revolutionary France proclaimed their devotion to the nation. (The Declaration of the Rights of Man states, "The principle of all sovereignty resides essentially in the nation. No body nor individual may exercise any authority which does not proceed directly from the nation.") Yet they also declared their support for other revolutionary movements that would rise up to throw off the chains of monarchy, feudalism, and Christianity. In the Proclamation of the Convention to the Nations (December 1792), they declared: "We have conquered our

---

6. For the universal acceptance of the revolution in France, even by the French right, see François Furet, *Penser la Révolution française*, 18 ff.

liberty and we shall maintain it. We offer to bring this inestimable blessing to you, for it has always been rightly ours, and only by a crime have
our oppressors robbed us of it. We have driven out your tyrants. Show
yourselves free men and we will protect you from their vengeance, their
machinations, or their return." In other words, the universal rights of
men were seen to justify the French conquest of Europe.

In the nineteenth century, the revolutionary ideal separated, temporarily, into nationalist and internationalist channels, the one leading
to the formation of centralized nation-states in France, Germany, Italy,
and the United States, and the other inspiring the Marxists' project of
establishing economic justice in an international order.

Marx and Engels viewed the nation-state (along with the family and
private property) as an institution that had been created by patriarchal
men solely for the purpose of oppressing women and the poor. In the
Communist Manifesto, they wrote the blueprint, not merely for communist revolutions, but for an international order that would ultimately
replace communist nation-states. Arguing that the working classes had
no nation, they concluded that the proletariat would finish the job begun
by the bourgeoisie: the elimination of nations. This would end not merely
the exploitation of the poor by the rich but even the exploitation of
poor nations by rich nations. It would also mean an end to the whole
system of nation-states.

Marxist theory, however, has done little to alleviate ethnic and national
hostilities. Marx's own ethnic prejudices were confirmed, rather than
weakened by, his progressive view of history. He viewed Highland Scots,
Africans, and Jews as primitive and retrograde peoples and as so many
obstacles to progress that had to be eliminated. In their correspondence,
Marx and Engels frequently used the English word *nigger* to refer to
people (including Jews) with dark skin. Marx, who supported the North
in the American Civil War but who initially opposed the emancipation
of American slaves, frequently described his son-in-law and disciple,
Paul Lafargue, who was perhaps one-eighth African, as "the negrillo"
and "the gorilla," observing that his daughter had contributed to solving the race problem "by marrying a nigger."[7]

Though Marx was himself ethnically Jewish (he was the grandson of
a rabbi), and Jews predominated in the leadership of most communist

7. Nathaniel Weyl, *Karl Marx: Racist,* 74–77.

parties, Marx and Engels were openly anti-Semitic in their writings. (The Soviet Union under Stalin eliminated most of the Jewish leaders of the party during the purge trials.) Marx's repulsive bigotry, combined with the record of communist states in persecuting ethnic groups (Ukrainians, Lithuanians, Mongols, Tibetans, and others) and in engaging in aggressive wars even with other communist states (for example, Vietnam and Cambodia), does little to strengthen the Marxist case for an international order.

On the question of political violence, most socialists and leftists part company with revolutionary Marxists and have been content to advocate a gradual movement within states toward a more perfect system of social justice. There is, however, a common thread (visible already in Saint-Pierre) that runs through liberal (and socialist) nationalism and internationalism: the perceived duty to provide "social justice," either to the citizens of a nation or to citizens of the world. The brotherhood of man promised to Christians living in the kingdom of God is now to be delivered by force to the denizens of the commonwealth of man. But even though the genie of human brotherhood cannot be locked up in the bottle of a nation-state, the effect of Marxism to date has been the growth of socialism within nation-states and an enhancement, rather than an elimination, of the nationalist spirit.

Nationalism

Love of country is a natural outgrowth of the love of kith and kin, but the modern concept of nationalism is largely the creation of the French Revolution, which implemented Rousseau's theory of the general will and continued the process of centralization inaugurated by the Bourbon monarchy. According to French nationalists, the will of the nation, defined as an historic community of blood and tongue, had to find expression in a common and unified state. Hence, the Italian nationalist Mazzini, whose political lineage goes back to the revolution, spoke always of the twin principles of unity and nationality.

Most nineteenth-century liberals were sympathetic to patriotic and nationalist movements of liberation and unification, and even John Stuart Mill, an arch-individualist, embraced the notion that every discrete nation should have its own state. However, other liberals, such as Jacob Burckhardt, condemned the nationalist state as spiritually and culturally mortifying. A divided Germany had produced Haydn and Goethe, but the nation-state, in its desire for power, would regard such dismemberment with shame, and Burckhardt noted "the hopelessness of any attempt at decentralization, of any voluntary restriction of power in favor of local and civilized life."[8]

In England, Lord Acton condemned nationalism as the principle most inimical to human liberty (which, liberals claimed, by definition was the great object of all their policies). Acton, who was descended on his mother's side from the aristocratic Dalbergs of Bavaria, was an admirer of the Holy Roman Empire, and he argued that the mixture of competing nations under one crown served to prevent the tyranny of the centralized state. He viewed a federal system, such as that of Switzerland or of the early American republic, as the best solution to ethnic conflict. States built on the national idea were, he felt, too confining to inspire the generous, cosmopolitan civilization that had been characteristic of European man.

If the nationalist point of view narrows the human outlook, it also implies (though it does not always express) a willingness to divide the human race into the categories of "us" and "them," and to define *them* as an enemy to be eliminated or subjugated. Nationalism, as George Orwell pointed out, stems from, first, "the habit of assuming that human beings can be classified like insects and that whole blocks of millions or tens of millions of people can be confidently labelled 'good' or 'bad'" and second, from "the habit of identifying oneself with a single nation or other unit, placing it beyond good and evil and recognizing no other duty than that of advancing its interests." Orwell distinguished this nationalist habit of mind from patriotism, which he defined as "devotion to a particular place and a particular way of life, which one believes to be the best in the world but has no wish to force on other people."[9]

Although nationalist ideology was born in the French Revolution, which was the "church militant" of the Enlightenment, the aspirations of European peoples to free themselves from the Ottoman, Hapsburg, and Russian empires was not based on theory. Poland had once been a great nation, and its partition among the great powers was a cynical expression of the imperialist urge to eliminate historic nations. The back-

8. Jakob Burckhardt, *Reflections on History,* 139.
9. George Orwell, "Notes on Nationalism."

lash was inevitable, and not just among Poles: Czechs, Serbs, Croats, Greeks, and others all had a legitimate desire to live within a state that allowed their language, culture, and religion to flourish.

Nationalism, although it often has its origin in so innocent a source as the desire for national liberation, can take ugly turns, developing into a theory of the racial uniqueness and superiority of one nation over all its rivals. All peoples tend to hate the conqueror and to look down upon the conquered, but such natural feelings do not always result in implacable resentment or bitter contempt. Ancient Greek cities banded together to oppose the invading Persians, who sacked cities, destroyed temples, and killed noncombatants, and yet Aeschylus, who fought them at Marathon and Salamis, portrays them sympathetically in *The Persians*, and later writers, such as Herodotus and Xenophon, were perfectly frank about the courage and virtues (as well as the vices) of the Greeks' greatest enemy. Serbs, though brutally oppressed by the Ottoman Turks and their Slavic and Albanian allies, were respectful toward the sultan and freely acknowledged, in their folk poems, the heroism of their enemies. "Alas," cried the Serbian hero Prince Marko after killing an Albanian brigand, "for I have killed the better man." Ivo Andrić's *The Bridge on the Drina*, written when the memory of Islamic oppression was still fresh, is nothing if not a sympathetic and respectful depiction of Muslim life in Bosnia.

Such respectful sentiments would be unthinkable coming from the mouth of a radical nationalist, who, at his worst, depicts the imperial Russians or Austrians as savages and the neighboring Slovaks or Serbs as canaille.[10] While soldiers in the two world wars were sometimes willing to look upon each other as human beings, their governments, which enlisted distinguished writers in their propaganda campaigns, were not. The Germans, who were portrayed as savage monsters by the Allies, ridiculed the effeminacy of Britain and France and portrayed Jews and Slavs as subhuman. The United States, in ridiculing the Japanese, resorted to the most sordid racial stereotyping.

Although such propaganda is often associated with right-wing nationalist movements, it is equally common among leftists and progressives, who are willing to demonize any opponent as racist or retrograde. This technique of propagandistic stereotyping, on the part of the American

10. See Thomas Fleming, *Montenegro: The Divided Land*, 126–29.

government, goes back to the Civil War, when a progressive government and its newspapers depicted Southerners as cruel and inhuman slave drivers who deserved no sympathy. Such propaganda can be used to justify any actions undertaken by a superior government, whether it is Sherman's march to the sea, the bombing of undefended cities, or the elimination of the Jews. It is the hallmark of the nationalist to justify every crime committed by his own people and to impute no honorable motives or actions to rival nations.

Patriotism

In general usage, *patriotism* signifies a person's willingness to take risks and make sacrifices for the sake of his country and his fellow citizens. Although his devotion may spring from an instinctive "devotion to a particular place and a particular way of life," the patriot does not merely feel loyal to a spot of ground, he is willing to defend it with his life, even if he feels no particular hostility toward the enemy who wishes to take it from him.

Patriotism, as Acton understood, can transcend the blood-and-soil passions of primitive man and become an ethical force that calls for self-sacrifice.

> Our connection with the race is merely natural or physical, whilst our duties to the political nation are ethical. One is a community of affections and instincts infinitely important and powerful in savage life, but pertaining more to the animal than to the civilized man; the other is an authority governing by laws, imposing obligations, and giving a moral sanction and character to the natural relations of society. Patriotism . . . is an extension of the family affections, as the tribe is an extension of the family. But in its real political character, patriotism consists in the development of the instinct of self-preservation into a moral duty which may involve self-sacrifice.[11]

Acton is not alone in regarding the highest form of patriotism as ethical rather than instinctive,[12] but such a conception is liable to misconstruction.

11. John E. D. Acton, "Nationality," 1:427–30.
12. Roger Scruton writes that *patriotism* should be "construed as the individual's sense of identity with a social order" (*The Meaning of Conservatism*, 25).

The state, as St. Thomas understood, exists to make virtue possible and not to impose virtue upon the people,[13] and his refusal to attribute moral purpose to the state is similar to the distinction made between individual charity and a government-imposed system of welfare. When a man is called "patriotic," the implication is that he has made a moral choice to risk his own self-interest for the good of his country, which is viewed as something that includes but can transcend blood and soil, as a constitutional order grounded in morality and law. And yet, as a moral individual, he can have little influence over life-and-death decisions made by the semidivine state, which may go beyond inspiring or requesting such loyalty: it may command it, backing its command with all the resources of the modern state. At that point, patriotism is so far removed from instinctive loyalty as to be almost indistinguishable from nationalism. It is not always easy to distinguish a war veteran who flies his country's flag to honor its heroes and its resistance to aggression from the chauvinist who waves the flag as a sign of the superiority and invincibility of the nation; indeed, the patriot and the chauvinist may often be the same person.

Rodoljublje

We can, however, draw a valid distinction between patriotism as an ethical and political virtue, originating in natural attachments but formed and directed by the state, and nationalism as a statist ideology that opposes and excludes other loyalties, whether those loyalties are to an international religion and civilization or to the province or region of one's birth. A patriotic German from Hanover might have no quarrel with Catholics in Bavaria, but a German nationalist will more typically dislike a religion that divides some Germans from others and unites them to people of other nations and races. Such distinctions are often, however, more theoretical than real. If patriotism can merge into nationalism, then perhaps we are dealing with a distinction without a difference, a question of gradation and degrees. At the opposite extremes of sentimental loyalty and rabid chauvinism, however, patriotism and nationalism seem poles apart. The problem lies in the concept of patri-

13. See also Thomas Molnar, *Politics and the State.*

otism itself, which in everyday speech seems to designate a transitional phase that may pass into nationalism but that derives from something more primitive, which has no name.

Patriotism is not simply an ethical devotion to a constitution or legal order, and even where such higher sentiments come into existence, they may not entirely escape the more primitive passions of love and loyalty. What Acton failed to understand, with his mind lodged securely in eighteenth-century rationalism, was that the stages of human social development can never be transcended; they can only be incorporated into more complex communities. The family was not eliminated for being incorporated in a tribe, and a tribal or provincial identity can be destroyed only at grave peril to the moral health of the people.

Jacobin nationalists, in attempting to build an abstract and artificially unified French nation, made war on all other, more real loyalties: They destroyed the Church, waged a war of genocide against Catholics in the Vendée, and did their best to obliterate the regional civilizations of Provence and Brittany that were responsible for the vitality of French culture. The predictable results of such efforts, in France, Britain, and the United States (to name only three examples), is a mass culture in which the only "national identity" is that created by commercial entertainment and state propaganda. Sheltered by the stultifying effects of communist misrule, the nations of Eastern Europe were able to preserve some of their cultural traditions; exposed to the virulent forces of free trade and global commercialism, they may sink into the morass of Americanism.

A deeply learned aristocrat, as at home in Italy or Germany as he was in England, Lord Acton did not grasp the fundamental and enduring importance of the instinctive attachment to family and tribe that has no name in English or in most European languages. However, Edmund Burke (a strong influence on Acton), in opposing the French Revolution, referred to the "little platoons" that command our loyalties. And we sometimes speak in English of "local patriotism" when referring to the attachment to neighborhood celebrated in G. K. Chesterton's *The Napoleon of Notting Hill*, but we are fumbling to express a concept for which we have no word. Serbian does have such a word: *rodoljublje*, which means love of kith and kin, or love of the stock *(rod)*. If we were to coin a technical term to describe such an attachment, it might be something like *genophilia*. This instinctive loyalty, which lies at the root of patriotism, is something quite different from—indeed, opposed to—nationalism.

To understand such loyalty requires a more anthropological approach. The historian of Sicily, Edward A. Freeman, following the work on kinship done by Sir Henry Sumner Maine, clearly distinguished the sentiment of attachment from ideological nationalisms such as German race theory or Russian Pan-Slavism. The ties between Russia and the Balkan Slavs would exist, with or without the ideology of Pan-Slavism. Such love of kith and kin is not based in race, but in language, culture, and tradition, and while the process of loyalty begins with the family, it culminates in the commonwealth which fulfills, without superseding, lesser loyalties. As Freeman observes: "Kindred, real or artificial, is the one basis on which all society and all government have grown up."[14]

The love of kith and kin does not require a nation-state. It is possible to be loyal to one's people even when separated from them, as Serbians, Montenegrins, and the Serbs of Bosnia and Krajina were in the nineteenth century (and as Greeks were until the Roman conquest). Separate ethnic groups may also be unified under a crown—as the Scots and English were under James VI of Scotland/James I of England or as the peoples of Spain were for many centuries. There are undoubted advantages, for a multiethnic state, in having a symbol of unity that transcends politics.

The difficulty comes when a multiethnic monarchy or empire begins to force assimilation, as happened in Austria-Hungary, which degenerated from the more inclusive ideal of the Holy Roman Empire into a dual monarchy, which, at the mercy of dual nationalisms (Hungarian and German), made it difficult if not impossible for Slovaks, Croats, and Serbs to preserve their identities. The Hungarian liberals, who had noisily and violently demanded their national rights, were unwilling to take on the Croats even as junior partners. Hungarian nationalists such as Louis Kossuth portrayed themselves as enlightened patriots interested only in the good of humanity, but Kossuth's attacks on Pan-Slavism as a Russian plot and his generous declarations of support for Slavic ethnicities (made to ignorant foreigners) make interesting reading when one is aware of the role he and his allies played in suppressing the Croats' and Slovaks' legitimate desire to defend their interests and preserve

14. Edward A. Freeman, "Race and Language."

their identity.[15] Like a true nationalist, Kossuth favored the Magyarization (that is, Hungarification) of ethnic Slavs.

The National Language

One chief feature of Magyarization was the campaign to eliminate national languages such as Slovak and Croat. The German Romantic Johann Gottfried von Herder, though often described as an early German nationalist, grew up in Latvia, where he learned the importance of a national language for the nations subjected to the Austro-Hungarian Empire.[16]

Language is not always the vehicle of national identity, but national movements in Ireland, Wales, Quebec, and Brittany (to say nothing of the spectacularly successful Zionists who resuscitated Hebrew) have usually seized upon the language question as a key to establishing national identity. In the United States, Southern nationalists make a point of using a regional pronunciation and vocabulary, and some have affected British spellings as a means of combating Northern dominance. The temptation to mock such eccentricities ought to be resisted. Language is the most essential of human arts, and it is through language that we construe the world. An Israel that spoke English or Arabic, as opposed to Hebrew, would be a very different proposition, and Ireland's expensive failure to reestablish Gaelic may, in the end, spell doom for Irish independence.

Language can simultaneously unite and divide peoples that are closely related to each other. Ancient Greeks knew that they were bound by ties of language and culture that separated them from the rest of the world inhabited by *barbaroi,* and, although the differences between the Attic and Doric dialects were far greater than the differences between most dialects that have survived in modern European countries, Athenians and Spartans were able to make common cause against the

---

15. Louis Kossuth, *Proceedings, Speeches, &c., at the Dinner Given to Louis Kossuth, at the National Hotel, Washington, Jan. 7, 1852.*
16. Johann Gottfried von Herder, *Outlines of a Philosophy of the History of Mankind.*

Persians. Spartans grew up listening to Homer in the Ionic dialect (of which Attic is a variant), but most choral lyric poetry—even in Athens—was written, more or less, in a form of Doric. Aristophanes could count on his Athenian audiences to understand dialogue designed to parody Spartan and Theban dialects, but not many years later, a company of Greek mercenaries stranded in the heart of the Persian empire could resolve their differences and pick Spartan and Athenian officers to lead them against the *barbaroi*.[17]

The Ethnic Point of View

Patriotism, in Dr. Johnson's famous phrase, is the last refuge of a scoundrel. Nothing so illustrates the dishonesty of the liberal attack on national loyalty as the systematic misrepresentation of this quotation. Johnson was proud of being a patriotic Englishman, and, in his essay "The Patriot," he praised the patriot as a man motivated by love of country rather than self-interest.

What Johnson objected to was the cynical misappropriation of the word by Whig politicians who wished to enhance the power of Parliament at the king's expense. No one who knew anything of England's greatest moralist could possibly suspect Johnson either of disloyalty or cynicism. His generous appreciation of the clan loyalties of the Scottish Highlanders was a good indication of his medieval attitude, though he was well aware that such loyalty was often accompanied by violence.

Patriotism of any kind may be drenched in blood, and, perverted into nationalism, it may be held partially accountable for many terrible wars in the nineteenth and early twentieth centuries. All good impulses, however, can be turned to evil ends, and the ethical distortions and hatreds engendered by nationalist movements should not blind us to the moral significance of ethnic and national identity. The cosmopolitanism advocated by Stoics and Marxists has never been a reality, except for a tiny part of the international ruling class. It was not the national point of view that turned the Soviet Union and Cambodia into slaughterhouses. The spiritual unity of mankind preached by saints and taught by philosophers is an ideal to be pursued and cultivated; it cannot be

17. The story is told by Xenophon in the *Anabasis*.

imposed by any government or combination of governments except by the most tyrannical means.

An international state is, in fact, entirely incompatible with the widespread diffusion of authority that has always been one of the goals of democratic life. As Gaetano Mosca makes plain in his great work on elite classes, the greater the extent of political authority, the smaller the proportion of the ruling class to the general population.[18] A shopkeeper might occasionally have his way within his *contrada* (neighborhood) in twelfth-century Siena and, through more powerful friends, even influence decisions made by the city. A shopkeeper in sixteenth-century Florence might hope to bribe an administrator, but as a citizen of twentieth-century Italy (much less of the European Union today), he would count for nothing. Nation-states, it can easily be argued, are already too big—or at least too top-heavy in the structure of authority—and strong movements for devolution have made rapid strides in Britain, Belgium, and Italy.

Italian Lessons

Italy in the early nineteenth century presented a special case of a people that had not been unified since the fall of the Western Roman Empire. Divided into competing principalities, some of which were ruled by foreign dynasties (for example, the Bourbons of Naples) or directly controlled by foreign powers (particularly Austria), Italy was only, in Metternich's famous phrase, a geographical expression. Since at least the end of the Middle Ages, Italian thinkers such as Dante, Petrarch, and Machiavelli had dreamed of unifying the peninsula, though more often than not their conception of Italy was based more on the Roman Empire than on the concept of a nation-state.

In the textbook version of Italian history, the Risorgimento was a campaign, parallel to the American Revolution, to liberate and unify Italians in a national state.[19] There is considerable truth in this version of the story, particularly in the early phase of the Risorgimento, during

---

18. Gaetano Mosca, *The Ruling Class (Elementi di Scienza Politica)*.
19. For the standard assessment of the Risorgimento, see the influential works of William Roscoe Thayer, G. M. Trevelyan, and Denis Mack Smith.

which northern Italy was liberated from Austrian rule. However, there is another version of the story, sometimes told in the South, according to which French-speaking liberals from the North[20] conquered both the Kingdom of Naples and the estates of the Church.

Unification and, therefore, centralization was the goal of Italian nationalists, a goal that naturally overrode all the local patriotisms of Sicilians, Venetians, Latins, and Tuscans—to say nothing of Catholics loyal to the pope, whose estates were rudely stripped away by a political class dominated by nonbelievers and anticlericalists, who wanted to strip the Church of its social and political functions. Even before the conquest of the estates of the Church, the Piedmontese government outlawed the Jesuits and confiscated Church property. Although the vast majority of the Italian people were Catholic, the political class was made up predominantly of liberals and freemasons—a term that had considerably more significance in nineteenth-century Europe than it does today. Even Garibaldi's admirers cannot disguise that freethinking revolutionary's ferocious hatred of the Church, and some Italian Catholic historians have gone so far as to portray the entire Risorgimento as a war against the Catholic Church.[21]

In forming the new Italian kingdom, some political leaders (such as the Lombard radical Carlo Cattaneo) argued for a federal model of unification, along the lines of the United States or Canada. After all, Italy's greatest glory had been gained by small, independent city-states and principalities. The small Tuscan town of Pisa or Siena has probably contributed more of value to world culture than all of the United States throughout its entire history. And Sicily, thought of as the most backward region, produced Italy's first poets and a series of important artists and composers; even in the twentieth century, the island was Italy's Mississippi—deplored for its poverty and sloth and yet admired for the literary geniuses to which it gave birth.

And yet, instead of recognizing the vitality that had come from regional diversity, the nationalist leader Count Camillo Cavour pushed hard for

20. Garibaldi came from Nice, and Cavour preferred to speak either French or his native Piedmontese dialect.

21. An argument made recently by Angela Pellicciari in *Risorgimento da riscrivere: Liberali & massoni contro la chiesa.*

a unitary centralized state of the type that French Jacobins and Bona-partists had established. In the name of building an Italian state, nation-alists were prepared to sacrifice all that was most real and vital in Italy: regional distinctiveness and the social authority of the Church.

Even for conservatives like Gaetano Mosca, the state became the ful-fillment of man's ethical purpose, and the creation of fascist Italy was not a large step to take for philosophers such as Giovanni Gentile, much less for the ex-socialist Benito Mussolini. Under Mussolini, the Italian state went further than ever in centralizing the government and elimi-nating local and provincial peculiarities. As a result, the Sicilian language, the first literary language of Italy, has become almost extinct, decaying into a mere dialect that is ridiculed by other Italians.

The nations adored by nationalists do not actually exist but are something to be realized in the future, and Italian nationalists were no exception. Mussolini, it is said, dreamed of changing the Italian climate to harden the character of his people, and after the war, the fascist Giulio Evola openly voiced his contempt for the Mediterranean character of Italy, the land of strumming mandolins and "O Sole Mio," and wanted to restore the virtues of ancient Rome, little realizing that Romans in the age of Cicero were far more "Mediterranean" than conventional historians admit.[22]

Divided, subjugated, and impoverished, nineteenth-century Italy had produced Bellini and Verdi, Leopardi and Mosca. The cultural contri-butions made by united and progressive Italy are a good deal less impres-sive, and it is significant that the most "backward" region of Italy re-tained so much of its cultural vitality down to the end of the twentieth century. Burckhardt's prediction of a similar fate for Germany has also been fulfilled. It would appear that Mosca's observation—the greater the state, the smaller the ruling class—can also be applied to literature and music: The greater the extent of direct political authority, the punier the literary and artistic output. Florence produced Dante and Michelan-gelo; united Italy must be content with Moravia and Modigliani. As part of the global cultural order, Italy can muster nothing more uplift-ing than Umberto Eco and Roberto Benigni.

---

22. Julius Evola, "Latin Character—Roman World—Mediterranean Soul," chap. 14 in *Men among the Ruins: Post-War Reflections of a Radical Traditionalist.*

Subsidiarity

There was little coherent opposition, in the nineteenth and twentieth centuries, to either revolutionary nationalism or revolutionary internationalism. In Britain and the United States, individualist liberals and conservatives did attempt to mount a defense of private property, marriage, and the nation-state, but their appeals to common sense, pragmatism, and tradition lacked the sweeping vision of Marxists and national socialists. The most successful effort was the Catholic response put forward by Popes Pius IX and Leo XIII, who defended a hierarchical social order that emphasized the importance of rooted institutions such as the family, the community, and the nation. This position, summed up in the word *subsidiarity*, was stated clearly in a famous passage of an encyclical of Pius XI *(Quadragesimo anno)*. Conceding that large-scale associations were necessary, the pope declared:

> [T]hat most weighty principle which cannot be set aside or changed remains fixed and unshaken in social philosophy. Just as it is gravely wrong to take from individuals what they can accomplish by their own initiative and give it to the community, so also it is an injustice and at the same time a grave evil and disturbance of right order to assign to a greater and higher association what lesser and subordinate organizations can do.

This is the Christian (not only Catholic)[23] response both to socialism and to internationalism: not an undifferentiated mass of the globe's peoples "sharing all the wealth" without the benefit of a coercive state, but a pyramid of natural associations within which men and women inherit identities that shape their character and in which they cooperate for the common good.

For many peoples, this pyramid culminated in a nation-state, but not necessarily or ideally in a state that destroyed all lesser loyalties. Nationalism—that is, the glorification of an ideal nation and the exaltation of state power—is a false and destructive theory that leads a people to sacrifice what is real and vital in favor of an illusory future.

---

23. Althusius, a German Calvinist, was the greatest exponent of the federalist vision that is encapsulated in the term *subsidiarity*. See Thomas Fleming, *The Politics of Human Nature.*

Nation-states may well represent an important obstacle to the globalization of the human race and the homogenization of all human culture, but they are not an end in themselves. What is precious, however, is the "ethnic perspective," sometimes expressed in a nation like France, a region like Sicily or Lombardy, or even within a small town or neighborhood. As foolish as some of its manifestations might have been, there was genuine sanity in the New Left's dream of neighborhood government, as well as in E. F. Schumacher's rallying cry that "small is beautiful" and in the opposition of Greens to globalization of the economy.

Small Is Beautiful

The Napoleon of Notting Hill (1904) is perhaps the wisest political novel of the last century. In Chesterton's futuristic tale, England is ruled by a bureaucratic machine in which the king is chosen by lot. When the lot falls on a practical joker named Auberon Quin, the new king decides to recreate the old London boroughs and invest them with a medieval pageantry of his own invention. No one takes Quin's prank seriously except the nineteen-year-old provost of Notting Hill, Adam Wayne, who loves the drab and familiar streets of his neighborhood. In the interests of progress and their own personal gain, the leaders of the other boroughs decide to run a thoroughfare through Notting Hill's Pump Street, and Wayne rallies the inhabitants to resist. When the politicians seeking to buy him off deprecate the size of Pump Street, Wayne fires back: "That which is large enough for the rich to covet . . . is large enough for the poor to defend," and when King Auberon tries to make him see the ludicrous side of Notting Hill patriotism, Wayne explains that "Notting Hill . . . is a rise or high ground of the common earth, on which men have built houses to live, in which they are born, fall in love, pray, marry, and die. Why should I think it absurd?"

To help defend his borough from aggression, Wayne appeals to the professional imaginations of the shopkeepers. "I can imagine," he tells the Pump Street grocer, "what it must be to sit all day as you do surrounded with wares from all the ends of the earth, from strange seas that we have never sailed and strange forests that we could not even picture." At first, his only convert is a toy merchant fond of war games, and together they plan the revolt of Notting Hill. Their very success, however, is almost their undoing, as the businessmen and bureaucrats succumb to bloodlust and patriotism. In the final struggle, a working-man tired of having cries of "Notting Hill!" flung in his face exclaims, "Well, what about Bayswater? . . . Bayswater forever," to which the provost responds: "We have won. . . . We have taught our enemies patriotism."

Chesterton's fable delighted its first readers, but his prophetic insight has taken longer to be recognized. It is partly the playful spirit of the book that prevents us from taking him seriously, but an even greater obstacle is our stupid conviction that history moves in a straight line. If, we say, the tendency since the Renaissance has been the agglomeration of little powers into great powers—of Florence into the Duchy of Tuscany into the Kingdom of Italy into the European Union—then it does little good to speak wistfully of the days when an independent Florence was at war with Siena and Arezzo and the very neighborhoods of Florence had their own names, their own flags, their own costumes, and—above all—their own honor for which the inhabitants contended in street fights. Even the United States, when they were a republic, more resembled medieval Siena or Adam Wayne's London than they do the mass-produced population that is sent to fight under the flag of the United Nations. But that, as we say, is history.

It is only after the end of the twentieth century that we can fully appreciate Chesterton's prophecy, not only because nations of the world are becoming more and more every day like the lifeless bureaucracies that he predicted, but because we are beginning to see the first flickers of resistance. In America, the western states are passing Tenth Amendment resolutions; in Italy, the Northern League (whatever its political future) has been successful in recreating a Lombard identity; and in Eastern Europe, the old nationalities are lifting their heads up out of the rubble of empire, singing their old songs, and reopening the ancient wounds whose very throbbing shows they are still alive.

One of Chesterton's hunches was that a New World Order would not tolerate particularity. At the beginning of his novel, Quin meets the president of Nicaragua. When told that Nicaragua is no longer a country, the old president declares: "Nicaragua has been conquered like Athens. Nicaragua has been annexed like Jerusalem. . . . The Yankee and the German and the brute powers of modernity have trampled it with the hoofs of oxen." One of Quin's civil-servant friends explains that Nicaragua was a stumbling block to civilization: "We moderns believe in a great cosmopolitan civilization, one which shall include all the talents of all the absorbed peoples."

The unabsorbed little nations and the movements they have inspired—however incoherent and self-contradictory they may be in their philosophy or ideology—contain a germ of truth and represent a wholesome antidote to the Marxist dream of a global state, without heaven or hell, without nations or countries, of "all the people living life in peace." National-socialist states, under Hitler, Stalin, and Mao, made the world a nightmare for the people. A global state could only be a global hell from which there would be no escape.

TOO MUCH REALITY

3

Let observation with extensive view
Survey mankind from China to Peru.

—Samuel Johnson, *The Vanity of Human Wishes*

Agrarian peoples are rarely sentimental about nature. Hesiod, giving advice to farmers ca. 700 B.C. in the hinterlands of Greece, did not pause to sigh over the beauties of landscape. Plato's Socrates, living in urban Athens three centuries later, did speak (in the *Phaedrus*) of the charms of nature, but only as a source of distraction from philosophical thought. It was not until the Hellenistic world, with its large cosmopolitan cities of mixed population, that pastoral poetry began to be a popular genre. Alexandrian Greeks, Romans of Vergil's day, and the refined courtiers at Louis XIV's Versailles all loved to imagine themselves in a golden age of shepherds and shepherdesses, singing their songs beneath the shade of a tree.

It is easy to poke fun at the artificiality of the pastoral tradition or at the delusions of Wordsworth (or Thoreau or William Morris or hippies living in a commune), who pretended to "go back to nature." Getting back to nature and "living the simple life" can be only a hobby for inhabitants of a modern industrialized society. Chesterton once quipped that

69

he would have liked to live the simple life, but he could not afford it, and it is precisely the rich who have the money to spend on rustic retreats and wilderness experiences. For the most part, it is only affluent people who can indulge the desire to live in a village, albeit a village with gates and armed guards to keep the pitchfork-wielding peasants out.

There is, nonetheless, something real in the desire to get back to nature and to live in a community on the human scale. Peter Laslett describes the world of his British ancestors as "a society of 300, 400 or 500 strong, perhaps more often in a hamlet separated from other hamlets which made up the parish, than in a village which was one group of houses side by side. From their earliest years they must have been conscious of the standing of the family into which they were born, within a group of other families."[1]

Living in a village of a few hundred, everyone can expect to be something—the best poet, the best cook, the worst liar, the laziest worker. In a country of three hundred million strangers, no one can be *anything*, unless his picture is on the cover of *People*. This partly explains the importance of celebrity in modern society. More than money, more than power, more even than sex, celebrity is the ticket, so we imagine, to becoming a real human being. The rest of us are so many ants in a global hive, and at best we can hope to be somebody in the tiny niche of the local Rotary Club or a society of comic-book collectors.

The Global Village

Many people who actually prefer to live in a traditional society have nonetheless come to believe that life on the human scale might be selfish and immoral. Taking care of our families, doing our jobs well, giving alms to beggars, and being loyal to our friends is not enough. We are called upon to cultivate global awareness and to accept responsibility for the entire world.

All the institutions of our cultural life—Church, television, schools, magazines, even what we now call "the arts"—tell the same story: However restricted the concerns of our private life, the rest of the world has a claim on us, and not just on our attention. Each one of us now has

---

1. Peter Laslett, *The World We Have Lost: England before the Industrial Age*, 79.

moral and political obligations that connect us with starving villagers in Peru, rebels in Afghanistan, aborted girl babies in China.

Small-town American libraries are filled with books and pamphlets that explain "what you can do to save the planet," and once every year on Earth Day, hundreds of thousands of people link hands to express their solidarity with all living things. Global awareness intrudes even into sports and entertainment. Popular musicians and athletes gather periodically to raise money for AIDS victims, black nationalists in Africa, debt-ridden American farmers, and prisoners of conscience. The solution to all of these problems, it would appear, is global awareness, the recognition—particularly in the developed world—that each of us owes an obligation to all mankind. As the anthem for the Live Aid concert put it, "We are the world, we are the children."

For most of us, this obligation can be discharged only by giving support to international charity. The spirit of international humanitarianism was best described by Raymond B. Fosdick, president of the Rockefeller Foundation from 1936 to 1948. Echoing the organization's charter, Fosdick proclaimed our debt as human beings to "the spirits of men who never thought in terms of flag or boundary lines and who never served a lesser loyalty than the welfare of mankind."[2]

Many people (perhaps most) in the United States and Europe acknowledge some responsibility to make charitable contributions out of their surplus and abundance. But how much to give, to whom, and how—these are questions to which there are no easy or obvious answers, although some philosophers and theologians have made it sound as if there were. All men are brothers, say the theologians, and Christians have an obligation to play the Good Samaritan everywhere and at all times. From each according to his abilities, to each according to his need, say some philosophers (Marx, for example), while others (like John Rawls) argue that we are positively obligated to do anything we can to alleviate suffering as long as it does not entail our sacrificing something that is as morally significant to us. Friendship or even proximity might once have counted for something, others (like Peter Singer) say, but the instant communication and swift transportation of the global village have transformed our moral universe.

2. Raymond B. Fosdick, *The Story of the Rockefeller Foundation*, 281.

The global village is a powerful image that makes everyone one another's next-door neighbor. If my neighbor's house burned down in the middle of winter, it would be worse than uncharitable to refuse to take in the family and provide them with food and warm clothing: it would be unjust. In the world of international philanthropy, the same argument applies to the global village. From this perspective, relief of a distant stranger's poverty is not what philosophers would once have called "supererogatory"—that is, something good to do but not obligatory. As defined (and condemned) in the Thirty-nine Articles of the Anglican Church, works of supererogation are "voluntary works besides, over and above, God's commandments" or, in the secular phrase, actions that "go beyond the call of duty." Our duty to the world's poor is not, we are told, of this kind, because we are all, individually and collectively, obliged to give, and not just of our excess.

Philanthropy by Fiat

Internationalism, as it is currently understood, is the contribution of Marx, both in the general sense of a movement to end or minimize state sovereignty and in the more narrow sense of the obligation of people in wealthy nations to contribute to poor nations. The claims of international philanthropy are, therefore, quite distinct from charity, which presupposes a voluntary contribution and not a politically imposed transfer of wealth.

To understand the difference, it may help to consider the question of poverty relief within nations. The idea of a national system of wealth transfer to help the poor did not originate with Marx. Some English liberals, despite their defense of private property, argued in favor of what we would now call "social justice." There is no way of escaping the fact, though, that a socially or politically imposed obligation to give until it hurts diminishes traditional notions about private property:

> Suppose . . . that it is right for one man to possess a greater portion of property than another, whether as the fruit of his industry, or the inheritance of his ancestors. Justice obliges him to regard this property as a trust, and calls upon him maturely to consider in what manner it may be employed for the increase of liberty, knowledge, and virtue. He has no right to dispose of a shilling of it at the suggestion of his caprice. So

far from being entitled to well earned applause, for having employed some scanty pittance in the service of philanthropy, he is in the eye of justice a delinquent, if he withhold any portion from that service.[3]

The liberal William Godwin was addressing this argument only to the people of eighteenth-century England, and similar arguments would be made in the nineteenth century by left-leaning liberals such as T. H. Green. Marx derided all such plans as mere reform, but the border between Marxist internationalism and social welfare is an infinitely receding line. If there are sound moral reasons for redistributing wealth within a society, then the same or similar arguments can be used to justify redistribution between societies. If, for example, a caste system is unfair because it hands out benefits according to morally arbitrary principles, then we might also "view the natural distribution of resources as morally arbitrary. The fact that someone happens to be located advantageously with respect to natural resources does not provide a reason why he or she should be entitled to exclude others from the benefits that may be derived from them."[4]

Christian theology did not recognize national boundaries as limits on charity, but in the classic view, such an obligation was between states and did not impose a burden on individuals of one state to assist those of another.[5] In obliterating the distinctions between mine and thine and in erasing international boundaries, internationalist philanthropists can no longer consider themselves American or French or Croat. They are citizens of the world, and their neighborhoods are linked by computers, fax machines, and mass media into a universal consciousness that feels "a special providence in the fall of a sparrow."

In the secularized vision of the human brotherhood, as it is represented by international agencies for relief and development, all the world's resources should be shared by all the world's peoples in a

3. Godwin, *Political Justice*, 174.

4. Charles R. Beitz, *Political Theory and International Relations*, 139–40. Beitz denies that the natural distribution of resources applies directly to politics or leads inevitably to world government, but argues that if communities—families, provinces, and nations—are stripped of the moral boundaries that justify unique obligations, they are also deprived of their legitimacy.

5. Fr. Austin Fagothey, S.J., preserves the standard Catholic view that "[t]he duties of charity between states are about the same as the duties of charity between individuals" (*Right and Reason: Ethics in Theory and Practice*, 551).

collaboration for the common good. The obstacles to fulfilling this dream are not lack of resources, the culture of Third World nations, or even common human frailty. As president of the World Bank, Robert S. McNamara perennially waged verbal combat with provincial pride, ethnic resentments, localism, nationalism, and all other obstacles to global justice.

McNamara and other internationalists invoke the language of community to justify what amounts to a global economic order. It is a natural fallacy to assume that what can be done by members of a family or residents of a village can be done better—or even simply done—by the government of a great nation, as if there were such a thing as a "national community," and it seems an easy matter to go from a sense of national obligation to one of international or global responsibility. Barbara Ward, in a very influential book, took the equation Family = World for granted: "[T]he task before us is the positive task of building a peaceful home for the human family."[6]

But states and international agencies can be treated as individuals only by analogy. A man can write a poem and a family can rear children, but it is not at all clear that a nation or union of nations can do either. A neighborhood is able to regulate itself with little government apparatus, but large nations require armies, police, and elaborate legal codes. A community of saints may abjure marriage, private property, and social distinction, but such a rule cannot be easily imposed upon a nation of peasants and shopkeepers. Fathers and mothers are bound to look after their children's welfare with a devotion bordering on fanaticism; a village or parish may be willing to assume a weaker responsibility for widows and orphans; but the family metaphor is strained beyond the breaking point when politicians speak of a "national family" with responsibilities owed by everyone to everyone else, and it is drained of all vitality when it is applied to the whole world.

The underlying conception of global philanthropy is that of the national welfare state applied internationally. Because of injustices committed by previous generations of Europeans, the current inhabitants of developed nations are positively obligated, according to dozens of declarations, charters, and manifestos, to promote the economic and social progress of all countries, especially developing countries. One

6. Barbara Ward, *The Rich Nations and the Poor Nations*, 154.

could cite any number of documents, for example, the United Nations' 1974 Declaration of the Establishment of a New International Order, which proclaims a "united determination . . . to correct inequalities and redress existing injustices . . . to eliminate the widening gap between the developed and developing countries," or its 1984 Charter of Economic Rights and Duties of States, which recognizes the rights of states "to nationalize, expropriate, or transfer ownership of foreign property."

The language of international justice and development is not confined to United Nations declarations and congresses of Third World leaders; it is the everyday language of World Bank presidents and American secretaries of state. And while we as individuals have little (if any) power over the decisions made by national and international leaders, we are expected to pay taxes and abide by declarations in ways that may increasingly intrude upon private life.

Secretary of State Cyrus Vance told a meeting of Organization for Economic Cooperation and Development ministers in 1977 that the "new era of cooperation" would mean a "firmer focus on people. . . . [T]he individual and collective hopes of people, their rights and needs deserve the fullest measure of our dedication." The logical deduction, according to an internationalist who quotes Vance approvingly, is that "it is the individual rather than the nation whose interests are of primary concern."[7] The growing international concern with the rights of individuals has two sides. Most obviously, it includes the various UN declarations on human rights and children's rights, which implicitly take precedence over national sovereignty and national legislation. A child mistreated or neglected in Detroit may now become the concern, not just of the United Nations, but of the member nations and (presumably) the citizens of those member nations, and a custody dispute (such as the famous case of Elian Gonzalez) can be turned into a global incident. But if we are all, as inhabitants of the world community, collectively responsible for one another, this also seems to imply a duty to provide for one another's welfare, to redress imbalances and correct injustices.

Similar language, after all, is used to justify the transfer of wealth and opportunities from rich to poor and between ethnic groups within

---

7. Miriam Camps, *Collective Management: The Reform of Global Economic Organizations,* 25–26.

the United States and other developed nations. It is precisely the argument used to justify programs aimed at achieving equity in school financing. Why, it is asked, should rich school districts be able to provide better education than poor districts? The solution is a statewide (or national) tax that can be used to equalize funding, and, since the 1880s, some form of an international tax has been proposed repeatedly as a remedy for inequities between nations.[8]

International taxation, even if carried to an extreme, would still fall far short of the dramatic measures urged by philosophers and philanthropists. Practically speaking, a system of the most minimal international compassion would have to be a matter of state compulsion; it could not be left up to individuals. For good or ill, few people are willing to sacrifice their second car, much less ride the bus to work, in the interest of either charity or justice. But if alleviating hunger and poverty is a duty that the individuals of advanced nations must discharge, not in the name of charity or compassion, then simple justice requires an *automatic* transfer of wealth between nations, since neither individual citizens nor individual nations have sufficient wisdom or impartiality to make the right decisions in the common interest of the world.[9]

On the face of it, the argument seems paradoxical: How can a person be just, if he is acting out of compulsion? If I rescue a drowning man only because his friend has a gun aimed at my head, no one will laud my heroism. But what if I am a member of a large group whose representatives vote to hire a lifeguard who saves the drowning man? My group (or nation) might be praised for its public spirit or the good sense it showed in picking its representatives. But if, while the lifeguard was off duty, the members stood by and watched another man drown, their public spirit or good sense would not excuse their indifference.

Most people believe that for moral actions to be truly moral, they must be freely undertaken, and that we deserve only limited credit for good works done in the name of governments or international agencies. It is the soldier risking his life on the battlefield who wins medals,

8. For an early example, see James Lorimer, "The Ultimate Problem of International Jurisprudence," book 5 of *The Institutes of the Law of Nations: A Treatise of the Jural Relations of Separate Political Communities*.

9. For the principle of "automaticity" as opposed to "totally voluntary acts of periodic generosity," see Karl Borgin and Kathleen Corbett, *The Destruction of a Continent: Africa and International Aid*, 53–54.

not the voters and taxpayers who support the government that sent him to fight and die.

We run serious risks in speaking the language of justice and not charity. It is not for nothing that the ancient pagans put the ultimate courts of justice in the land of the dead. "Use every man after his desert, and who should 'scape whipping?" Christians have always believed that human nature, at its best, is too frail and corrupt to deserve, under the law of justice, anything but condemnation and death. Man's salvation did not come as an act of justice but as a supreme gesture of divine charity.

Charity, caritas, agape, love—these words have different emphases, but a central point connects them all. Under the old law, so Christians believe, every man is condemned, but the spirit of love gives salvation. Therefore, for any kind of Christian, the requirements of justice—however exacting and grave—must take second place to the obligation to perform works of charity. The responsibility for love cannot be delegated or reassigned; it must be discharged by individuals who, in doing good, are becoming, while not good in themselves, more nearly good. In this sense, the charitable man receives more benefits than he confers.

The Jewish and Christian scriptures command us to look after ourselves and our dependents and to practice charity. As Augustine put it, charity is the "virtue that joins us to God in love," and it is, as St. Paul tells us, a greater gift of the spirit even than faith. But charity under the duress of taxation is not charity at all, even if the taxes are voted by a majority.

One of the worst effects of national welfare systems is that they diminish our capacity and our desire to perform voluntary works of charity. Until modern times, the rulers of Europe provided relief to the poor only in times of great necessity or only to the widows and orphans of veteran soldiers. The Roman emperors, it is true, distributed grain and bread within the capital, but this was a sure indication that the population of Rome had lost its independence and looked to the emperor as its ultimate patron.

In Christian Europe, it might be supposed, rulers would be tempted to exercise charity toward their peoples, and, in cases of emergency, a prince might open his granaries to his subjects—as did the Egyptian pharaoh who, on the advice of Joseph, sold the grain to his starving subjects (at a profit, admittedly). The Christian Gospel commands those who accept it to do good, as they are able, to widows, orphans, and the destitute, and throughout Christian England, before Henry VIII nationalized the Church, parishes provided charity to the needy.

What we might now call welfare—food, clothing, shelter, medicine—was distributed by the Church to members of the local parish. The monasteries, on the other hand, gave emergency relief to strangers and beggars. The Church in medieval England can be seen as a vast network of nonpolitical associations providing relief and welfare to those in need. On the eve of the Reformation, at least 3 percent of monastic income was devoted to relief of the poor, and the wills of well-to-do Christians specified what moneys should be spent on food and clothing for the poor. These were often quite significant, although few could match Richard II's uncle, John of Gaunt, whose will provided 300 silver marks on the eve of his funeral, 500 more on the day of his burial, and 50 a day for forty days after his death—a staggering fortune.[10]

The religious arguments for charity are significant, because even nonbelievers, in making a case for national and international poverty relief, have appropriated religious language. On the other hand, it is obvious that theological arguments will carry little weight with non-Christians who accept neither the authority of scripture nor the duty of charity (as opposed to social justice). However, many philosophers who are not orthodox Christians have insisted upon the moral autonomy of human individuals. A follower of Sartre or Kant, as much as St. Paul and St. Augustine, would have to reject any argument that transferred moral decisions from individuals to vast impersonal agencies. For good or ill, free men and women must make their own decisions, commit their own blunders, discharge their own obligations. To surrender the power to do good or ill, right and wrong—even if the surrender is only in the mind—is to give up an essential part of our humanity.

The Global Philanthropy Racket

Whatever vehicles or agencies we choose, the exercise of charity remains an individual act. But even if he were to retain (or regain) the power to dispose of his own assets, the citizen of an advanced nation

10. J. C. Dickinson, *The Later Middle Ages from the Norman Conquest to the Eve of the Reformation*, 345–60.

might nonetheless choose to endorse a program of international wealth transfer to which he could make voluntary contributions, either through his church or by checking a box on his income-tax return. However, before writing a check or supporting a political movement, he would still have to sort through another set of moral and practical problems. How could he know that he was doing the right thing? Could he really be sure, for example, that it is a good idea to transfer, say, $1,000 per year from consumer luxuries to the starving children of Ethiopia? Before making such a decision, he would first have to find out a few things about Ethiopia and about the organizations to which we (either as individuals or as taxpayers with votes) contribute our funds. It is not, after all, a matter of a few hundred lire but of millions and billions of dollars that have the most far-reaching effects upon entire nations and continents.

Unfortunately, all too much of the money sent by Western nations to poorer countries is squandered by inefficient and corrupt organizations, both public and private. In his book *Lords of Poverty*, Graham Hancock documents the waste, fraud, and mismanagement of the international aid business. His indictment takes in the UN and Red Cross officials who administer relief while living in luxury hotels; religious organizations (such as International Christian Aid and World Vision) whose "overhead" costs can exceed 50 percent; and the record of rotting food, inoperative equipment, and unusable (and potentially lethal) medicines that have been inflicted upon the objects of international charity.[11]

The politics of humanitarian aid are more complicated than is generally imagined. In the case of Ethiopia, or Angola, or any number of impoverished countries, the recipient government is, in large measure, the source of the problem. Under their present and recent regimes, many African countries have ruined their agricultures along with their economies. Such governments routinely seize food and supplies sent for humanitarian relief, and Western food aid sometimes serves as bait in a trap that lures starving villagers into deportation centers and disguised labor camps.

---

11. Graham Hancock, *Lords of Poverty: The Power, Prestige, and Corruption of the International Aid Business*, esp. 79–110. As far back as 1954, the Tompkins Committee of the State of New York concluded that "the public is being mulcted of millions of dollars each year" by fraudulent charities (Scott M. Cutlip, *Fund Raising in the United States: Its Role in Philanthropy*, 343, 441–76).

Western relief efforts have contributed to the success of this and other brutal dictatorships. Idi Amin in Uganda, Pol Pot in Cambodia, Hacim Thaci in Kosovo are only three of the notorious thugs to have received substantial Western aid. Such aid contributes to what the late P. T. Bauer termed "the disastrous politicization of life in the Third World."[12] Much aid money is stolen or squandered, and some of the rest is used to increase the power of government, which devotes labor and resources on profitless industries and "show projects" to advertise the regime.[13]

What effect has the World Bank had upon the Third World countries it has attempted to "develop"? Anyone who is willing to take upon himself the depressing task of reading through the annual addresses made by former World Bank president Robert S. McNamara will soon notice a pattern of recurring themes. In speech after speech, McNamara lauded the bank's "very impressive record of development," while conceding that the bank had failed either to close the gap between rich and poor nations or to reduce poverty.

Although the bank's defenders speak warmly of the progress that is being made, both free-market and socialist critics have held the bank responsible for at least some of the economic and agricultural disasters that have overtaken many poor nations in recent decades. Leftists have cited the destruction of traditional social structures and farming practices (in some cases traceable to International Monetary Fund/World Bank policies) as contributing to the impoverishment of Third World nations. In the capitalist critique, easy money has encouraged Third World countries to engage in reckless spending on money-losing projects, to discourage the start-up of profitable and productive businesses, and to undertake the sort of centralized economic planning and controls that have failed everywhere they have been tried. Robert Ayres, who has received grants from the Council on Foreign Relations and served on the Overseas Development Council, has made the best case possible for the World Bank, but for all his efforts to cite only documents that put the bank in a good light, he lamely concedes that it is

12. P. T. Bauer, *Equality, the Third World, and Economic Delusion*, 103.
13. See J. Bruce Nichols, *The Uneasy Alliance: Religion, Refugee Work, and U.S. Foreign Policy;* and "Infiltration Charges Dividing Salvadoran Churches, State," *Washington Post*, August 16, 1986. The problem goes back at least to the Spanish Civil War; see Merle Curti, *American Philanthropy Abroad*, 391–409.

difficult to analyze the effectiveness of the bank's rural-development projects, largely because the bank has never studied its own effectiveness.[14]

Leftists have charged that the West's insistence upon development is a form of neocolonialism whose real object is to reduce independent farmers to the level of cogs in the giant machine of international business. Even improvements in agricultural methods—the so-called Green Revolution—have come under fire. New strains of wheat and rice, for example, require more intensive cultivation and higher amounts of chemical fertilizers and pesticides. The results are profits for the more advanced farmers who can take advantage of the loans and advice proffered by foreign experts; failure and bankruptcy for smaller, traditional farmers who cannot compete; and enormous profits for international agribusiness.[15]

The Global Market

The goal of "integration into world markets" is not a conspiracy theory invented by the left: it is the language of the World Bank, the Brandt Commission, and other proponents of international aid. Whatever the merits of the case for market integration, such language obviously begs the question of what is best for people. It is not self-evidently true, as Bauer points out, that an industrial laborer in the West is happier than a subsistence farmer in Central Africa, and there is no reason to believe that modernization of Third World cultures will be uniformly welcomed by the peoples themselves. The developers would like traditional peoples to trade a secure daily round of simple labor within a family-centered community for the dependent status of an employee subject to the vicissitudes of international markets. It may prove to be no great bargain.

Defenders of capitalism, however, are convinced that, in breaking down all tariff restrictions and in building a global free-trade zone, they are lowering prices for consumers around the world and increasing

14. Robert Ayres, *Banking on the Poor: The World Bank and World Poverty.*

15. See, for example, A. J. M. Van de Laar, *The World Bank and the World's Poor;* Jose R. Vivencio, ed., *Mortgaging the Future: The World Bank and IMF in the Philippines;* and Al Gedicks, *Resource Rebels: Native Challenges to Mining and Oil Corporations,* for the negative impact of development projects on indigenous peoples in the United States.

employment opportunities for billions of the planet's workers. "Green" critics of free-trade agreements cite evidence of lowered environmental and health standards and glaring cases of exploitation of workers in the Third World: Mexican autoworkers who do not earn in a day what their counterparts in Detroit make in an hour; sweatshops in emerging Asian nations; slave labor in China. Conservative opponents of free trade (especially in the United States) emphasize the loss of sovereignty, the erosion of the industrial job base, and the tens of thousands of technical regulations in the documents establishing NAFTA, GATT, and the WTO—a strangely complex bureaucracy for policies supposedly doing no more than lowering and eliminating tariffs.

The debate over free trade has gone beyond logic and statistics in the streets of Seattle, Quebec, and Genoa, but the protesters who are setting cars on fire do not actually have a fundamental quarrel with the politicians protected by riot police. Both sides are committed to the concept of global responsibility, both are working for world government. Their disagreements (where they are sincere) are over strategy and tactics. The state capitalists who represent developed nations are not plutocrats: for the most part they are democratic socialists. The rebels in the streets are not Marxist theorists or disciples of Pol Pot, only suburbanites who are seeking an alternative to the suburbanization of planet Earth.

A few of them (following in the footsteps of Ralph Nader and Kirkpatrick Sale) may actually have an agrarian vision of life on a small scale, but virtually all of them are prey to the continuing leftist delusion that saving the planet requires a global socialist state. A traditional agrarian, however, would be forced to point out to the rioters that it is paradoxical to think that small-scale societies can be rescued by vast governments, whether of nation-states, the European Union, or a planetary state. One might as well expect government to defend "family values" or protect religious liberty.

The debate should not be over ideal tariff levels, but over who is entitled to decide the question. One set of globalists puts its trust in multinational corporations and the governments they control; their opponents want to give universal power to philanthropic bureaucrats who will decide the best interests of the planet. The fact that most of these global philanthropists, like Robert McNamara, have passed their lives in the service of multinational corporate interests seems to escape the dreamers of the green dream. James Buchanan won a Nobel Prize in economics for pointing out what should be plain to everyone: that public servants, just like everyone else, spend their time increasing their own wealth and power and the wealth and power of the entities that employ them. This acquired power, whether it accrues to a national government, a multinational corporation, an international relief agency, or a charitable nongovernmental organization, is always at the expense of ordinary people leading everyday lives away from the centers of power.

Sinking the Lifeboat

Imagine the best possible case of international aid, where food and medical aid has rescued thousands, perhaps millions, from death by disease and starvation. In the most successful examples of food aid to the Third World, the known result is an increase in population, that is, a growth in poverty. On the strength of this evidence, ecologist Garrett Hardin concluded that we owe no obligation to the Third World and likened the condition of wealthy nations to that of a lifeboat. We owe it to ourselves, he argued, not to take on more passengers either as immigrants or as consumers. Hardin called his basic principle Gregg's Law, after Alan Gregg, the vice president of the Rockefeller Foundation, who worried that increased food production would cause a cancerous growth of human population. This would mean diminishing material, environmental, and aesthetic resources for future human beings, especially in countries like India, if Western aid caused a dramatic increase in population.[16]

Hardin's evidence and reasoning do not necessarily lead to his rejection of all moral responsibility. One medical ethicist has, in fact, gone Hardin one better, arguing that we are obligated not to practice any philanthropy that damages, either now or in the future, a people's ability to survive and sustain itself. Our society, says H. Tristram Engelhardt, does have obligations to backward societies, and one of those obligations is to do no harm to their future generations. Therefore it is ethically permissible to refuse aid to societies that do nothing to reduce their population.[17]

16. Garrett Hardin, "Living on a Lifeboat."
17. H. Tristram Engelhardt, "Individuals and Communities, Present and Future: Toward a Morality in a Time of Famine."

A donor who cannot predict the most likely results of his gift is in the awkward position of the practical joker who means only to bring amusement but whose prank causes a traffic accident or heart failure. We can never be certain about the results of any action, but we are obliged, especially in our gratuitous acts, to behave prudently. It is not generosity to give wine (or the money to buy it with) to an alcoholic, and it is not charity (much less justice) to send aid to a foreign country where, for all we know, it may do more harm than good.

In extreme cases of life or death, the possible benefit may outweigh the probable harm. A physician might prescribe chemotherapy, for example, weighing the small chance of prolonging the patient's life against the near certainty of painful side effects. This argument can be applied to international charity only if most of the options are known. Even saving individual lives is not sufficient justification, if the end result is famine and war.

The humane person does have other options. One might, for example, practice charity closer to home, where it is possible to become personally involved and where it is much easier to monitor the honesty and effectiveness of relief programs. Mother Teresa, when a Milwaukee woman volunteered to assist her in India, told the woman to do good in her own hometown, to find Calcutta in Milwaukee.

Unfortunately, the private efforts of charitable individuals in their own neighborhoods and cities will never attract newspaper headlines or have the effect of a photograph of an emaciated child. Newspapers and advertising have a legitimate mission, the communication of information to interested persons, but for several decades the primary objective of the media has been to arouse strong feelings in their audiences. These feelings are not directed toward familiar objects—the reader's parents, spouse, children, or neighbors—but toward complete strangers.

The Pornography of Compassion

The passion most commonly appealed to is sexual desire. The attempt to arouse desire or stimulate passion for strangers by use of words and images goes by the name of pornography. The original word, *pornographia,* refers to the depiction of prostitutes and acts of prostitution, and pornography is the aesthetic or imaginative dimension of prostitution, a business devoted to promoting the illusion that one human being is having an erotic relationship with another. The reality of the "relationship" is simpler: a cash transaction without emotional or moral attachment.[18]

"Money can't buy me love," but the man who hires a prostitute can buy the illusion of love or passion or innocence, and it is this illusion that he is willing to pay for, not the mere act of fornication. If a discharge of surplus erotic energy were the only point, he might find safer and less costly alternatives. No, at least part of what he is paying for in hiring a prostitute is the illusion of attachment, and, on a lower level, the purchaser of pornography is pursuing the same fantasy.

There are other desires, other interests, other passions: pity, fear, anger, and hatred, to name only a few. Aristotle believed that the object of tragedy was the purgation or discharge of pity and fear for those who participate as observers in the experience. The object of pornography and of the "trash journalism" produced by the television networks and newspapers is not purgation but merely stimulation, and while the stories on *Oprah, Jerry,* and *Jenny* may be as fictional as the ancient Greek tale of the witch who murders her rival and her own children in order to punish her lover, we watch these fables as if they were real events whose participants are known to us. Someone else's child, trapped in a well, monopolizes the attention of millions of Americans who neglect their own children or entrust them to the care of strangers, and an airline disaster is celebrated as a major news event, even though the two hundred people killed represent only a tiny fraction of the people who die, from various causes, every day throughout the world. This is information only in the sense that an exact count of the pop bottles found on the sand of Myrtle Beach on a given day is information.

Even the terrible slaughter of several thousand innocent people on September 11, 2001, was insignificant, when compared with the grisly figures for traffic fatalities and abortions. NATO's little war against Yugoslavia inflicted more civilian deaths as a percentage of population. Americans cared about the victims of the World Trade Center attacks not because they were generic human beings but precisely because they were Americans. Nonetheless, there was something unsettling about the apparently unending series of celebrity memorial concerts. What began

18. Walter Burkert, *Creation of the Sacred: Tracks of Biology in Early Religions,* 133.

as sincere mourning seemed to degenerate into an orgy of compassion in which showmanship took precedence over grief.

Recent films have portrayed the degradation of the news business as something new, but already in the 1950s Billy Wilder's film *The Big Carnival* portrayed a cynical reporter who not only exploits a tragedy—in this case, a man trapped in a cave-in—for his advancement but even helps to perpetuate it. One might receive a similar, if unintended, impression from a cursory scan of the nineteenth-century yellow press, which Thackeray and Trollope (especially in his two Phineas Finn novels) ridiculed. In fact, the illegitimate manipulation of sentiment has been the object of the press for as long as there has been a press.

Many, if not most, "human interest" stories are reported without any object other than the arousal of passions for strangers, and to that extent they are pornographic. Although there is a fine line between the nightly news programs and the commercial interludes that pay for them, most advertising is overtly pornographic, even in the ordinary sexual sense. Advertising depends for its success on powerful images that stir the emotions of greed, envy, sexual desire, and compassion, but the success comes at a price. Commercial ads, whether they are celebrating detergents or publicizing starving Somalis, are always fantasies that distort our perception of reality. In reality, most people in underdeveloped nations are not starving to death, nor are they the helpless victims of natural disasters or colonial exploitation. They are men and women and children struggling to make a life for themselves under sometimes adverse circumstances.

Charity Begins at Home

The mark of genuine charity is (in Greek) *storge,* or loving-kindness, and while such love may be bestowed upon objects that seem utterly alien to the giver, it is not the strangeness that attracts but the recognition of some common bond, whether it is common humanity or, in the case of lower animals, some resemblance to human qualities.

Charity does begin at home, and the burden of charity is most easily discharged toward those with whom we are already connected by bonds of blood and experience. Charity toward strangers requires effort, and the more foreign the stranger, the greater the effort required. I am speaking now of the natural charity that grows and expands with the maturing conscience of the individual, as distinguished from what is generally meant in politics by "compassion," which is the artificial sense of benevolence we are taught to feel in doing good deeds by long distance. In the latter case, the reverse is true: Americans who will not take a bowl of soup to a sick neighbor will weep over the fate of starving Albanians whose pictures they see on television, and even in their own country their concern with poverty and family dissolution is inevitably limited to inner-city blacks or to the poor of the Appalachians, their desire to propagate the Gospel confined to Asians and Hispanics; their zeal to improve public education directed primarily at minority advancement.

All these goals are laudable in themselves, and worthy men and women may well choose to devote themselves to pursuing the welfare of foreigners as a sort of special vocation, but what seems to be far more common is the "telescopic philanthropy" of Mrs. Jellyby in *Bleak House,* whose eyes—so farsighted that "they could see nothing nearer than Africa"—overlook the needs of her own children, friends, and neighbors.

Telescopic philanthropy is not charity. Call it social justice or anything else you like, but not charity, a virtue that springs from the loving character of the giver. Where the cause is guilt or national self-hatred or only a formal duty learned by rote in catechism, the impulse springs from sources quite distinct from charitable love, and while we may admire the cold sense of duty that calls people to send checks in to telethons, we cannot, in most cases, attribute their zeal to charity.

St. Thomas puts the question of charity in the context of both grace and natural obligation. As a gift of the Holy Spirit, charity connects us to God. Rather than lavish our wealth on the evil (for example, thieves, confidence men, and child molesters), St. Thomas tells us that we should will the greatest good to those who are closest to God. But from the natural perspective—and much charity concerns the satisfaction of natural necessities—closeness to ourselves must also affect the degree of our charity: "In what concerns nature we should love our kinsmen most, . . . and we are more closely bound to provide them with necessities of life."[19]

If there is a natural priority of obligation toward our kinsmen and neighbors, then charitable assistance to foreign countries would be at the bottom of the scale. Until modern times, this was certainly the com-

19. St. Thomas Aquinas, *Summa Theologiae,* 2.2, 26.

mon perception. Wealthy Greeks (and the Hellenized non-Greeks of the ancient Middle East) took it for granted that they should spend some of their surplus on their native *polis*. The system of "liturgies" was institutionalized in Athens, but it is observable even in the later Roman Empire. One of the Greek complaints against Jews was that they did not contribute money locally to build theaters or assist the poor but sent it to Jerusalem. For a good Jew, however, such a decision had nothing to do with a desire to practice international philanthropy and everything to do with his sense of primary obligation to his own people. Greeks, thinking exclusively in terms of the city, could not or would not understand the nature of Jewish loyalty, which was, in fact, very like their own.

On the face of it, the sense of universal obligation is not only an impossible ideal but absurd. (If pigs could fly, they would no doubt fly on rescue missions to the Third World.) If our highest obligation is to all mankind or to a higher law, then what is the status of all those "lesser" obligations we grow up believing in and accepting? Should we, for example, take the bread out of our overfed children's mouths and send it to Africa? Perhaps the lawyer should give up his corporate practice in Ohio and devote himself to aiding Islamic dissidents in the Soviet Union or, better still, lend his talents to the struggle for world peace. The classic modern statement came from E. M. Forster, in a controversial passage of *Two Cheers for Democracy*. In affirming the priority of personal relationships and the need for trust, Forster decried the rise of movements and causes:

> I hate the idea of causes, and if I had to choose between betraying my country and betraying my friend, I hope I should have the guts to betray my country. Such a choice may scandalize the modern reader. . . . It would not have shocked Dante, though. Dante places Brutus and Cassius in the lowest circle of Hell because they had chosen to betray their friend Julius Caesar rather than their country Rome.[20]

Forster's statement has sometimes been taken as evidence of the "treason of the intellectuals," when, in fact, he was defending rooted loyalties against the claims of universal and abstract political philosophies. His

20. E. M. Forster, *Two Cheers for Democracy*, 68–69.

novel *The Longest Journey* gives a better idea of his position. When a Cambridge student makes the case for loyalty to "the great world," his friend delivers the argument that might serve as the thesis of the book:

> "There is no great world at all, only a little earth, for ever isolated from the rest of the little solar system. The earth is full of tiny societies, and Cambridge is one of them. All the societies are narrow, but some are good and some are bad—just as one house is beautiful inside and another ugly.... The good societies say, 'I tell you to do this because I am Cambridge.' The bad ones say, 'I tell you to do that because I am the great world,—not because I am "Peckham," or "Billingsgate," or "Park Lane," but because I am the great world.'"

Since Forster's time, the great world has been making headway against Cambridge and Billingsgate, and the results would appear to include the sort of moral paralysis that afflicted Forster's young hero. When human beings are consistently subjected to conflicting commands from different (and opposed) sources of authority, they may, of course, choose to obey one set and ignore the others. Forster, without reflecting too deeply, concluded that people mattered more than principles, loyalty and friendship more than nations and parties.

Internationalists ask us to sacrifice family and friends and all our lesser loyalties to the global idea. Josiah Royce, by contrast, made the principle of loyalty the basis of his moral philosophy. Although Royce was a Harvard philosopher, he had learned a great deal from his mother, whose diary of a westward trek he published. On that trek his mother noticed that even strangers on a wagon train or in a mining camp could develop into a little community whose members, loyal to the group, treated one another with respect.

According to Royce, we begin by accepting the various petty responsibilities that may be thrust upon us and, in the course of our lives, assume more and more loyalties. The ultimate principle he called "loyalty to loyalty," by which he meant a sort of Golden Rule of obligation: In making decisions, we are to consider whether our acts will augment or diminish the loyalty not just of ourselves, but of other people, even our adversaries.

At the very beginning of American philanthropy, Royce applied his principle to the Carnegie Foundation's effort to raise the standards of American colleges, and he rejected the foundation's universalism in favor of "a wise provincialism in education." He was all in favor of high standards, but there was no need for all the colleges in America to have the *same* standards.[21]

Royce feared the centralization of standards and power that would inevitably subvert the lesser provincial loyalties that are always (whether in classical Greece, medieval Italy, or frontier America) the foundation of a robust moral and cultural life. From this point of view, there is an inevitable clash between loyalty to tradition and family and the obedience that is owed to the state, especially when the state is bent on increasing its power.

Compassion Fatigue

Antigone, the protagonist of Sophocles' play, is faced with just such a decision. Her brothers have killed each other in a war over their city, but while one brother, a defender of his native Thebes, has been buried with state honors, the other (an attacker) has been declared a public enemy and left to rot. This is Antigone's dilemma: Should she obey the dictates of her uncle, Creon, the king of Thebes, or should she bury her brother, thus fulfilling the divine commandments and exercising her responsibility as a surviving member of her father's family?

Antigone chooses God and family over the state and dies a heroine. But there is another possibility: Unable to decide on the merits of different claims, some people become incapable of making any important ethical decisions. Antigone's sister, Ismene, cannot decide until it is too late. Claiming belated credit for the burial of her brother, she earns her sister's scorn without avoiding the wrath of her uncle, who regards her as insane for implicating herself in a criminal act in which she did not take part.[22]

Many people in the modern world are caught, like Ismene, between conflicting loyalties: job and family compete for time and attention; ideology and nation put forth opposing claims; parents and spouse can drag one back and forth between warring households and antagonistic

21. See E. C. Lagemann, *Private Power for the Public Good: A History of the Carnegie Foundation for the Advancement of Teaching*, 180–83.
22. For a fuller discussion of *Antigone*, see chap. 6.

affections. Children caught up in a divorce are forced to choose, not between good and evil, but between good and good; they realize that to support one party means that they must repudiate the other. The frustration that children experience in a divided home has much in common with what is sometimes called job-related stress or burnout: a phenomenon that is most frequent in such occupations as nursing and teaching, where employees are caught between the needs of the people they serve (patients and students) and the demands made by their superiors and by those who make the rules the superiors are supposed to enforce. Add in the sense of helplessness that comes with repeated failure in important duties (saving lives, teaching children), and you have a formula for the moral paralysis that all too often afflicts the cogs of bureaucratic machines.

The most ominous symptoms of burnout are emotional exhaustion and depersonalization. Teachers, social workers, and nurses, who often begin their careers on a note of moral heroism and emotional commitment, can end up exhibiting a numbness to the needs of others that is the functional equivalent of autism. Florence Nightingale, who established the nursing profession, was also a pioneer in international relief, and yet, in her personal life, she was a coldhearted monster. Although she became deeply involved in the politics and administration of British public medicine, she was increasingly a recluse who had neither patience nor time for her family. Invariably suffering from one or another mysterious ailment, she summoned a married aunt away from husband and children and became furious when the aunt, after two years of constant attendance upon the ailing nurse, returned to her family. She literally drove to death her warmest friend and supporter, Sidney Herbert, by insisting that the very sick man retain his post in the Cabinet, and she treated her other supporters, including the poet A. H. Clough, with similar kindness. When friends like Clough and Herbert died, she felt betrayed, and she constantly complained that her mother and sister were hypochondriacs who did not understand how greatly she suffered. Outliving all her friends and supporters, Florence Nightingale died at the age of ninety.

The best remedy for this moral disease is an active social and family life. If we experience a sense of helplessness as cogs in a bureaucratic machine, we must find ways of humanizing that machine.

Wherever the technocratic attitude of mind gains strength, so will this evil of depersonalization.... The real problem is that of knowing to what degree an administrative machine can be informed with spiritual values; and it is very hard not to feel very pessimistic when dealing with this problem. There seems to be a chance of a positive solution only in the case in which what looks from the outside like a mere administrative machine in reality conceals a structure of a quite different sort ... something of limited size ... a small team of men of good will who have intimate links with each other.[23]

An American nurse wrote that when she saw her own child under the care of an uncaring nurse, she became "extremely conscious of all I did and said around my patients. I imagined them to be my father, or one of my brothers."[24] A similar experience is at the heart of one of the most powerful scenes in literature. Near the end of the *Iliad,* Achilles, mad with grief and rage over the death of his friend Patroclus, kills Hector and drags the corpse behind his chariot, outraging even the gods, who are afraid to confront him. He does not relent until he finds himself face to face with Hector's aged father, Priam, who reminds him of what his own father would feel if the situation were reversed.

Single workers appear to experience the most dehumanization; married workers, the least. Having children is an additional asset. Married workers, with a network of friends and family to whom they can turn for moral support, are less likely to give way to job-related stress. When someone is having a bad time at work or school, we routinely blame his problems on difficulties he may be having at home. Most people, if they are to carry out their public duties, must have their private lives in order; even more important, they must *have* a private life.

We know, from the common sense writ large which we call history, that man was not made to live in a vast, impersonal society, surrounded by hundreds of thousands of strangers (or, in this electronic age, hearing the voices of billions of people we will never meet). Early man lived in small, kin-centered communities in which all the members were personally known to one another, and we, his descendants, still need the comfort of stable marriages and familiar faces, especially if we are to face the rigors of this urban and cosmopolitan world.

23. Gabriel Marcel, *Man against Mass Society,* 153.
24. Echo Heron, *Intensive Care: The Story of a Nurse,* 324.

Unfortunately, we moderns have mucked things up badly. So far from "the history of ethics . . . just beginning" (as one recent Dr. Pangloss has put it),[25] our modern moral reasoning has turned out to be more like H. G. Wells's "mind at the end of its tether." The unconscionable destruction of civilian life that has marked twentieth-century wars—World War II, Vietnam, the Gulf War, the NATO attack on Yugoslavia—demonstrates clearly that civilized European man has made himself capable of the brutalities of an Attila or a Genghis Khan. Television audiences were scandalized by the Vietnam War; the Gulf War—and the hundreds of thousands of civilians who died after the war as a result of the embargo—was experienced as part diversion, part tedium. We have grown morally numb, universal paymasters of the universal soldier.

To adopt a computer metaphor commonly used by psychologists, human beings are "programmed" and "wired" for certain kinds of experiences. The life of a peasant village or a primitive tribe is more congenial to our nature than the life of a Wall Street lawyer. Why else do the rich escape, whenever they can, to exclusive resorts in (carefully manicured) natural settings? If it takes effort to make oneself at home in a city, how much more effort is required to live, morally, in the global village! Universal commitments, if they are not grounded in the everyday life of family and friends, run a serious risk of overloading the circuits and burning out the system. T. S. Eliot wryly took the measure of man in the first of his *Four Quartets:* "Human kind / Cannot bear very much reality." How much is very much will vary from time to time, from human to human, but this much is certain: Without the aid of those we love, we cannot bear the weight of the entire world.

25. Derek Parfit, *Reasons and Persons,* 453.

GROWING UP UNABSURD

4

"Excuse me, I'm a virtuous person now."

—W. S. Gilbert, *Ruddigore*

"How someone may realize that he is making progress in virtue" is the title of a moral essay written in Greek at the height of the Roman Empire (*Mor.* 75). The moralist, Plutarch, proposes a variety of answers, but several of them seem to come down to one principle: In making moral progress, we gradually give up the conceit that we are better and wiser than other people. To illustrate his point, Plutarch tells the story of the amateur philosopher who calls in his servant to say, "Look, I've quit being conceited" (*Mor.* 80f). In a similar vein, Ben Franklin put humility at the bottom of the list of virtues he wanted to attain, on the grounds that it was the most difficult.

For professional intellectuals of any age, the greatest source of pride is the conviction that they have privileged access to technical information and intellectual methods that confer a profound understanding of human life and its problems. The temptation to mistake an arcane terminology for actual knowledge was as compelling to ancient philosophers as it is to modern social scientists. Plutarch regards it as a sign of progress when a student gives up "disputes, conundrums, and sophistries" and, passing

94

from pretentious and technical language, turns to "discourse that deals with character and feeling" (*Mor.* 78–79). He takes it as a bad sign when a student is more interested in language than subject and, in reading philosophy, concentrates on passages that contain exotic and difficult matter as opposed to what is useful, substantial, and helpful.

Moral Heroism

The pretensions of philosophers were a subject for satire throughout antiquity. According to a Greek legend, Thales fell down a well while he was speculating on the nature of the universe, and Socrates is memorably ridiculed by Aristophanes for having his head in the clouds. Later writers were particularly fond of emphasizing the contrast between, on the one hand, philosophers' claims to moral superiority and their air of indifference to material things, and on the other, their everyday habits of greed, gluttony, and lust.

> Their book says that one must despise riches and fame and think only the good is beautiful, and that one must be free of anger and look down on these big shots and talk with them on the basis of equality.... But they teach these very principles for pay, they stand in awe of the rich, and are gaga for money; they are worse-tempered than curs, more cowardly than rabbits, more obsequious than monkeys, randier than jackasses; they are worse thieves than ferrets and quarrel more than fighting cocks. (Lucian *Anabiountes* 34)

It is not just high-minded philosophers who have feet of clay. Many of the great crusaders for social and political justice betrayed their wives, scrounged off friends, and behaved in general like contemptible scoundrels. Karl Marx persuaded Friedrich Engels to acknowledge one of Marx's bastards as his own; Jean-Jacques Rousseau, who wrote the most beautiful book on the education of children, abandoned his own family; Mahatma Gandhi, in his long career, went from being a loyal servant of British imperialism in Africa to a nationalist leader willing to sacrifice both friends and family for his personal cause; and Martin Luther King, Jr., was a notorious philanderer who plagiarized much of the writings and speeches that made his reputation. An idealist's personal weaknesses do not necessarily detract from his ideals or discredit his accomplishments, but such contradictions do call into question the practicality of moral or political systems that seem impossible to live up to.

Some writers have attempted to link leftist ideologies with bad character,[1] but there have been as many sinners among conservatives and reactionaries. The moral shortcomings of French reactionaries (such as Céline) are at least on a par with Rousseau's, and many of America's conservative religious leaders have been exposed as swindlers and adulterers, plagiarists and frauds. Senators Barry Goldwater and John McCain consorted openly with swindlers and crime lords; former president Ronald Reagan, who spent his second term promoting free trade and opposing sanctions against unfair Japanese trading practices, accepted a $2 million speaking fee from a Japanese business; and more than a few leading conservative journalists have abandoned their wives for younger women. Some leaders of "cultural conservatism" have dubious credentials: a foundation head with a storefront Ph.D., a foreign policy expert who lied to Congress, a Christian Right leader who misrepresented his military service. The credentials of William Bennett, former secretary of education and exponent of the virtues, are based on a brief and sophomoric doctoral dissertation and a series of ghostwritten publications. Bennett's moral code apparently does not exclude losing millions of dollars through compulsive gambling. Hypocrisy is no leftist monopoly.

Part of our unease with people like Marx and Rousseau and Bennett is their colossal hypocrisy. Professing the loftiest motives and goals, they cannot manage the minimal self-restraint of the nine-to-five worker who comes home to watch television with his children and drink a beer. I have used the word *hypocrisy*, but it is worse than that. Many decent people find it difficult to live up to the moral standards they believe in, though their standards are those of everyday life: fidelity in marriage, hard work on the job, honesty in business and personal transactions. The ideals of Marxism and global philanthropy, on the other hand, are heroic. Political and spiritual leaders call upon others to sacrifice their comforts and pleasures and common decencies in order to construct a more perfect world, but, as it so often turns out, our heroes cannot live up to the minimal standards they despise as insufficient.

1. For example, Paul Johnson in *Intellectuals*. The conservative Johnson himself has been revealed to be less than admirable in his personal life.

Most of us do not pretend, even to ourselves, that we are brave heroes or noble statesmen. But when we, as private citizens, begin to assume responsibility, if only in our own minds, for the welfare of the whole world, we may lose sight of our private obligations and come more and more to resemble Agamemnon, who sacrificed his daughter Iphigenia for a business trip, or Dickens's Mrs. Jellyby, whose telescopic philanthropy took notice of nothing closer than Africa.

A contempt for everyday life seems to be an inevitable component of the religion of humanity that has replaced Christianity as the dominant way of understanding moral obligation, and the impossible ideals of universal compassion are echoed in high-school civics classes, Sunday schools, YMCAs, Boy and Girl Scout meetings, and commercial advertising. "We shall overcome" has merged into "I'd like to buy the world a Coke and keep it company," and—without knowing why or how—we have become ashamed of any loyalty that cannot be summed up in a universal declaration.

What all this generalized good feeling about the human race sometimes conceals is a widespread failure to form deeper attachments. Popular films and music are full of characters who are desperately in search of even a temporary commitment. Such sentiments are also pervasive in popular magazines, and it is hard not to find some truth in the Marxian argument (going back at least to the 1920s) that the West in general and America in particular has laid too heavy a burden on the individual. The pursuit of success at any cost scatters family members across the continent, dissolves community into "networks" of associates, and reduces love and friendship to a bond of mutual exploitation.

Read the singles pages of any newspaper: Lonely and isolated strangers, apparently without the usual resources of friends and family, have resorted to marketing themselves as commodities. I chose two "personals" at random from my local newspaper. In the first, a young woman lists her assets: "Intelligent, attractive, financially secure, divorced white female professional with blue eyes and blond hair, college degree." In the second, a man uses the terminology of real-estate brokers and used-car salesmen to pitch himself: "READY TO UPGRADE? Single white Christian male, 40's, seeks single white Christian female, 30–37, who has morals, family values, sense of humor, and enjoys sports, travel, antiques, and most anything else." A younger woman with "morals" and "family values" will presumably be willing to ditch her current lover in order to move up to a higher-priced model.

To seek out the company of strangers is a risky business. In earlier periods, marriages were arranged between families, or at least took place between members of a community in which people knew one another's character. In a market-driven society, however, individuals are expected to make the best deal with whomever they can, and by the end of the 1980s, American films began to depict the dangers: a murderess seducing her lawyer, a nanny trying to murder her employer and steal her husband and kids, a young woman answering an ad for an apartment share and attempting to take over her roommate's identity. In film as in life, one theme at the turn of the millennium was obsessive love for strangers. Popular celebrities were stalked by adoring fans who believed they had a personal relationship with their idol and occasionally turned very nasty when the reality of the situation was revealed.

This unhappy loneliness, although it is probably not so pervasive in real life as it is in films and music, is the darker side of the individualism we usually regard as admirable and heroic. Our novels and films are filled with alienated individualists who feel alone in the midst of crowds and who spend their lives in splendid isolation. From Shelley in his tower and Byron's Manfred to Camus' stranger, the Angry Young Men of the postwar era, and Clint Eastwood as the Man with No Name, our heroes have been loners.[2]

There are societies in which Manfred and Martin Scorsese's taxi driver would be regarded as psychopaths. The Chinese apparently read the story of Robinson Crusoe with horror, and in classical antiquity exile was regarded as a reasonable substitute for capital punishment, because for an ancient Greek or Roman, detachment from community was virtually inconceivable.

Learning to Be Human

The best Crusoe story of antiquity concerns Achilles' friend, Philoctetes, whose festering snakebite caused the Greeks to lure him away from the siege of Troy and leave him on an abandoned island. In Sophocles'

---

2. For American ambivalence toward loners, see David Riesman, *The Lonely Crowd: A Study of the Changing American Character,* 155 ff.

play on the subject, the Greek leaders realize that they cannot win the war without the bow of the late Hercules, which just happens to be in Philoctetes' possession. They send Achilles' son, Neoptolemus, to retrieve the bow.

When Odysseus first tells Neoptolemus that he must lie to win the confidence of his father's friend, the naive young man is horrified and proposes, instead, a more straightforward approach: combat. Odysseus explains that this will not work, since the bow of Hercules never misses. The young man persists: "Don't you think it is shameful to tell lies?" "No," replies Odysseus with a sophistry common in late fifth-century Athens, "not if lying saves your neck" (Soph. *Philoctetes* 108–9). Neoptolemus gives way when he realizes that Troy cannot be taken without this ignoble stratagem, and he is reassured that, after one day's dishonor, he will be called noble the rest of his life. The Greeks, like most people, could not easily divorce the sense of shame from public opinion, and Neoptolemus is young enough to be swayed by the opinion of his seniors and superiors. As Philoctetes observes after he has been cheated of his bow, Neoptolemus is a man "who knew nothing except to do as he was bidden" (*Phil.* 1010).

But, overwhelmed by pity for Philoctetes, Neoptolemus changes his mind, much to the disgust of Odysseus, who accuses him of foolishness. The son of Achilles answers in the spirit of his father: "But if what I do is just, it is better than wisdom" (*Phil.* 1251). What seems to be an irreconcilable conflict between two allegiances (the army and a family friend) and two values (justice and political necessity), as well as between the sense of shame and the sense of loyalty, is resolved only when the deified Hercules appears to tell his old comrade-in-arms Philoctetes that he must use his bow in the Greek cause. Philoctetes is healed of his wound—and of his poisonous resentment. Friendship, for the Greeks, trumped, or rather subsumed, other loyalties, and it is friendship and not logic that resolves the dilemma.

In addition to portraying moral conflict, Sophocles' play also raises questions of moral development. We see in Neoptolemus a young man, a teenager, really, who at the beginning of the play identifies morality with obedience. His conversion and rebellion are motivated not only by compassion for the suffering Philoctetes but by the recognition that there are standards of decency that transcend authority. He learns his lessons not from textbooks or sermons but out of his experience with friends. All the years alone on an island taught Philoctetes very little, and the inexperienced Neoptolemus would have learned even less under the same circumstances. It is by living with other people that we learn to be fully human. The great hero of the Trojan war, Achilles, is a classic loner who quarrels with his commander over a point of pride and honor and withdraws to his tent. It is only when his best friend is killed that he agrees to return to the battle—and then, only to wreak revenge.

Most of us do not face the stark dilemmas of Homeric heroes or Sophoclean tragedy, and none of us can count on a deus ex machina to sort out our loyalties. We are, however, every day faced with difficult choices: Should a young mother take a job to increase the family income, do volunteer work for charity, or stay home and take care of the kids? Should a man concerned about the environment spend his free time trying to save the whales, or do a good turn for his neighbors by cleaning up his backyard? Should a teenage boy inform the police that his parents are growing something more than African violets under the lamps in the basement?

One ancient philosopher went further, posing a question that goes to the heart of the matter: Suppose a father were robbing a temple or digging tunnels into the treasury; should a son give information to the government? The philosopher's answer, according to Cicero, was: No, that would be wrong. Instead, he ought to defend his father in court. But, someone would ask, doesn't one's country take precedence over other responsibilities? Yes, indeed, but it is in the country's interest to have citizens loyal to their parents (Cic. *Off.* 3.89).

Obviously, what the philosopher, Hecaton of Rhodes, had in mind was the notion that a healthy state could not exist without healthy families. This principle strikes many modern readers as nothing worse than conventional piety, but the elevation of family loyalty over lawfulness shocks many Christians, including Catholics. And yet, the most comprehensive moral theologian, St. Alphonsus de Liguori, said that "a son gravely sins against the reverence [due to parents] if he accuses them in a public forum even of an actual crime . . . when there is another way of correcting them." The only exceptions are for heresy, treason, and conspiracy against the ruler.[3]

3. St. Alphonsus de Liguori, *Theologia Moralis*, 1:601–2.

Hecaton seems to have believed that all such conflicts in loyalty could be resolved by examining the individual interests involved. At the same time, he understood that individuals do not live in a moral vacuum: "A wise man does nothing against the customs, laws, and institutions, while he is taking care of his personal interests. For we do not want to be wealthy for the sake of ourselves alone, but for our children, relatives, friends, and especially for the commonwealth. For the resources and riches of individuals are the wealth of the commonwealth" (Cic. *Off.* 3.63).

This comparatively obscure philosopher was hardly alone in his concern for the special obligations imposed by family, friends, and country. Cicero, who preserved this passage, declared the family to be the seedbed of the commonwealth and, throughout his varied works, displayed an awareness of particular responsibilities. Aristotle went so far as to wonder if a man could be counted happy if, after his death, his family and nation suffered disaster.

This hierarchy of obligation, far from being limited to the Greco-Roman world, was even more strongly emphasized in China. In a famous passage of the Confucian classic *Ta Hsueh* (The great learning), the modern West's priority of values is turned upside down:

> The ancients who wished clearly to manifest illustrious virtue throughout the world would first govern their states well. Wishing to govern their states well, they would first regulate their families. Wishing to regulate their families, they would first cultivate their own persons. Wishing to cultivate their own persons, they would first rectify their own hearts. Wishing to rectify their hearts, they would first seek sincerity in their thoughts. Wishing for sincerity in their thoughts, they would first extend their knowledge. The extension of knowledge lay in the investigation of things.[4]

From careful observation of the world, one proceeds to sincerity—a refusal to deceive oneself about perceptions—and then to gain control over personal behavior, which allows one to set a good example within the household, and so on. Rather than imposing order on the world, the ideal ruler sets an example within his own home.

4. Ch'u Chai and Winberg Chai, ed. and trans., *The Sacred Books of Confucius and Other Confucian Classics*, 295.

Confucius was later attacked by Taoists for presuming to meddle in the affairs of other people instead of leading a more natural life according to the *Tao*. Taoists emphasized natural obligations as opposed to the Confucian insistence on rigorous fulfillment of moral duty. But even Taoists, despite their tendency to speak in universal terms, supported the ordinary categories of the social structure. In the *Thai-Shang,* a popular tractate on moral cause and effect, the list of crimes includes lack of respect toward rulers and teachers, mistreatment of relatives, and thwarting the will of parents.[5] In other words, both Taoists and Confucianists upheld the traditional obligations imposed by the special relationships of kinship and authority.

Today, however, the sentiments of Confucius and Aristotle seem very strange to moral philosophers and political commentators who work within the dominant liberal tradition that encompasses nearly the whole political spectrum, from conventional radicalism to mainstream conservativism, both of which Alasdair MacIntyre has described as "mere stalking horses for liberalism."[6] There are, it goes without saying, many differences of opinion among the various shades of liberal, and their shadowboxing constitutes the ideological struggles of Western political life. But most of the contestants agree on certain principles and modes of argument: that the individual and his welfare is the basic unit of analysis; that rationality is the only mode of inquiry; and that moral principles, to be genuine, must be universal.

One sign of the mainstream liberal (which distinguishes him from the defectives or dissidents that inhabit the fringes of right and left) is the naive conviction that, so far from working within a tradition, his basic set of beliefs are self-evident truths. This assumption needs to be spelled out occasionally, when the liberal mainstream is challenged by the responsible left or the respectable right. Why, asked an editor of the *New Republic,* do most journalists turn out to be liberals? The answer, he said, is obvious: "Since most journalists I meet are reasonable, intelligent people, the mystery to me is not why journalists tend to be liberals but why so many other reasonable, intelligent people are not."[7] QED.

---

5. James Legge, trans., *Texts of Taoism,* 2:238 ff.
6. Alasdair MacIntyre, *Whose Justice? Which Rationality?* 392.
7. Michael Kinsley, *New Republic,* December 14, 1992, 6.

There should be nothing mysterious in the notion that other people do not always agree with me. They might be right; we both might be wrong; and we are all, right or wrong, subject to the whims and foibles of our temperament and feelings. While ancient and medieval writers often emphasized the influence of both character and the passions upon moral and political life, modern philosophers have frequently treated morality as if it could be reduced to decisions arrived at by an entirely rational process of applying abstract rules to particular situations. This has meant, among many other things, that the older doctrine of the virtues had to be eliminated, if only because courage and charity could not be boiled down to mathematical formulas.

To replace the untidy lists of virtues that used to be a major part of ethical treatises, philosophers devised neat and elegant principles like Kant's categorical imperative, a sort of dry reformulation of the Golden Rule that requires us, in making decisions, to act as if we were legislating for the human race (including ourselves). Another popular device was the notion that one should make decisions as if one were not an interested party but an impartial observer, or as if one were operating behind a veil of ignorance. In these schemes, our moral decisions are to be made in the same spirit as a secretary of defense whose investments have been put into a blind trust: We should act as if we did not consider our own interest (or that of our friends and relatives). This impartiality prompted Robert Frost's caustic observation that a liberal was someone who would not take his own side in an argument.

Despite the many varieties of liberal thought, there is a consistency of tone, a certain universal high-mindedness that is impatient with distinctions and disdainful of irrational attachments. Sentiments of loyalty, because they are not entirely rational, do not yield their secrets to analysis or measurement. The more intensely they are felt, the less precisely can they be quantified. Mother love can be an all-consuming passion in which there is little hope for reward, and without reciprocity between parent and child, it makes little sense to speak of the rights of parents or the rights of children. Because love is commitment and has no business with rights and claims, it must be amoral or, at best, premoral.

Lofty principles of right and public good, when they enter into the relations of friends and family, are nearly always harmful. A reformer who conducts a campaign to correct some social abuse can end up harming his dearest friends. Anthony Trollope, in his novel *The Warden,* wrote just such a story, in which the liberal John Bold is bent on reforming a small, church-run home for elderly men. He cannot do so, however, without injuring the feelings—and the livelihood—of Septimus Harding, the warden of the hospital and the one man who has befriended Bold since his youth. It does not help matters that Bold is in love with Mr. Harding's daughter. Early on in Bold's campaign, his sister attempts to dissuade him by pointing out the consequences of his rash interference in matters that do not appear to concern him. Asked why he must take up this case, Bold explains it is his duty. But, his sister asks, what of his friendship with old Mr. Harding? "Surely, John, as a friend, as a young friend . . ." Bold responds: "That's a woman's logic all over. . . . What has age to do with it . . . ? and as to friendship, if the thing itself be right, private motives should never be allowed to interfere." His sister finally begs him to give it up, if only for the sake of the girl he loves: "You are going to make yourself, and her, and her father miserable; you are going to make us all miserable. And for what? For a dream of justice."

"A dream of justice"—the phrase is the perfect characterization of so much political philosophy since the eighteenth century. An ordinary person attending a conference of liberal philosophers (as I have) finds himself in a strange world of unexamined assumptions in which it is taken for granted that the only moral actors are individuals, national governments, and (it is hoped some day) international governments. Families and neighborhoods, towns and states, churches, clubs, and fraternal societies are hardly ever mentioned. There are only individual dilemmas that require national and universal government actions carried out according to strictly rational rules.

Mechanical Moralities

At the foundation of liberal ethics is John Locke's conviction that moral behavior is really a question of rational decision-making: "[T]he great principle and foundation of all virtue and worth is placed in this: that a man is able to deny himself of his own desires, cross his own inclinations, and purely follow what reason directs as best."[8] This self-restraint

8. John Locke, *Some Thoughts concerning Education*, 33.

derives from a rational understanding of certain clear and abstract principles, which

> would . . . if duly considered and pursued, afford such foundations of
> our duty and rules of action as might place morality amongst the sciences
> capable of demonstration: wherein I doubt not but from self-evident
> propositions, by necessary consequences, as incontestable as those in
> mathematics, the measures of right and wrong might be made out to
> anyone that will apply himself with the same indifference and attention
> to the one as he does to the other of these sciences.

Morality, concedes Locke, may be a more complex matter than geometry,
but this is partly owing to the imprecision of language, and the problem
"may in good measure be alleviated by definitions."[9] Someday, Locke
hoped, the symbolic methods of algebra might be used to simplify ethical questions, and this hope was realized within a generation in the
moral equations drawn up by Scottish philosopher Francis Hutcheson.
Hutcheson was, in many respects, a wise man who looked back to older
ethical traditions, but his "let *G* stand for goodness" approach (derived
from Leibniz and Descartes) is no less comical than the symbolic formulas of more recent academic philosophers.

In Locke's own lifetime, however, some moral philosophers were still
studying, case by case, the sorts of dilemmas that ordinary people might
conceivably face, and this branch of philosophy, known as casuistry,
had become a highly technical art. But in Locke's view, a rational morality does not require the professional skills claimed by the practitioners
of casuistry; even the simplest men and women can make sense of their
obligations, if they will only attend carefully to the meaning of words.

Locke's carefree assumption that mathematical methods could be
applied to moral questions would have alarmed thinkers of an earlier
age. Aristotle had carefully distinguished between the exact sciences,
which are capable of demonstration, and the fuzzier disciplines that
study human life (such as ethics and politics), where we must be content
with partial truths and rough outlines: "It is the mark of an educated
man to seek precision only so far as the nature of the subject admits. To
demand logical proofs from rhetoric is the rough equivalent of expecting mathematics to use the language of persuasion" (*Eth. Nic.* 1094b).

9. John Locke, *An Essay concerning Human Understanding*, 4.3.20 (2:211).

More recently, Howard Gardner, in summing up recent researches in cognitive psychology and anthropology, came to a similar conclusion: "Pure logic . . . which developed long after our survival mechanisms had fallen into place . . . may be useful under certain circumstances. . . . But logic cannot serve as a valid model of how most individuals solve most problems most of the time."[10]

It was Descartes who laid the foundation for a scientific construction of ethics, likening philosophy to a tree "whose roots are metaphysics, whose trunk is physics, and whose branches . . . are all the other sciences . . . medicine, mechanics, and morals."[11] Just as he was able to construct geometry out of arithmetic and derive physics from mathematics, Descartes was confident that the same precise methods could be applied to human morals.

Although the tree metaphor is organic, Descartes seems more fond of mechanical models of human nature. He explains the body in mechanical terms, comparing it to a machine whose parts correspond to bones, nerves, muscles, and so forth.[12] The human passions he reduces to interactive processes of soul and body that are as mechanical as anything imagined by the behaviorists. The soul, for example, is said to induce passions by causing "the little gland to which it is closely united to move in the way requisite to produce the effect," while tears are a form of condensation, groans are produced by excess blood in the lungs, and so on.[13] At the beginning of his *Treatise on Man,* Descartes adopts the conventional view that man consists of soul and body, but he proceeds to ignore the former and to explain the functioning of the latter by imagining the body as a mere machine, and this analogy extends to perceptions, dreams, and feelings. The reduction of man to a "meat machine" (as the inventor Nikola Tesla later put it) reached an almost classical perfection in La Mettrie's *L'Homme machine.* It seemed an inevitable progression, after Descartes and Hobbes (who also employed an extended machine metaphor to describe man and society), to go from

10. Howard Gardner, *The Mind's New Science: A History of the Cognitive Revolution,* 370.

11. René Descartes, preface to *Principles of Philosophy,* in *The Philosophical Works of Descartes,* trans. E. S. Haldane and G. R. T. Ross, 1:211.

12. René Descartes, *Discourse on Method,* in *Philosophical Works,* 1:115–16.

13. René Descartes, *Des passions de l'ame,* 351 (gland), 479 (tears), 426 (groans).

a mechanical explanation of human feelings and thoughts to treating man as nothing more than a machine.

La Mettrie's disciple, the Marquis de Sade, took the argument to its logical conclusion: If human passions are mere physiological itches, man's proverbial dignity is a fraud, and there is nothing—not even our normal revulsion against rape and torture—to stand in the way of treating other human beings as sex tools. From the materialistic perspective, nothing can be entirely unnatural.[14]

What Descartes sketched out and his successors elaborated is a bells-and-whistles, Rube Goldberg model of passion and behavior that makes it seem easy to establish a science of ethics. In the twentieth century, behaviorists like B. F. Skinner applied these simplistic theories to real human beings. Skinner actually put his daughter into a modified Skinner box called the Baby Tender, which obviated the need for blankets and diapers. According to legend, the daughter grew up insane and sued her father.

In fact, she grew up to be a fairly normal person who admired her father, but there is a grain of truth in the legend. Mothers ruined children, the behaviorists wrote in their popular articles, and human beings could be brought up sane only if they were put into a laboratory setting and deprived of human contact. The Baby Tender was a step in that direction. Skinner's mentor and the founder of behaviorism, John B. Watson, dedicated his book on children to the first mother to raise a happy child. One of Watson's sons remembered his father as cold and inhuman; his eldest son committed suicide. The most famous "expert" on child rearing, Benjamin Spock, was ridiculed in his later years for telling parents to be too permissive, but his original importance lay in the challenge he posed to the behaviorists: Mothers are not always wrong, Spock argued, and a mother's natural affection for her children is a more reliable guide than theories that seem to work only with rats and pigeons.

Scientific arrogance toward all things human did not begin with John B. Watson. Such arrogance was present at the very beginning of modern ethical and political theory. With his emphasis on the power of reason, Descartes was inclined toward an ethic of rationality and voli-

14. See Neil Schaeffer, *The Marquis de Sade: A Life*, 71.

tion, and he seems to come close to the Socratic belief that to know good is akin to doing it, and that evil is the result of ignorance.[15]

Such radical assumptions become particularly dangerous in an age in which revolutionary simplicity is desired. Although Descartes more than once professed his adherence to Catholic theology and conventional morality—and his disdain for reformers—the bent of his mind was against both tradition and authority. The sublime individual counted most, both as judge of all things and as creator. For example, Descartes thought a city constructed by one man would be more beautiful than the product of historical accretion—even if the latter had more beautiful buildings—and that it would be better if a state's legal and political system were designed by one man at the beginning rather than produced by a gradual evolution in response to changing circumstances. Admitting that it may not be possible to tear down an entire city to rebuild it anew, he thought it could be done with a single house.[16]

The whole cast of the Cartesian mind is an arrogant self-confidence in an individual's ability to set aside the wisdom of experience and to recreate all of philosophy "from scratch." Descartes speaks of himself, over and over, as a man of modest ability, only to take it for granted that his own contributions to philosophy supersede all that has ever been written. In the *Discourse on Method,* he insists that he has accepted all the conventional morality of his society, but it is hard to square this protestation with the radicalism of his city-planning discussion, which he concludes with the general observation that "as regards all the opinions which up to this time I had embraced, I thought I could not do better than endeavor once for all to sweep them completely away, so that they might later on be replaced, either by others which were better, or by the same, when I had made them conform to the uniformity of a rational scheme." His resolution is not limited to science and mathematics: "By this means I should succeed in directing my life much better than if I had built on old foundations, and relied on principles of which I allowed myself to be in youth persuaded without having inquired into their truth."[17]

15. Descartes did, however, express agreement with Cornelis Jansen on the problem of will and predestination.
16. Descartes, *Discourse on Method,* 1:87 ff.
17. Ibid., 1:89.

It is safer, though, to begin by treating conventional views with respect, while all the time subjecting them to radical skepticism. Although Descartes is best known for the skeptical chain of reasoning culminating in his "*cogito ergo sum*," from another perspective he is less a skeptic than a naive and utopian revolutionary, ready to tilt at any windmill, even those that grind the wheat for his daily bread. The results of such sophomoric questioning in the realms of morals and politics are disastrous, both for inciting unstable characters to kick over the traces and for encouraging even thoughtful people to transfer moral questions from the everyday world of action to the ethereal kingdom of speculative reasoning.

If correct moral decisions are arrived at by a process of reason and analysis, there must be some process of development by which morally irrational creatures become rational and the irresponsible become responsible. If the ability to think rationally is the touchstone of our morality, we should be interested in the question: How is it that we come to let reason affect what we do at all? Stephen Toulmin, who poses the question in these terms, thinks it was important only in a logical and philosophical sense—what sort of reason would justify ethical decisions? He adds: "It cannot matter to us exactly what Socrates said, what attitude the sect of Thugs adopts toward ritual murder, how this or that degree of malnutrition affects individual moral standards or at what age one first sees that there is a difference between 'wrong' and 'what Daddy forbids.'"[18]

But all these questions, however irrelevant they are to a discussion of Toulmin's subject—the place of reason in ethics—matter to us a great deal. Any moral philosophy, if it is to persuade us that some decisions are better and higher than others, must include some account of how men and women become virtuous. Without such an explanation, there is no well-marked route from worse to better conduct and hardly even a sufficient reason for escaping the moral hedonism of a child. In fact, most educators speak and act as if they had some idea of how to form a good moral character (however they define *good*).

Plutarch, in his essay on awareness of moral progress, was really concerned with refuting the Stoic philosophers who taught that men were either absolutely good or simply evil, "putting the injustice of Aristides

18. Stephen Toulmin, *The Place of Reason in Ethics*, 131.

(nicknamed 'the just') on par with the injustice of Phalaris," the tyrant proverbial for torturing his enemies to death (*Mor.* 76). On the contrary, there are degrees of good and evil, and it is only by studying our progress and regress in each that we can confidently make our way toward a more virtuous life. In his essay "On Moral Virtue," Plutarch declares that the ethical is a quality of the irrational. He does not deny that reason plays an important part in moral life; its role, however, is not to eliminate the passions, but to moderate them (*Mor.* 443).

One of Plato's central concerns—it sometimes seems like an obsession—was how virtue can be acquired. Is it taught *(Protagoras)?* Inherited *(Laches)?* Or is it inspired by a god *(Meno)?* Plato devoted a significant part of both the *Republic* and the *Laws* to the formulation of an educational process designed to produce virtuous citizens, and while he was inclined to overestimate the significance of rational understanding—confounding knowledge of the good with practice of the good— he realized that the totality of a community's social and political institutions is responsible for forming the character—good or ill—of its citizens.

Liberals, with their emphasis on an individual's ability to apply rational rules universally, treat moral development as virtually the same thing as development of the power of ethical reasoning. For Descartes, morality consisted of the subjugation of the passions by the rational will, and the only progress he seems to have conceived of is rational. Locke, more a man of the world, was not so blind as to suppose that self-denying rationality could be taught exclusively by proofs and maxims: "This power is to be got and improved by custom, made easy and familiar by an early practice."[19] But it is a small step from Locke to the theories of moral development in children that presuppose a progressive development from irrational to rational, from particular to universal, from acceptance of imposed authority to individual autonomy.

Thinking Our Way to Virtue

To a great extent, these assumptions are manifest in the work of Jean Piaget, Erik Erikson, and Lawrence Kohlberg. Piaget believed that a human being's moral and intellectual development was a natural process,

---

19. Locke, *Some Thoughts concerning Education*, 38.

prescribed and carried down through the generations in our genes, more or less like the rules that govern physical maturation. If a person is normal, his moral development proceeds through a series of phases—although not all individuals go through these phases at the same rate.

Piaget's approach was largely intellectual and concentrated on the child's growing ability to abstract general rules and form hypotheses. By adolescence, the child has developed "the capacity to reason in terms of verbally stated hypotheses and no longer in terms of concrete objects." This means that the fifteen-year-old not only can entertain an opposing point of view but can also interest himself in problems that arise from outside his own experience.[20]

Piaget was interested primarily in the stages of childhood and adolescence. Erikson and Kohlberg attempted to improve upon his account by including the whole of human life. But after adolescence, Piaget's parallel with physical development becomes much less relevant, since by adulthood the major physiological processes of growth are complete.[21]

The most celebrated theory of moral development was that of Kohlberg and his colleagues. Kohlberg published his research on the subject over a twenty-five-year period, and his thinking inevitably underwent many changes and refinements, which would be a distraction to discuss. In essence, Kohlberg outlined three broad phases of moral development through which every individual in every culture proceeds, although many do not get much more than halfway through the course.

In the "pre-conventional" phase, an individual goes from being motivated by blind obedience and the fear of punishment (Stage 1) to a more selfish stage of a naive hedonism in which he seeks to get his own way (Stage 2). In the "conventional" phase, he begins by desiring to secure approval from others (Stage 3) and ends up recognizing the need for social order and authority (Stage 4). The "post-conventional" phase finds the more enlightened individuals passing from an understanding that contracts and agreements are the basis of any democratic social order (Stage 5) to an ultimate affirmation of a sort of golden rule. At this highest level (Stage 6), the individual becomes a sage who is interested neither in processes like justice nor in his own self-interest. His

20. Jean Piaget, *The Moral Judgment of the Child*, 26; Jean Piaget, "Intellectual Evolution from Adolescence to Adulthood."

21. See John C. Gibbs, "Kohlberg's Moral Stage Theory: A Piagetian Revision."

moral conscience encompasses the fate of all mankind and even the entire universe, and he applies his abstract principles as if the fate of the world depended on them.

The most obvious problem with Kohlberg's theory is that such sages do not exist. Kohlberg, at least, never interviewed one, and the biographies of most historical candidates—the moral and political heroes with whom we began this discussion—disclose a layer of clay that rises well above the ankles. How useful, we have a right to ask, is a moral scheme that culminates in an ideal that is not merely difficult to reach but apparently unrealizable? One answer might be that it constitutes an ideal to strive for. But it is scarcely helpful to tell people that if they tried harder, they could fly by jumping off a tall building and waving their arms. Religious teachers, it is true, may tell their followers to give away all their possessions or even to face death, but these demands derive from superhuman sources. A strictly secular and natural ethic is in no position to make such demands.

Even Kohlberg's "democratic" Stage 5 is little more than the historical product of modern society and an artifact of liberal education in the West. Members of traditional societies simply do not think that way, or, if they do, it is because they have been indoctrinated by a long process of Western education. In the United States, only a few reach the penultimate stage, and those few are predominantly white, middle-class, college-educated, and male.

It is this last restriction, maleness, that Carol Gilligan has criticized. Men, argues Gilligan, tend to view moral questions in terms of abstract rights and duties, while women respond to the human needs of people to whom they are connected. She calls this latter approach an "ethic of care." Originally viewing these two moral perspectives as divergent—a sexual dichotomy—Gilligan and her colleagues later came to realize that they were overlapping and complementary strategies. Depending upon circumstances, an individual of either sex might choose one or the other. How we view a situation depends upon point of view, and moral dilemmas resemble the ambiguous figure which, depending upon our perspective, can be seen either as a duck or a rabbit.[22]

---

22. Carol Gilligan and Grant Wiggins, "The Origins of Morality in Early Childhood Relationships." For "ethic of care," see Carol Gilligan, *In a Different Voice: Psychological Theory and Women's Development.*

The two perspectives, however, are not quite equal. In the parallel case of sexual development, we all start out more or less female, and it requires the infusion of male hormones at key periods of development (before and after birth) to create a male. The female appears to be the basic theme, the male the variation. A similar claim might be made for morality—that the female element in human nature is more or less generic, and the male a derived variant. Concern and affection are universal and necessary, while the more abstract rules devised by men fond of contests, power struggles, and battles are useful only in the situations that gave rise to them. We do not "reason" our way into caring for children or respecting aged parents or being good neighbors. We can imagine a ruleless society based on kinship and affection and self-defense— or rather, we do not have to imagine it, because most premodern societies were of this type—but it is terrifying to conceive of a society based on no principles but those invented by liberal philosophers in pursuit of perfect justice.

Gilligan's work represents a useful step backward in the retreat from theoretical ethics. The significance of her approach, however, has sometimes been obscured by her political commitments. A *New York Times* feature described her research group as committed "to extending beyond abstract clinical research . . . seeking ways to intervene in the developmental process."[23] The problem of the observer in scientific experiments goes back at least to Heisenberg, but Gilligan's group does not even treat it as a problem.

Much of Gilligan's work involves telling stories and fables to adolescent girls and recording their responses. Unfortunately, the feminist emphasis puts additional strains upon a methodology that is already somewhat remote from everyday reality. This can be seen in the use of beast fables by Gilligan's colleague Kay Johnson. Children were told the story of the porcupine taken in by a family of moles who find they cannot endure the continual pricking of his quills.[24] The fable in its original form teaches a simple lesson: Kindness to strangers is all very well,

23. Francine Prose, "Confident at 11, Confused at 16," *New York Times Magazine*, January 7, 1990, p. 23.

24. See Carol Gilligan et al., eds., *Mapping the Moral Domain: A Contribution of Women's Thinking to Psychological Theory and Education*, esp. Kay Johnson, "Adolescent Solutions to Dilemmas in Fables: Two Moral Orientations—Two Problem Solving Strategies," 49–69.

but family comes first. This did not satisfy the researchers, who evidently follow Kohlberg in despising notions of private property and family commitment. Thus, when the children took the moles' side in the argument, the researchers gently urged them to come up with more cooperative solutions. For Gilligan, in the end, Kohlberg's rationalist democratic values and universal principles trump the feminist's primary attachments.

Kohlberg's naive faith in moral progress is a cultural artifact, a residue of nineteenth-century progressivism. For John Stuart Mill, the progress of civilization was inevitably echoed by the moral progress of individuals who more and more considered the welfare of others:

> This mode of conceiving ourselves and human life, as civilization goes on, is felt to be more and more natural. Every step in political improvement renders it more so, by removing the sources of opposition of interest, and leveling those inequalities of legal privilege between individuals or classes, owing to which there are large portions of mankind it is still practicable to disregard. In an improving state of the human mind, the influences are constantly on the increase which tend to generate in each individual a feeling of unity with the rest; which, if perfect, would make him never think of, or desire, any beneficial condition for himself, in the benefits of which they are not included.[25]

Mill's faith in the progress of individuals and of civilization, combined with his manifest contempt for the lower classes (he concedes that "differences of opinion and of mental culture" makes universal sympathy difficult),[26] lend his essay on utilitarianism a messianic air that may inspire derision in postmodern readers who have savored the bitter fruits of progress: political repression, genocide, environmental degradation, nuclear warfare against civilians. Mere change does not necessarily constitute progress, either in the individual or in society, and the mere fact that one stage comes later than another does not make it, prima facie, higher. The Third Reich followed the Weimar Republic, which followed the stable and affluent Wilhelmine regime. Decay and entropy are at least as characteristic of human societies as progress and enlightenment.

The same goes for individuals. There is a grain of truth in Wordsworth's statement that "the child is father to the man" or in the Taoist celebration of infancy. While many of us, as the years go by, may gain

25. John Stuart Mill, *On Liberty,* 54.
26. John Stuart Mill, *Utilitarianism,* 139–48.

in prudence and knowledge, we also lose our sincerity in the pursuit of selfish interest and in the disappointments of love and ambition. The young Ebenezer Scrooge was capable of loyalties and affections that, as a mature liberal capitalist, he eventually despised.

Many people, when they are told of the various schemes of Kohlberg or Erikson or Gilligan, reply that it sounds like a fine idea but, in their own case, development did not proceed in so regular a fashion.[27] Like love, the course of morality never did run smooth. Where to put, for example, Neoptolemus? At first glance, *Philoctetes* might seem to be about the transition from a recognition of social order to the "contract" mentality of democracy. But the young man's initial obedience is direct and "pre-conventional," unconnected to any larger vision. When he revolts against authority, that too is very personal, although there are elements in it of the final stage of sainthood.

With few exceptions, however, Greek moralists refused to apply pure reason to ethics and saw life as a sometimes snarled tangle of duties and virtues, and none of the terms they used to discuss this tangle can be successfully translated into English. How are we to grapple with their sense of virtue, when the word we are translating *(arete)* means pre-eminently "manliness" or "courage"? And what are we to make of the Homeric notion of friendship, when the root word *friend/friendly (philos)* is used by a hero primarily "to demonstrate the persons and things on which his life depends"?[28] This is not to say that Greek morality is opaque to modern readers or even that it is radically different in every respect, but an abstract analysis of the use of moral terms in twenty-first-century English does not advance our understanding of ethics much further than a polltaker contributes to the understanding of a complex political issue. As sociologist John Shelton Reed likes to say, a survey tells you what people think they ought to say when a stranger knocks on the door and begins asking suspicious questions, and language is as often used to conceal as to reveal an individual's moral opinions.

It is a strangely ethnocentric view of moral life that not only sets a wildly impossible goal but also sees all human history and all personal

27. See Lawrence J. Walker, "The Sequentiality of Kohlberg's Stages of Moral Development."

28. The classic discussion (albeit overstated) of these issues is M. R. Adkins, *Merit and Responsibility: A Study in Greek Values.*

development as culminating in a professor of philosophy who reasons his way to correct decisions. He may desert his wife and children, evade every obligation to his country—he may even betray it—but so long as his decisions are rational and based on a universal scheme of values, he is considered superior to the ignorant savage who takes care of his family and defends his people. Child psychologist Robert Coles confessed he became angry at the suggestion that poor black children, because they could not reason their way through a dilemma, were incapable of high ethical behavior, and he insisted that "moral life is not to be confused with tests meant to measure certain kinds of abstract (moral) thinking, or with tests that give people a chance to offer hypothetical responses to made-up scenarios."[29]

This is not to deny the obvious merits of all their years of patient interviewing and analysis, but what Kohlberg and like-minded psychologists describe is not a process of moral development so much as stages of cognitive development seen from the peculiar perspective of a liberal philosophy that sets itself at the pinnacle and views all other ways of living and thinking as, at best, inchoate strugglings toward the light of revelation. Kohlberg, who believed that a properly informed and free society would inevitably evolve toward "recognition of human rights," expressed impatience with the rate of moral progress in the 1970s: "Watergate is a reminder that the Stage 5 social contract still waits for the majority to evolve."[30] In this sense, the ordinary men and women who voted for Richard Nixon are a lower form of almost-human life.

The Socratic Fallacy

Kohlberg's basic fallacy goes back to Descartes and ultimately to Socrates, who argued repeatedly, according to Plato, that no one knowingly acts unjustly. Vice is ignorance, which (presumably) can be eliminated by a thorough course in dialectic. In the case of some of Socrates' friends and disciples, the course did little good. Alcibiades profaned his

29. Robert Coles, *The Moral Life of Children*, 286 ff., 27–28.
30. Lawrence Kohlberg, "The Future of Liberalism as the Dominant Ideology of the West," 67.

city's religious rites and betrayed his country; Critias and Charmides staged a coup and established a dictatorship in which they killed innocent Athenians for the sole purpose of stealing their property; and Meno the Thessalian, so charmingly portrayed by Plato in the dialogue that bears his name, turned into the treacherous scoundrel described by Xenophon: "Eager to get rich and eager to have power in order to get richer, eager to be honored in order to profit more. He wanted to be a friend to the very powerful so that, when he did wrong, he would not have to pay. For accomplishing his desires he thought the shortest way was through perjury, lying, and deception" (*Anabasis* 2.6.21–29).

Even Socrates, apparently, could not teach his students to reason their way toward goodness. Socrates and Plato were suspicious of the moral influence of poets, but it was a poet who first revealed Socrates' mistake. In his play *Hippolytus,* Euripides portrayed a passionate woman in the act of making up her mind to seduce her stepson: "In my opinion people do not do wrong because of their mind's nature. For many people can reason well. But we have to look at the matter in this way. We know and recognize what it is best to do, but we do not work at accomplishing it, some from laziness, others by putting pleasure above goodness" (377–82). St. Paul made the point more directly: "I can will what is right, but I cannot do it" (Rom. 7:19).

Plato himself eventually realized that dialectic alone was no guarantee of ethical improvement. Some of this lesson he apparently learned—if we believe his Seventh Letter to be genuine—in the school of hard knocks. In Sicily, where he hoped to try out some of his political ideas, he came to realize that the problems of the Greek cities there did not derive from a faulty constitution. What could be done, after all, with people who think happiness consists of "stuffing themselves twice a day and never sleeping alone at night"? As a result of such habits, practiced from youth, "no one under heaven could be wise or temperate or capable of any of the virtues, nor could a city be at rest, no matter what laws it had, when all the citizens think they have to spend all they have on their excesses, and when they agree upon the necessity of being idle, except when it comes to feasting, drinking, and sex."

In two of his later works, Plato devoted a great deal of attention to child rearing and education as a means for avoiding the Sicilian character. This was not an innovation on his part so much as a return to the conventional Greek (and American) view of the matter. What rationalists minimize—or even ignore—is the context, the environment in which moral development is fostered or repressed. Common opinion tells a different story: "As the twig is bent, so grows the tree" and "Spare the rod and spoil the child" are proverbs that emphasize the importance of training and chastisement in the development of character. Bookstores are filled with how-to books on child rearing (the equivalents in human terms of *No Bad Dogs*), and, despite the vast differences among the various schools of pop psychology and human development, they all guarantee results. By subjecting our children to the right series of experiences (as opposed to logical training or thought experiments), we can, so they claim, turn out healthy and productive human beings.

Obviously, there are limits to the effects of environments. You can't make a silk purse out of a sow's ear, or a Nobel laureate in physics out of a child who inherits no aptitude for math or analytical reasoning. Character traits also run in families, and while their transmission is partly the result of training and environment, there are qualities that pop up very early in life and prompt us to say, "Like father, like son," or "The apple never falls far from the tree."

Setting aside these genetic limitations, both general (in the sense that they are universally human) and particular (belonging to a specific blood line), the proverbs and the psychologists are right to emphasize the significance of environment on moral development. Aristotle, in his accounts of how people become virtuous, described the virtues as states of character that result from practice as opposed to intellectual training. Anticipating (and resolving) the nature/nurture debate, he wrote, "The virtues do not come into being from nature or against nature, but we are born capable of receiving them and we develop them through habit." The task of legislators, therefore, is to make good and responsible citizens by instilling good habits, "for it is by what we do in our interchanges with other human beings that we become just and unjust" (*Eth. Nic.* 1103a).

For Aristotle, the study of ethics is not a theoretical science—first, because the nature of the evidence does not admit of precision (*Eth. Nic.* 1094b) and second, because the object is practical (1103b–1104a). Ethics is therefore of no use to children or to persons of bad character who have failed to develop a rudimentary sense of right and wrong.

What distinguishes Aristotle's approach from that of modern philosophers is his attempt to combine psychology with ethics.[31] His concern, in other words, is both to justify ordinary perceptions of right and wrong and to give an account of how people become morally responsible.

Philosophers of the Scottish Enlightenment, although they differed sharply from Aristotle in many respects, shared his concern with the development of "moral sentiments." David Hume, in *A Treatise of Human Nature,* locates the source of natural virtues in the pleasure and pain we receive in performing a vicious or virtuous act, and ascribes the "artificial virtues" (such as justice) to the sympathy we feel for the pleasure or pain of other people.[32]

For Aristotle as for Hume, moral reasoning is an aspect of moral development but not a sufficient explanation for why some people behave more responsibly than others. Some criminals resemble Sherlock Holmes's nemesis, Professor Moriarty, "a man of good birth and excellent education, endowed by nature with a phenomenal mathematical facility.... a genius, a philosopher, an abstract thinker," who, on the strength of his great talents, became "the Napoleon of crime." Moriarty would have been no less immoral had he confined his viciousness to the narrow world of an academic department. If higher reasoning is the basis of morality, then why is the academic world periodically rocked by scandals involving fraudulent research and plagiarized articles? These failings are not unknown even among philosophers; the author of a recent discourse on honesty was discovered to have made up the endorsements for his book.

The greatest "sinners" of history have been the tyrants who used the resources of government to gratify their passions, but the moral failings of dictators from Critias (the ex-student of Socrates) to Stalin (a theology student with a taste for poetry) are not primarily intellectual, and there is no reason to suppose that, controlling for differences of class and income, college graduates are more moral than men and women who go to work at the age of eighteen. There are, it goes without saying, numerous psychological studies that have been designed to show a correlation between higher education and an increased ability in moral

31. See Miles Burnyeat, "Aristotle on Learning to be Good."
32. Hume, *A Treatise of Human Nature,* 2:37–38.

reasoning.[33] One researcher even claimed to have found a strong correlation between political ideology and Kohlberg's higher stages—not surprisingly, the progression is from conservative to liberal to radical. Conservatism, for example, is defined as an authoritarian view of rules that corresponds with Kohlberg's authoritarian stage.[34]

Kohlberg himself was forced to wrestle with the problematic connection between moral logic and moral action in response to a critique by two psychologists who pointed to the obvious paradox that young people who have attained the conventional, law-and-order stage of moral reasoning "are capable of deceitful conformity, vandalism, and indifference to life-and-death problems of strangers who ask for help, [and] are capable even of endangering others." Kohlberg's response was to make a connection between moral reasoning and "deontic judgment"—that is, a judgment that regards an action as morally obligatory, independent of consequences. His only evidence came from studies showing what students *say* they would do under certain circumstances.[35]

Interviews and discussions, however, do not begin to address the question of why educated and rational people of all ages behave, on occasion, irresponsibly to the point of committing serious crimes. On college campuses, the same campuses where research on moral progress is conducted, attacks against women have become routine, along with vandalism, racial violence, cheating on tests, and pilfering. "Morally advanced" students and professors are capable of trading sexual favors for grades, insulting people from different backgrounds, and shouting down visiting lecturers whose opinions they dislike.

In fact, there is no evidence that high status, income, and level of education are, in this age of the world, moral assets. In the 1920s, two affluent college students, Nathan Leopold and Richard Loeb, murdered a young man in cold blood. Their motives were partly sexual, partly thrill-seeking, and partly panic, but at the trial, their lawyer, Clarence Darrow, argued that they were victims of a higher education that included Darwin and

33. See, for example, James R. Rest, Mark L. Davison, and Steven Robbins, "Age Trends in Judging Moral Issues: A Review of Cross-Sectional, Longitudinal, and Sequential Studies of the Defining Issues Test."

34. Evan Simpson, "The Development of Political Reasoning."

35. Roger Brown and Richard Herrnstein, *Psychology,* 289; Lawrence Kohlberg and Daniel Candee, "The Relationship of Moral Judgment to Moral Action."

Nietzsche.[36] While Darrow's argument ought to receive serious consideration from a committee on curriculum, it is hard to see a necessary connection between the theory of natural selection and a pointless killing (William Jennings Bryan cited the argument to show Darrow's hypocrisy at the Scopes trial). It was not Leopold and Loeb's understanding that was flawed but their characters, as friends and acquaintances testified. The lawyer and novelist Erle Stanley Gardner, in his introduction to Leopold's memoir, wondered if the murderers' teachers and parents had failed to include in their educational diet "certain moral vitamins," with the result that "there was mental growth but spiritual apathy."[37]

If habits, as Aristotle says, make all the difference between virtue and vice, then the environment in which good habits are acquired is an essential aspect of moral development. For more than 99 percent of the time in which man has been developing on this planet, he has lived within the narrow orbit of families and small-scale communities. What is the point of a moral system that leaves these facts of life out of the picture? Unlike modern rationalists, most ancient philosophers recognized the special demands of blood and nationality. Aristotle remarks that it is worse to cheat a comrade than a fellow citizen, that to fail to help a brother is worse than to fail to help a stranger, and that striking a father is a more terrible crime than any other assault. (St. Alphonsus regarded it as a mortal sin for children to provoke their mothers by calling them "crazy, drunk, beast, witch," or even "old, dizzy, ignorant.")[38] Kinship, of course, was the most special relationship, and Aristotle describes family relationships in almost sociobiological terms. Parents, he says, love children as their very selves, and brothers love each other as being born from the same parents: Their identity with their parents makes them identical with each other (*Eth. Nic.* 1161b).

Aristotle's family-and-village morality is not limited to the Greeks. On the contrary, it is Lawrence Kohlberg's higher stages of moral reasoning that are culturally limited. "Only Kohlberg's lower moral stages

---

36. Meyer Levin retold the story in his novel *Compulsion*. At the Scopes trial, William Jennings Bryan used Darrow's argument against him to maintain that Tennessee was right to ban the teaching of evolution.

37. Erle Stanley Gardner, introduction to *Life plus 99 Years*, by Nathan F. Leopold, 1.

38. St. Alphonsus, *Theologia Moralis*, 1:600.

have been proved to be universal to the cultures thus far sampled.... The higher stages appear to be culture specific."[39] Indeed, since no two cultures have exactly the same moral codes, no two cultures will treat moral development in the same way. Societies based on kinship will prize loyalty to clan, perhaps, above other recognized virtues such as honesty, while democratic-capitalist societies will encourage competition and success, perhaps at the expense of the "family values" that they also espouse. This is an obvious point. Serious Catholics and Protestants do not agree on such questions as marriage, contraception, and the grounds for war, and, even among conservative Catholics, Americans frequently part company with Europeans, siding with more purely American values at the expense of their Church's teachings.

Family Values

Far from being the exclusive preserve of rational individuals, morality is, for all practical purposes, a social phenomenon, as Durkheim noted: "Morality begins . . . only in so far as we belong to a human group, whatever it may be. Since, in fact, man is complete only to the extent that we feel identified with those different groups in which we are involved—family, union, business, club, political party, country, humanity."[40]

The first, the primary one of these groups, is the family, the social context in which we learn to be human. The process begins with the infant's growing attachment to its mother,[41] and this attachment gradually expands to embrace the entire household:

> Characteristically young children come to love the people who care for them, desiring to be near them, wanting to know them, being able to recognize them, and being sad when they leave. In the context of attachment the child discovers the patterns of human interaction and observes the ways in which people care for and hurt one another.... The experience of attachment profoundly affects the child's understanding of how

39. Carolyn P. Edwards, "Societal Complexity and Moral Development," 509–10; cf. the same writer's "Moral Development in Comparative Cultural Perspective."
40. Emile Durkheim, *Moral Education: A Study in the Theory and Application of the Sociology of Education*, 80.
41. The classic study is John Bowlby's *Attachment and Loss*.

one should act toward other people and the child's knowledge of human feelings.[42]

Small children who have a strong bond with their mother are less likely to cry when she leaves the room and can face strange situations with comparative equanimity. They are also more cooperative and outgoing.[43] Good character and good citizenship are forged in the nursery, where children learn to rely on the affectionate attention of a mother who is constantly accessible.

The family is also the setting in which moral rules are learned. Small children (two to three years old) learn their moral code both from siblings and parents (especially mothers); during the second year, they develop an interest in teasing and "show an increasing interest in what is permitted or prohibited behavior" by observing and joining in conflicts. Children develop most rapidly in families where the mother makes frequent reference to family rules and to the feelings of others.[44] Family life is, therefore, the social context in which moral progress takes place.

The process of attachment is natural but not inevitable, and not all children are born into a stable family setting. Failure in the early stages of development may mean a permanent moral disability. Orphans and even children deprived of one parent are more likely to pose social problems than children brought up in intact families. Truancy, delinquency, drug and alcohol use, sexual promiscuity, illegitimate pregnancy, depression, and suicide among teenagers have all been linked to broken or never-formed marriages. This is no more than common sense. Growing up human is a difficult process that absorbs the efforts of parents, kinfolk, friends, and neighbors. Single-parent families in traditional societies can fall back on the reserves, but many Americans lack the advantages provided by extended families and close-knit communities. Besides, boys and girls need to learn, at close quarters, what men and women are really like, and those lessons can best be learned at home. Some of these lessons are nothing more nor less than the habits of affection, responsible behavior, and trust.

42. Gilligan and Wiggins, "Origins of Morality," 280.
43. See Mary D. Salter Ainsworth, Mary C. Blehar, Everett Waters, and Sally Wall, *Patterns of Attachment: A Psychological Study of the Strange Situation,* 23–28.
44. Judy Dunn, "The Beginnings of Moral Understanding: Development in the Second Year," 100–101.

Leaving the Nest

The family is not a self-contained, discrete unit, and few human societies consist exclusively of warring kindreds: Households are joined together in tribes and villages, which in turn coalesce into nations. But at the base of all this higher social order is the one truly natural institution. Since families need to replicate themselves, the child cannot remain forever locked within the familiar prison of the household. Most societies have rituals to mark the transition from childhood to adulthood.[45] Where the process is complicated by customs that hinder contact between fathers and sons, the rituals are often particularly violent, as in the case of gang initiations that include violent crimes or games of Russian roulette.

These rituals of transformation are nearly universal. In the modern West, they take the form of college and military training, but there are older and deeper customs, such as First Communion and the bar mitzvah. Traditional superstitions such as tales of werewolves have been explained as a ritualized exile of teenage boys, driven out of the village and educated in a sort of deer-camp survival course.[46] In Boy Scouts, on the football team, at boot camp, in the frat house, young males learn to view their families with some detachment and to see themselves as part of a group that will someday be in charge. Young women face a parallel set of initiation rituals, sometimes more daunting than those of the male. These run the gamut from coming-out parties to the barbarous cruelty of female circumcision.

In the standard view of development, early adolescence is the period in which children earn autonomy by freeing themselves from their dependence upon the household. This is certainly the view advanced by teachers who emphasize the child's right to establish his own code in matters of sexual morality and politics. But is the young adolescent really becoming autonomous or merely "trading . . . dependency on parents for dependency on peers?"[47] A fourteen-year-old boy appears to be more of a conformist than his eight-year-old brother, as any parent can testify.

45. See Arnold Van Gennep, *The Rites of Passage.*
46. Walter Burkert, *Homo Necans: The Anthropology of Ancient Greek Sacrificial Ritual and Myth.*
47. Laurence Steinberg and Susan B. Silverberg, "The Vicissitudes of Autonomy in Early Adolescence," 848.

Adolescence is also marked by the growing proficiency in logic observed by Piaget, Kohlberg, and others, although the process is by no means so uniform as it is often described.[48] By late adolescence, children have commonly developed the ability to think abstractly, to generalize, and to transcend the personal dimensions of a problem. They begin to form a general conception of law as something functional rather than an arbitrary and absolute authority.[49] At the same time, their horizons are broadening to include neighborhood, school, and the wider world they are exposed to by way of rumors, including the electronically manufactured rumors of the evening news.

These wider social horizons are sometimes explained by the term *identity,* made popular by Erik Erikson, who insisted that personality development could not be understood without considering the environment in which it took place.[50] Identity is not innate or determined by biology; it is a social construction built out of the expectations of other people. Erickson also emphasized the importance of a wholesome early childhood in the family as a necessary precondition for continued development into the broader stages of neighborhood and school identities.

The slow emergence of a social identity is a complex and sometimes painful metamorphosis that is not well understood, but everyone who remembers starting kindergarten or changing schools can recognize the difficulty. We enter a new situation as an alien, knowing no one and not understanding the rules. It is as if everyone else is a member of a secret society; they know the passwords and can take part in the rituals. As the months go by, we are introduced little by little to the arcana of the tribe, until the day comes when being a Cooper School boy is second nature.

The once-popular Victorian novel *Tom Brown's School Days* chronicles just such a transformation. At first unable to live up to the high standards of Dr. Arnold's Rugby, Tom (or rather the author, Thomas Hughes) evolves into a model Victorian public servant. A more gradual and compelling description of this painful process is provided by Trol-

48. John Michael Murphy and Carol Gilligan, "Moral Development in Late Adolescence and Adulthood: A Critique and Reconstruction of Kohlberg's Theory," but for the uniform view, see, for example, David Moshman and Edith Neimark, "Four Aspects of Cognitive Development."

49. See Joseph Adelson and Robert P. O'Neil, "Growth of Political Ideas in Adolescence."

50. Erik H. Erikson, *Identity: Youth and Crisis,* 24.

lope in his depiction of Johnny Eames (another self-portrait) in *The Small House at Allington*. Eames is a young "hobbledehoy" who cannot put either his life or his career in order until a chance opportunity for heroism sets him on the path to wisdom and success.

The same process takes place when adults start a new job, and it is even more noticeable in retreats and conferences held in isolated settings. At the beginning, most people may be strangers, with no pattern of expectation to fall back on, but within three or four days—if the conference is small enough and intelligently planned—a unique group identity is forged, one that is hard to explain or even understand a few weeks later, once the intense intimacy of the experience has faded.

Sociologists and social psychologists who study group formation and group identity are familiar with this phenomenon and have devised a number of theories to explain it. The important thing, however, is not why it happens or how it happens but that it does happen. The ability to assume a group identity is an important part of the human condition; failure in the early stages, particularly failure to become part of a stable family, seems to presage a wider failure to become a good neighbor and a good citizen. It is also a self-replicating failure, since children who grow up in broken and unstable homes are less likely to become good spouses and parents.

The practical consequences should be apparent. If it is only in domestic and private life that children can develop morally, then governments are simply not capable of undertaking such responsibility. On this point, Plato and Aristotle were quite wrong; it is precisely because the moral education of the young is vital to the commonwealth that so important a task cannot be entrusted to slaves or mercenary strangers. Ethics, as it is taught in most public schools, aims only at moral reasoning of a type that is often inappropriate to a child's age, and where it has any success, the most it can do is unsettle the convictions that have been instilled by the parents.

The choice is not, as so many reformers seem to think, between the "primitive" moral and religious codes inculcated within homes and churches and the "higher" ethical understanding taught in the schools. Schools, as it is now apparent to anyone with eyes, cannot teach practical morality, even if that were the intention. As a result, whatever good lessons about honesty, chastity, and loyalty are learned from parents are undermined by teachers who show students how to doubt and question everything but what is learned in the classroom. Even liberals are appalled by the results when high-school teachers refuse to condemn theft, for instance, on the grounds that it is not their right to impose an ethical point of view.

The great mistake is to look at moral education from the wrong end. We teach the morality of saints to children who have yet to acquire the virtues of savages. The evolution of moral responsibility is more than progress in rationality and critical thought; it is also a steady broadening of moral contexts in which human beings recognize a larger and larger circle of fellow men and women.

The ancient Stoic philosopher Hierocles used the image of concentric rings, widening out from the family to the human race.[51] This image was part of an attempt to explain moral development as a progressive evolution that involved both a growth in reason and the fulfillment of functions or duties appropriate to a person's age. The first such function is self-preservation, implanted by nature as an instinct. In order to preserve his life, the child must next learn to hold on to the things that accord with his nature (for example, food) and repel those that are contrary and harmful. In the third stage, the child learns to make an active choice, and in the fourth, his correct selection becomes habitual. Finally, he is in a position to know and to do what is really good and according to nature (Cic. *De Finibus* 2.20–21). According to another ancient philosopher, Antiochus of Ascalon—an eclectic academic who sometimes borrowed from Stoic sources—it is parental love that is the source of the child's growth in social responsibility and affection:

> There is nothing so glorious nor more wide-spread than the unity of mankind, that partnership and sharing of interests, that dearness of the human race, which has its origin at birth, because parents love their offspring, and because the whole family is bound together by marriage and by parenthood. This sentiment gradually spreads beyond the household, first to blood relatives, then to relations acquired by marriage, then to friends and later to neighbors, then to fellow-citizens and to those who are allies and friends in public life, and finally comes to embrace the whole human race. (Cic. *Fin.* 5.65)

True citizens of the world, on this understanding, are the end products of a long process—beginning with a child's experience of parental

---

51. See Simon Pembroke, "Oikeiosis," 126 ff.

love—of forming attachments. It is as if moral ontogeny recapitulated moral and political phylogeny—that is, as if a healthy human being had to have gone through the steps of mankind's social and political evolution, that no one can be a citizen of the world if he is not first part of a family, a village community, a nation.[52] If parents repudiate the obligation to socialize their children (or merely fail in their effort), the consequences are perilous, both to the children and to society. Some responsibility must be laid at the door of those who lay down the moral guidelines for society—that is, the teachers, writers, and experts who have failed to convince parents of their responsibilities.

The sense of duty or conscientiousness taught by liberal philosophers is simply not enough. Parents owe their children more than conscientiousness; they owe them love. This is a problem for liberal philosophers, who tend "to be fairly silent on who has what obligations to new members of the moral community." There is simply no room in modern ethics for the traditional duty of parents to love and nurture their children, even though all the evidence we can muster suggests that children are as much in need of love as they are of food.[53] A child's absolute need for love is like an apple tree growing in the road that obstructs the philosopher's cart filled with theoretical apples that no one can eat.

Friendship

Human beings are not solitary creatures; man is a social animal who, both out of necessity and from causes within his own nature, is driven to seek out the company of his fellows. For any understanding of morality, therefore, friendship must be a key term, since it is the relationship between different types of friends (including relatives) that requires us to behave justly toward others (Arist. *Eth. Eud.* 1234b-35a).

In his discussion of friendship in the *Eudemian Ethics,* Aristotle starts with the general opinion that

> [j]ustice and injustice are chiefly a question of friends. . . . a good man is a friendly man . . . friendship is a state of moral character. . . . Therefore

---

52. For a biological argument for the genesis of the individual, see Antoine Danchin, "Stabilisation fonctionelle et epigenèse: Une approche biologique de la genèse de l'identité individuelle."

53. Annette C. Baier, *Moral Prejudices: Essays on Ethics,* 5.

justice and friendship are the same thing, or close to it. ... We spend our days with family, relations, and pals, children, parents, or wife, and our personal acts of justice directed toward friends are up to us, while just behavior directed toward others is established by law and not up to us. (*Eth. Eud.* 1234b)

By friendship *(philia)*, Aristotle means something like affection, concern, or love, and the most natural (as well as the most powerful) form is the love between parents and children. More broadly spread throughout the community, it is friendship, rather than justice, that holds the city together (*Eth. Nic.* 1155a16–25). Although most people would rather receive than give love, the hallmark of friendship is loving, and the strongest example is the unselfish love of a mother who may even be willing to give her child up, if that is in its best interest (1159a).

Friendship is the basis of all human associations that require sharing and mutual responsibilities. To the extent we have a "relationship," there is friendship to the same extent—and justice. In this sense, justice and friendship (or love) are concerned with the same things (*Eth. Nic.* 1159b25 ff.). Aristotle's arguments seem to lead to a conclusion that most Greeks would have readily accepted: It is only by loving others and by treating them as part of ourselves that we can behave justly toward them.

Modern readers are often puzzled by Aristotle's insistence that only the virtuous are happy. We have all seen apparently "happy" people who achieved success by immoral means or at the expense of friends and family members. But Aristotle insists that the successful immoralist cannot be happy, precisely because he has harmed his relatives, neighbors, and fellow countrymen.[54]

Love and friendship go by many names and derive from different sources, and no adequate account has ever been given. There are obvious differences between sexual desire *(eros)* and friendship *(philia)*, and still more obvious differences between a mother's intense and altruistic attachment to her children and her generalized feeling of benevolence toward an old but not especially close friend. There is a utilitarian aspect to many friendships which can function as a system of cooperation and mutual assistance. Man's nearest relatives, the primates, form alliances that benefit both parties: Baboon and chimpanzee males collaborate

54. See Jean Roberts, "Political Animals in the Nicomachean Ethics."

to establish a dominant position within their band, and in some species of baboons, the females cooperate in various ways as part of a larger hierarchy which their offspring inherit. Such "friendships" are adaptive, because they enable the parties to gain access to greater resources, such as more food, more matings and offspring, and to provide more resources to their children.[55]

If the friendships of beasts can be reduced to self-interest and utility, human affections—although rooted in the same ground—can rise to an appreciation of the other party. As is the case in all human things, there are degrees of seriousness, levels of intensity. Aristotle distinguishes between the lower forms of friendship, in which the friend is valued largely for the pleasure or enjoyment he gives, and higher forms, in which the friend is valued for his own sake. For Aristotle, "the central and basic kind of friendship . . . is friendship of character. Such friendships exist when two persons, having spent enough time together (1156b25–29), come to love one another because of their good human qualities."[56]

At the root of any serious attachment must lie an acknowledgment that the friend or beloved is a separate person, an autonomous self with his own character and "first-person" identity. Anything less is narcissism.

We do not come to know the world by reading about it but by living in it, and to live with other people, to grasp their reality, requires love. A man might apprehend the principles of a Bach fugue or understand the structure of a sonnet or be an expert in viticulture, but until he enjoys the music, the poetry, the wine, he does not really know them. It is love that wakes us up to the world and to the reality that was created, so Christians believe, by an overflowing of divine love. "The best way to bring a clever young man, who has become skeptical and unsettled, to reason," said Coleridge, "is to make him feel something in any way. Love, if sincere and unworldly, will in nine instances out of ten, bring him to a sense and assurance of something real and actual; and that sense alone will make him think to a sound purpose, instead of dreaming that he is thinking."[57]

55. Dorothy Cheney, Robert Seyfarth, and Barbara Smuts, "Social Relationships and Social Cognition in Nonhuman Primates."

56. John Cooper, "Aristotle on Friendship," 308.

57. Samuel Taylor Coleridge, *Specimens of the Table Talk of the Late Samuel Taylor Coleridge,* 169 (May 17, 1830).

Justice, as much as judgment, requires love, and love is rooted in erotic desire and the attachment between parents and children. To love the whole world, we must begin by loving our parents, our spouse, and our children. Charity, so it is said, begins at home. It then radiates outward in ever broader and weaker concentric rings until it encompasses the widest human horizons a person is willing to acknowledge. For Edward Banfield's Calabrians, this may be the village; for many moderns, it may be the nation; and there may even be saints capable of loving the entire human race. But if such general love is not based on more specific and local attachments, it amounts to little more than whim, a narcissistic love that basks in its own superiority without acknowledging the personhood of other human beings.

The ancient sophists were the progenitors of the modern philosophers who legislate for the world without setting their own affairs in order. When one of them, Gorgias of Leontini, went to Olympia and delivered a discourse on *homonoia*—that is, concord or social harmony—one of his auditors remarked that he had "given advice on concord, but he could not persuade the members of his own household to live in peace." Gorgias, it seems, was part of a love triangle involving his wife and his maidservant, and Plutarch, who records the anecdote in "Advice to Bride and Groom," goes on to generalize: "A man intending to harmonize the city, the market-place [meaning commercial and political life], and his friends, ought to have his own household well-harmonized" (*Mor.* 144).

The ancient insistence upon the priority of particular relationships stands in marked contrast with modern moral philosophies that either ignore the claims of family and friends or even exclude them from the realm of morality. If genuine moral decisions are made rationally on the basis of rules that apply universally, then all the petty kindnesses and irrational sacrifices made by friends and lovers either go beyond or fall short of morality.

Reason may command us to perform acts of justice and charity, but if they are done grudgingly and out of a sense of duty, then the acts may themselves be morally commendable, but the doer is not. A religious man who does good only because it is commanded is scarcely better than a hostage to morality. For what is the difference between the threat of physical death and the threat of eternal condemnation? The skeptical rationalist fares hardly any better. Once he has constructed or accepted a moral system to which he gives his allegiance, his acts of justice—if they are no more than acts of obedience—may display the superiority of his will, but they reveal nothing of his character.

Ancient morality stressed the virtues of character and took it for granted that a man of good character would do the right thing, once he understood what was right. Plato and Aristotle may have underestimated the difficulty of doing good, but they recognized that goodness lies in the doer rather than in the deed. "All men mean by justice the sort of character state which disposes people to do what is just" (Arist. *Eth. Nic.* 1129a). In modern accounts of morality, a virtuous man who does good almost by nature is not even considered a moral person. But to whom would it be safer to entrust one's daughter, to a naturally virtuous man who hardly feels any temptation, or to a rogue who has rationalized and disciplined his behavior into a system of continence and puritanism? Good works are good in and of themselves, but those who do them are not necessarily good: "And though I give all my belongings to feed the hungry and surrender my body to be burned, but I have no love, I am not the least benefited."

"When I was a child," St. Paul concludes, "I spoke like a child, I thought like a child, I reasoned like a child, but on becoming a man I put away childish things." How was this moral transformation accomplished? By a growth in reason? By studying philosophy? No, for knowledge is fragmentary and will lose its meaning. But love "takes no pleasure in injustice," and it is a growth in love, from family to community, to nation, to mankind, and ultimately to love of God, that represents our true moral development (1 Cor. 13:3–11). For Aristotle, as for St. Paul, God is the ultimate object of our attention: "Since the prime mover in the cosmos moves as an object of love, we are left to conclude that the intellectual love of God is, for the *E[udemian] E[thics],* also the prime motive within the soul. The measure of virtuous living is, for the *EE,* the contemplation and service of God. . . . the key to virtue is to know, love, and serve God."[58]

Nothing is really valuable to us unless we love it, and no one appreciates a favor done out of obligation. We resent the condescension and quite rightly suspect the motives of those who profess to do things for

58. Anthony Kenny, "The Nicomachean Conception of Happiness," 80.

our own good. We require love and sympathy, not the unkind kindnesses that display the moral superiority of Lady Bountiful. Neoptolemus did not reason his way to a decision to help Philoctetes; he learned to love him as a friend, which means, in Stoic terms, to hold him almost as dearly as he held himself.

The greatest Greek heroes risked everything for friendship. Theseus was trapped in the underworld, where he had descended to help his friend Pirithous, who wanted to take Persephone, the queen of the dead, for his wife. In one version of the story, it is another friend, Hercules, who descends and rescues Theseus. And Achilles, who was given the tragic choice of long life or glory—how did he decide? Actually, he seems to have changed his mind twice. As an inexperienced youth, he opted for adventure and glory, but, like many headstrong young men who cannot get along with their leaders, he changed his mind, withdrew from the battle, and preserved his life. Ultimately, the death of his friend Patroclus brings him back into the fray, to win undying fame—and death.

For pagans, it is a tragic choice and a subject for sad songs. The stories of Protesilaus, who returns from the grave for one day a year to visit his wife, and of Alcestis, the young wife who volunteers to take her husband's place in death, show that, even for pagans, love could triumph over the grave. More typical is the tale of Orpheus's bride, Eurydice, whom the hero fails to rescue from hell.

> Night holds Hippolytus the pure of stain,
> Diana steads him nothing, he must stay;
> And Theseus leaves Pirithous in the chain
> The love of comrades cannot take away.

Horace and his modern imitator (A. E. Housman) were both pagans who sought the meaning of life in its brevity. For Christians, it is a different matter. It is love that confers immortality, God's love for His treacherous and faithless creatures and their love for one another, a dim reflection of the divine love. Rather than imitating the Father Who, outside of time and space, created the universe and all that is in it, Christians are called upon to imitate the Son, Who came down from heaven and was made man, and Who in His humiliation subjected Himself to that first-person perspective that philosophers would have us transcend.

To His followers, He left two commandments, both already a part of

Jewish scripture. After the first great commandment to love God, the second was "to love thy neighbor as thyself." These two commandments of love take precedence over any philosophical system or rules of law, because it is on love and friendship that all our systems and rules depend: "On these two commandments hang all the law and the prophets" (Matt. 22:40).

PROBLEMS OF PERSPECTIVE

5

... maps are of time, not place, so far as the army
Happens to be concerned—the reason being,
Is one which need not delay us. Again, you know
There are three kinds of tree, three only, the fir and the poplar,
And those which have bushy tops; and lastly
    That things only seem to be things.

               —Henry Reed, "Judging Distances"

We have all had the experience. We catch sight of a distant object that seems, unmistakably, to be a flying saucer, but as we come closer the alien spacecraft gradually reveals itself to be only the sun's reflection off a tin roof. Getting closer to things is a little like what happens when a myopic bird-watcher puts on his eyeglasses and can finally make out what lies beyond the end of his nose.

By changing the distance, we alter our perspective on what things are, but not always for the better. In Henry Reed's poem "Judging Distances," an English soldier experiences what we might now call cognitive dissonance as he undergoes artillery training during the Second World War. From the artillery's point of view, "things only seem to be things," and in the late afternoon sun "a pair of what appear to be humans / Appear to be loving." What really matters to the army, however, is not a couple making love but "in what direction are they, / And how far away...?"[1]

The significance of trees and lovers, apparently, depends on distance and point of view. "There is nothing either good or bad, but thinking makes it so," observes Hamlet, who illustrates his theory by teaching old Polonius to regard a single cloud as a camel, a weasel, and a whale. Point of view, it seems, is everything, or almost. Young people are often told by parents and teachers to "put things in the proper perspective," but in "Judging Distances" the proper perspective of the artillery reduces the fields, a white house, and the elm trees under which the lovers lie to a set of coordinates that would determine their destruction.

Impartiality

Sometimes the object of our attention is neither clouds nor lovers, but ourselves. Many moral philosophers, at least since the end of the eighteenth century, have urged us to view our own decisions objectively and impartially, to assume the perspective of a third person, an uninvolved party who can judge the situation dispassionately. This approach amounts to little more than common sense. Anyone, even a philosopher, can get so wrapped up in himself that he cannot think rationally about what he should do. In such a case, he might have recourse to the opinion of a friend, a priest, or a counselor. Even if there is no one to talk to, he could summon up the mental image of some wise relative, who may be absent or even dead, and imagine what he would advise.

The virtues and vices of our friends can also serve as a mirror in which to view our own moral progress. Plutarch offers the analogy of a painter who often steps back to contemplate his work: "Since it is impossible for a man to withdraw from himself and break off the continuity of his perception—which makes every man a worse judge of himself than of others—the next best thing would be to examine his friends from time to time and to offer himself to his friends' scrutiny...to observe whether or not time has added something good or taken away some piece of baseness" (*Mor.* 453a).

1. Henry Reed, *Collected Poems*, 50–51.

As a boy I often thought of what my cousin would think of me, while my cousin, on the other hand, used my father as the true north of his moral compass. One useful aspect of prayer, surely, is that when we pray, we are referring our problems to a being whom we believe to be supremely wise and supremely good. In this respect, Burns's prayer is still worth invoking:

> O wad some pow'r the giftie gie us
> To see oursels as others see us!
> It wad frae mony a blunder free us,
>   And foolish notion.

Objectivity, then, has its uses, but how far are we to go in judging ourselves and our friends objectively? A man would be reduced to complete impotence if he attempted to view his everyday actions—eating, drinking, going to work—from a universal perspective. He might conclude that the cattle being raised for the beef he eats are polluting the atmosphere with methane, and that the corn they eat should go instead to starving Somalis. He might decide to eat only texturized soy protein and content himself that he is doing little harm, but how can he be sure (if he takes a perspective *sub specie aeternitatis*) of the effect on future generations?

The state, which is, according to Hobbes, a "mortal god," can afford to take such long views and to regard individuals, groups, and entire generations of young soldiers as less important than a tussle over some piece of territory that will increase its power. Keynes's quip that "in the long run we're all dead" does not really apply to states, which outlive most of the "we's" who might make such a statement and which may well regard a cartographic inch as worth the lives of a hundred thousand men. No one could really have thought Verdun worth the price of so much blood, except, perhaps, the town's inhabitants who witnessed its complete destruction.

Making Up Our Own Reality

"The maps," says Henry Reed, "are of time, not place, so far as the army / Happens to be concerned," and one tendency of the third-person perspective is to reduce oneself to the level of one man among billions, one foot soldier in the army of the human race. Paradoxically, the same perspective can encourage a belief in one's omnipotence. What is solipsism, if not the delusion that the fate of the world hangs on the mind of a single man? And the delusion is hardly different when it is the collective belief that each citizen represents one–270 millionth of the state's omnipotence. One of the superstitions of democracy is that each citizen, by voting, has a share in the powerful "manna" of the general will, when in fact most of the really important decisions are made by special interests that care as much about election returns as they do about Greek prosody or the Ten Commandments.

Solipsism is an extreme case, but what if a person feels compelled, before making any decisions, to refer them to a set of abstract social rules that determines the economic and social outcomes of individual X under Y circumstances? And what if he had to imagine that he himself was in a position to draw up this set of rules, but—and here is the important part—he had to devise (or agree to) such a code without knowing how it would affect his own life? In crude terms, this is what many liberal philosophers assume in arguing for social justice and equality: that to make a just decision today—say on tax policy or law enforcement—we must refer to general principles that lie at the foundation of our social order, and that we are forbidden to take into account how these rules or their application will affect us personally.

Think of life as if it were golf and of justice as the rules. When the game was invented or when the country club was established, some founders would have had to draw up the set of rules or principles. Afterwards, all members, both new and original, would have to play according to these rules. For the sake of fairness, the creators of the game, the original members of a club, or the founders of human society would set up the rules from behind a Veil of Ignorance. This is to make sure that the principles will be just and established (as Rawls says of his imaginary society) "solely on the basis of general considerations." In deciding on the use of golf carts, for example, I would not be allowed to know that I had (or would someday have) a disability; in setting the qualifications for members, I could not know that someday I would be rich or poor or that my daughter would marry someone from an unfashionable ethnic or religious group; and in setting up the cash prize for the annual tournament, I could not know that I would turn out to be a poor businessman but a great golfer who would rely on his winnings to supplement his income. Similarly, in establishing a society—or government in general—the mythical founding fathers would not be able to know what status or wealth each would have under the new rules. They are in the position of two children dividing a piece of cake: One cuts, while the other chooses the portion he wants.[2]

Justice, viewed from this impartial perspective, is arrived at by applying a set of abstract principles uniformly and impartially to everyone including myself, whom I am supposed to look at as just another person. However, real human beings, as opposed to the mythical heroes who found cities and establish governments, have experiences that bias their taste and opinions, and it is hard to conceive of a set of ethical and economic principles that would win universal acceptance, much less a social code that would not reduce the diversity of human life to a dull and coerced uniformity.

These differences are not trivial quirks of taste and prejudice, which do not affect the necessary social consensus on what is good. If I am an aristocrat with inherited wealth and social position, I may be unable to imagine a just society where inherited rank and wealth are not recognized. There would be no grounds of agreement between me and the socialist who wants to eliminate people like the aristocrat from the social order. Of course, the philosopher can say that every just person agrees that inherited inequalities are unfair, but he would have a difficult time persuading the aristocrats and plutocrats, especially since there are no developed societies that have succeeded in eliminating inherited differences of social position and wealth. The Communist New Class described by Milovan Djilas did eliminate the old aristocracy and bourgeoisie, but they also looked out pretty well for their own interests and those of their children.

Of course, most liberals and socialists acknowledge the fact that different human beings want different things out of life. However, it is not enough to say (as Rawls, among others, does) that in a good society different individuals are free to pursue different life plans without following the dictates of other people's opinions, because those very plans may override any of the general rules of justice that have been agreed to. The architects of an impartially just society, before granting individual

2. These arguments are drawn from John Rawls, *A Theory of Justice*, 12 ff., 136–42, and 447 ff.

freedom to pursue a plan of life, would first have to make a fundamental distinction between things that I regard as good for me (like smoking a specific brand of cigarettes) and those things that we agree to regard as a necessary foundation of any good life (which for some people means the right to smoke). There is no escaping this dilemma. Any conceivable society that devotes itself to the aim of universal and impartial justice will be felt as coercive by some people, whether it is the rich who resent the loss of wealth, Catholics who want society to be organized by their Church, or libertarians who consider zoning laws and restrictions on pornography as infringements of their natural liberties.

Imagine two founding fathers of a religious body that is to function as a commonwealth. Paul is proud of his Jewish roots but, as a Christian convert, regards circumcision and kosher laws as unnecessary for gentiles. Peter, on the other hand, regards them as a necessary precondition for a justified life for all members of the Church. The dispute is not trivial, and until it was settled in favor of Paul, it divided the early Christian Church. Afterwards, Jewish Christians were free to preserve their traditions, but they could not impose them on gentiles. On this point, at least, a sphere of tolerance was seemingly created within which people were free to pursue different styles of Christianity. What happened, however, was that Jewish Christianity was doomed to wither and die. Tolerance meant persecution.

Many, if not most, of the peculiarities of an individual's definition of "the good" are related to the circumstances of his life and to the particular relationships in which he is entangled. An Italian might regard access to inexpensive drinkable wine as a basic part of any decent existence, while an American might regard all wine as, at best, a desirable luxury but not a necessity. (This distinction will seem trivial only to those who do not drink wine every day.) A more serious flaw in the objective point of view is that it ignores or eliminates the significance of basic social relationships. "The good," in a mother's definition, may be something quite different from what a confirmed bachelor perceives as good, and all the personal, social, and civic relationships of everyday life make their claims as well.

If we were to leave these particular relationships out of our ethical scheme, we should be closing our eyes to the actual problems that confront most people in order to focus attention on decisions that few of us will ever be in a position to make. Theories of universal benevolence may sound lovely, but they run aground on the reality of taxes. When American and European families are already contributing 50–60 percent of their incomes to government, they can hardly be expected to consider proposals for global economic justice (and the higher taxes to support wealth-transfer schemes) as an abstract proposition. Call them selfish and unjust, if you like, and tax them into the poorhouse if you can, but do not expect them to express their appreciation for your theory of justice.

Despite the rhetoric of patriotic speeches on the blessings of democracy, citizens of modern states have a very limited freedom to determine "their own good." In a liberal society, each individual may be left free to pursue his own vision of the good life, whether as a stamp collector or as a vegetarian, but only so long as he does not violate the fundamental rules, however they happen to be defined; and, even though we may attach more importance to, say, parental authority or the ability of our church to shape society, those things we value most may well be forbidden. In fact, liberal societies (both real and hypothetical) are generally set up to prevent the special privileges that arise from the particular relationships on which many people think their happiness depends. The son of a rich man is not permitted, either by political theorists or by the governments of the United States and the United Kingdom, to inherit all of his father's wealth and social position. A father who tries to act on the contrary principle will end up violating the laws of his country.

Far from being neutral on the ends of individuals, the hypothetically "just" society might well exclude the very qualities of life that many ordinary people prize above all others. During the French Revolution, some Jacobins proposed to remove children from the households of families *suspected* of harboring hostile thoughts to the regime, and in more recent years governments have taken children away from "undesirable" families: non-Western immigrants, fundamentalist home-schoolers, poor housekeepers. Some of those families presumably felt this intrusion into their private life as a deprivation of the liberal right to pursue their own interests, even if the social workers were pursuing a greater good or "the best interests of the child."

It is only natural for us to suppose that the basic rules we have devised for society must be imposed on every individual, even when they conflict with his definition of what is good, but it is difficult, sometimes impossible even for philosophers, to be neutral or objective. If, for example, we believe it is wrong for society to practice discrimination based on race or ethnicity, sex or religion, how is it permissible for an individual to find a way of doing just that? And if it is generally wrong for the rich to shower privileges upon their children, why is it not wrong in the case of a particular rich man? A liberal philosopher might reply that social discrimination and vast legacies would be excluded from a just society, but that only means that he would set up a government so powerful that it would not allow people to make unjust choices. Inheritance taxes would confiscate the wealth of the rich man's son, and private clubs and schools would not be able to exclude members of minorities.

Once we begin to apply such "objective" criteria to other people's moral choices, we may not stop until we reach the point where no individual would be free to make decisions about matters much more significant than ice-cream flavors (excluding, of course, macadamia nut, which may be too costly). If there are basic rules of fairness and equality on which society is based, then the society presumably has the authority to impose them in procrustean fashion on everyone. A modern vision of social justice may well be "higher" than a traditional social order that takes account of the petty attachments of blood and familiarity, but it is better not to pretend that it includes a large sphere of indifference in which people are free to pursue their own plans of life. In a liberal state, we are free to pursue only those life plans that are not inconsistent with the general liberal theories on which the system is based. Step outside the box—by refusing to vaccinate your children or send them to school—and you invite persecution. All societies impose a quasi-religious orthodoxy, but at least Islamic fundamentalists do not pretend to be building an "open society."

Most social and moral theorists do not argue explicitly against mother love or patriotism, but the key to understanding any ideology is to be found not so much in what is said as in what is left out. Look in the index of most modern works of political theory, and you will search in vain for such terms as wife, father, child, marriage, family, friend, and neighbor. The omission is not an oversight. If impartiality is to be made a primary requirement of moral judgment, then it becomes difficult to know how to deal with the irrational partialities entailed by kinship and friendship. Such a one-size-fits-all approach to ethics was explicitly rejected by Aristotle, who did not attempt to reduce justice to a set of universal propositions, because different kinds of virtue are required of different persons: "A father's or a master's justice is not the same as that of the citizens" (*Eth. Nic.* 1134b).

The Impartial Spectator

The ancient Stoics went very far in holding up an ideal of moral perfection that transcended local attachments, and proclaimed themselves "citizens of the world." Their impractical idealism exasperated Cicero, who complained that no mortal man had ever attained such wisdom (*De Amicitia* 5.18). The Stoic slave Epictetus even found it absurd that a man would mourn the loss of his own wife while remaining indifferent to the news of the death of another's wife. Adam Smith, who like Cicero was interested in a practical moral philosophy, deflated this Stoic platitude, observing: "The man who should feel no more for the death or distress of his own father than for those of any other man's father or son, would appear neither a good son nor a good father."[3]

Many of the paradoxes inherent in the practice of third-person moral judgment appear in Smith's *Theory of Moral Sentiments*. Since Smith is one of the founding fathers not only of classical economics but also of classical liberal ethics, it is worth taking the time to see where this brilliant man went wrong.

Beginning with the commonsense observation that morality is not invented by isolated individuals but constructed socially out of the judgments of parents, friends, and the little gods of "what people say," Smith goes on to describe the "impartial spectator" who comes to reside in our breasts and to judge our moral decisions. When, for example, we experience a powerful passion, we are to consider what a disinterested spectator would think. Even if he is sympathetic with our plight, his feelings would fall short of our own. Thus the sufferer, if he wishes to gain the sympathy that arises from a "concord of sentiments," must learn to lower his tone.

> In order to produce this concord, as nature teaches the spectators to assume the circumstances of the person principally concerned, so she teaches this last in some measure to assume those of the spectators. As they are continually placing themselves in his situation, and thence con-

3. Adam Smith, *Theory of Moral Sentiments*, 240.

ceiving emotions similar to what he feels; so he is as constantly placing himself in theirs, and thence conceiving some degree of that coolness about his own fortune, with which he is sensible that they will view it.[4]

When a man is angry, says Smith, we detest his passion if it is indulged in without restraint:

> But we admire that noble and generous resentment which governs its pursuit of the greatest injuries, not by the rage which they are apt to excite in the breast of the sufferer, but by the indignation which they naturally call forth in that of the impartial spectator.... And hence it is, that to feel much for others, and little for ourselves, that to restrain our selfish, and to indulge our benevolent, affections, constitutes the perfection of human nature.[5]

In pursuing "the perfection of human nature," the philosopher runs ahead of the commonsense intuition on which he based his theory and enters the perilous realm of moral theology. It was probably inevitable in Calvinist Scotland that his conception of moral perfection would be inspired by the New Testament: "As to love our neighbour as we love ourselves is the great law of Christianity so it is the great precept of nature to love ourselves only as we love our neighbour, or, what comes to the same thing, as our neighbour is capable of loving us."[6]

In this fateful sentence, Smith makes a wrong turn, in both logic and ethics, and the first step of his wrong turn is a lie. Love of neighbor is not "the great law of Christianity," as Smith well knew, but Christ's *second* great commandment. The entire passage from Matthew is worth a careful look. Jesus is being tempted by the Pharisees, who practiced the ritualistic rigorism that has become associated with their name. It was the Pharisees, for example, who reproached Jesus' followers for not keeping to Jewish rules on fasting.

> Then one of them, which was a lawyer, asked him a question, tempting him, and saying, Master, which is the great commandment in the law? Jesus said unto him, Thou shalt love the Lord thy God with all thy heart, and with all thy soul, and with all thy mind. This is the first and great commandment. And the second is like unto it, Thou shalt love thy neighbor as thyself. On these two commandments hang all the law and the prophets. (Matt. 22:35–40)

4. Ibid., 67.
5. Ibid., 71.
6. Ibid., 72.

For Christ, love of neighbor (meaning the people one knows and associates with on a regular basis, then the members of the Christian Church,
and finally, by extension, any human being one comes in contact with)
is rooted in love of God, but what makes sense as a divine commandment cannot have the same force when applied as a logical deduction
from observable behavior. Since no ordinary person does, or can, love a
neighbor as himself, it is pointless to base a naturalistic ethical system
on an impossible injunction. Smith leaves behind the commonsense intuition with which he began and argues for the "perfection" of human
nature—a thing which has never been and will never be, short of mirac-
ulous intervention. Along the way he manages to rewrite Christian
morality, which is made, ultimately, to serve social and political ends for
which it was never designed.

Even if Christianity were reducible to the second great commandment, it does not at all follow that we should love ourselves (and our
own) only up to the point that our neighbor can love us. Consider such
consequences as our treatment of our property and our children, if we
took care of them only on the scale established by an impartial neighbor. Smith might answer that our neighbor would want us to take care
of our children and maintain our property, but he would only desire
this, first, in the abstract, and second, insofar as it affected him (an un-
mowed lawn and vagabond children might lower the value of his own
property). Such cool calculations, however, are a far cry from what it
takes to inspire responsibility in a father and householder. The ecological catastrophe that results from common or governmental ownership
of lands, described by Garrett Hardin as "the tragedy of the commons,"
is a modern instance of Aristotle's dictum that when all are in charge,
no one takes responsibility.

In fact, Smith has got it exactly wrong. Christ's commandment is
that we should make the attempt to extend self-love to others. Just as
he urged the Jews to regard Samaritans and gentiles as fully human, he
enjoined his followers to broaden their sphere of affection. The philosopher, on the other hand, is telling us to limit our love for ourselves to
the low and rational level that another person would feel for us—which
is the direct opposite of Christ's commandment to extend our love.

Smith is aware of the dangers of any universal morality that lays too
heavy a burden on individuals, and he mocks those moralists who say
we cannot be happy so long as millions of strangers suffer: "This artifi-

cial commiseration . . . is not only absurd, but seems altogether un-attainable." He is, nonetheless, attracted by the first universalist creed, the ancient Stoic doctrine of world citizenship, and he concludes: "We should view ourselves, not in the light in which our own selfish passions are apt to place us, but in the light in which any other citizen of the world would view us."[7] He is too wise to carry his argument to the extreme advocated by Epictetus, but that only means that his heart and common sense are better than his philosophy.

Although Smith's process of reasoning leads him in the direction of the moral algebra advocated by Descartes and Locke, he is well aware that human beings are subject to conflicts of motives and loyalties. However, instead of recommending a careful analysis of the particularities involved in such conflicts, Smith turns all such questions over to the objective third-person point of view. A conflict between gratitude and friendship, for example,

> must be left to the decision of the man within the breast, the supposed impartial spectator, the great judge and arbiter of our conduct. If we place ourselves completely in his situation, if we really view ourselves with his eyes and as he views us, and listen with diligent and reverential attention to what he suggests to us, his voice will never deceive us. We shall stand in need of no casuistic rules to direct our conduct.[8]

In this apotheosis, Smith's impartial spectator, which began life as a wise friend correcting our excesses, ends up both as the voice of conscience and as someone outside ourselves, a person that is both self and other. At this point the spectator becomes something close to a pagan god. There is no need for "casuistic rules," because an all-knowing god (unlike a fallible human conscience) will always make the correct decision. Such moral certainty belongs only to saints and homicidal maniacs.

Homer dramatized such a dissociation of desire and moral conscience as a conflict between human impulse and divine intervention. At the beginning of the *Iliad*, Achilles, swayed by his passions (represented by an organ called the *thymos*), draws his sword to kill his commander, when the goddess Athena appears (only to him), pulls his hair, and urges him to seek a more disciplined revenge. In the everyday world

7. Ibid., 238, 239.
8. Ibid., 371.

that exists outside of epic poetry, such a split perception, between internal passion and externally imposed third-person discipline, would be regarded as a sign of psychotic dissociation.

How far can I go in stepping outside of myself to view my actions with objectivity? Dr. Johnson, who thoroughly disliked Adam Smith, understood that each man was a prisoner of his background and even his trade: "Two men examining the same question proceed commonly like the physician and gardener in selecting herbs, or the farmer and hero looking on the plain; they bring minds impressed with different notions, and direct their enquiries to different ends; they form, therefore, contrary conclusions, and each wonders at the other's absurdity." Johnson would have viewed the prospects for impartiality as very dim. At best, he thought, friends might criticize and help reform each other's vices, though he was quick to point out that "[i]t is not indeed certain, that the most refined caution will find a proper time for bringing a man to the knowledge of his own failing, or the most zealous benevolence reconcile him to that judgment by which they are detected."[9]

To put myself in my friend's shoes is not too difficult and to interpret the promptings of conscience as the voice of a god is not impossible; the further I depart from myself, however, the more likely I am to view myself (and other people) in the abstract. If a man succeeds in dividing his consciousness, as moral philosophers since the eighteenth century have recommended, he might have the feeling that there was another "I" roaming the streets, the *Doppelgänger* that haunted the imaginations of so many Romantic writers. This "false philosophy" (or, to use David Hume's expression, "refinement") "cuts the thinker off from custom, which is the source of all belief and action."[10]

Rising above Humanity

Are human beings even capable of sustaining an abstract objectivity that does not distinguish their own interests and concerns from those of all mankind? Lawrence Kohlberg, who held up such a standard as a

9. Samuel Johnson, *The Adventurer* 107 (November 13, 1753); Samuel Johnson, *The Rambler* 40 (August 4, 1750).

10. Donald Livingston, *Philosophical Melancholy and Delirium: Hume's Pathology of Philosophy*, 219.

moral ideal, was never able to find a sage who lived up to it. Most men, as Hume (another enlightened Scotsman and a friend of Adam Smith) points out, are interested in the "public interest" only to the extent that they obey the law and stay out of trouble: "There is no such passion in human minds, as the love of mankind, merely as such, independent of personal qualities, of services, or of relation to ourself."[11] Our sympathies, in other words, are particular, not universal.

But even if the problem of nonrational loyalties to home and country are set to one side, impartiality is not a self-evident requirement of all intellectual inquiry. Some questions, it seems obvious, demand impartiality and objectivity. My attachments are irrelevant when the point at issue is the sum of two and two or the color of your necktie or the date of the Battle of Gettysburg or the effect on prices that a specific policy will predictably have. I am, nonetheless, free to disagree with any conclusions drawn from the facts. A Virginian might, for example, consider Gettysburg a draw, militarily speaking, and a disaster for his country; I can cheerfully concede that your tie is green but deplore your bad taste in wearing such a color; and, though an economic analysis might prove incontrovertibly that free-trade policies lower prices without having an overall negative effect on wages, I might continue to oppose free trade on moral or political grounds.

These distinctions arise in the no-man's-land between what is and what we think ought to be, between fact and value, but the distinction is not always so clear-cut. Facts do not always come before the value judgments we make on them. Sometimes a value has to exist for a fact to mean anything. If the protection of innocent life is not a value, then abortion and carpet bombing will be regarded only as legitimate means to a worthy end and not by some as homicide or murder.

Some liberals reply by distinguishing between the fact of homicide and the value-based interpretation of that fact as an instance of murder. But the glibness of that reply overlooks the reality, which is that defenders of abortion have gone from justifying it on the grounds of expedient homicide to denying the scientifically self-evident fact that an embryo is nothing but an underdeveloped form of human life. The value—in this case, a woman's right to choose—determines the fact. Similarly, when the United States responds to terrorists or leaders of rogue states

11. Hume, *Treatise of Human Nature*, 2:213.

by bombing civilians or imposing embargos that starve them to death, political leaders and journalists do their best to pretend it never happened. Smart bombs, they say inevitably, preclude the possibility of substantial "collateral damage," and in using such expressions they deny the reality of the ordinary human beings who have been killed for reasons that have nothing to do with them.

Quite apart from questions of taste or value, different situations call for differing degrees of impartiality. If any common life is to be carried on at all, we must assume that statements of fact are subject to verification, and that all reasonable people would agree on the sum of two and two or on the closing price of a stock. When we are trying to make up our minds what to do, either individually or as a group, we cannot assume that most other people will agree with either our premises or our conclusions. We simply cannot divide ourselves up into compartment A that likes corn-fed beef and compartment B that writes checks to People for the Ethical Treatment of Animals, and it is much too simplistic to portray such conflicting desires as a contest between irrational appetites and a rational pursuit of duty. It is, after all, the same person who eats the beef and writes the check. "The I that stands back in rational reflection from my desires," writes Bernard Williams, "is still the I that has those desires and will, empirically and concretely, act. . . . [T]here is no route to the impartial standpoint from rational deliberation alone."[12]

Is the standard of impartiality really impartial? I have already brought up the example of maternal love, which can never be impartial. A mother is supposed to be biased in favor of her children, and in conventional, everyday morality we expect a man to help his neighbor and love his country. We might also expect him to be honest and truthful toward strangers, but that is not the same as saying he should treat a stranger as his neighbor, or vice versa.

The Independent Scholar

If everyday life is fraught with paradoxes that either blur or blunt the hard edges of impartiality, scholarship (and its inferior brother, journalism) would seem to present a clear case of "nothing but the facts" to be measured and analyzed according to objective criteria. But such im-

12. Bernard Williams, *Ethics and the Limits of Philosophy,* 68–70.

partiality is neither universal nor, necessarily, desirable in all cases. Setting aside the extreme cases—such as the demand that only African Americans teach black history and only women pursue women's studies—the attempt to construct objective history has been an abysmal failure. When historians still had pedagogic and patriotic ends in view, writers as diverse as Thucydides and Livy, Hume and Macaulay actually shaped the moral and political imaginations of ordinary people. Today, by contrast, history is a subject for debate between professionals (though ordinary people still read popular history and watch historical programs on television). An historian is not necessarily dishonest just because he confesses to having a point of view, and a modern historian who relies on facts and figures is not necessarily honest just because he is reticent about his prejudices. Even at the beginning of Western history and epic literature, Homer was clearly on the side of the Greeks in the *Iliad,* and yet he was more than fair to the Trojans, to the point that many readers have regarded Hector as the real hero of the work.

If human experience were a glacier, slowly accreting pebbles of fact and statistical debris in its course, a case might be made for writing impartial history, but much of what we call history is a conflict of wills between leaders and nations and religions. Who could write an impartial account of the Crusades? Not a faithful Catholic or Muslim, and certainly not an atheist who pretends to be neutral on the religious claims of the two parties: The atheist, in fact, has the biggest ax to grind. People in the northern United States may have a vague notion that the "right" side won the Civil War, but only an expert or an enthusiast takes the trouble to find out the facts. Many southerners, however, have taken a passionate interest in the war and preserved a family memory of houses burned, silver stolen, and women outraged. A Civil War historian from the South might feel it his duty to be scrupulous about the facts without sacrificing the point of view he has inherited. An African American might take quite a different position, the descendant of Midwestern Copperheads another, and an Irish American whose ancestor was killed in a struggle he found entirely alien to him, still another.

In a more candid age, American newspapers used to identify themselves as Democratic or Republican, frankly acknowledging the prejudices that their readers were considered able to discount. Today, when the overwhelming majority of journalists vote for liberal and Democratic candidates, they persist in the fiction that there is no liberal bias in the media. Conservatives insist on a parallel fiction, that they are interested only in an objective evaluation of the facts. This pointless debate only illustrates the difficulty of being objective.

G. K. Chesterton frequently ridiculed the pose of objectivity assumed by the type he called the "new bigot," who will not argue with you because he knows you agree with him. In *Orthodoxy*, he took up the case of modern liberal aesthetes who liberated themselves from all convention and tradition:

> The ordinary aesthetic anarchist who sets out to feel everything freely gets knotted at last in a paradox that prevents him feeling at all. He breaks away from home limits to follow poetry. But in ceasing to feel home limits he has ceased to feel the "Odyssey." He is free from national prejudices and outside patriotism. But being outside patriotism he is outside "Henry V." Such a literary man is simply outside all literature: he is more of a prisoner than any bigot. For if there is a wall between you and the world, it makes little difference whether you describe yourself as locked in or as locked out.[13]

Individuals have their own points of view, but so do groups and traditions. The history of the past five hundred years will be told in quite different language and emphasis, if the tellers are, say, an Icelander, an Orthodox Serb, and an African American. Imagine, for a moment, a history of the world narrated not from the shifting perspective of the Western capitals—Athens, Rome, Florence, Paris, London—but from the north. Suddenly the relations of Norwegians, Scots, and Russians come into focus, and the career of Harold Hadrada (mercenary commander of Byzantines and Russians, king of Norway, claimant to the throne of England in 1066) dwarfs that of William the Conqueror.

Of course such a history would be as partial as the history of Europe from the Polish perspective written by Norman Davies, but it would open up (as Davies does in *Heart of Europe: A Short History of Poland*) entire vistas that had been veiled. Frequently, it is only by adopting a point of view (if only temporarily) that a scholar or journalist can catch a glimpse of the truth that eludes all those whom impartiality has made blind.

13. G. K. Chesterton, *Orthodoxy*, 176.

Tradition!

Points of view are not, in most cases, adopted capriciously by free-thinking individualists. Human beings grow up within traditions of manners and thought (what Hume called custom) that shape their taste and attitudes. The point has been made not only by classical reactionaries, such as T. S. Eliot in his essay "Tradition and the Individual Talent," but also by postmodern relativists such as Hans-Georg Gadamer. Tradition is a powerful influence, but it would be too much to say that our mental outlook is entirely determined by the traditions in which we have been reared. People have been known, after all, to rebel, though even rebellion can be conditioned by the very institutions the rebel seeks to overthrow. The cult of objectivity, as Alasdair MacIntyre has pointed out in *Whose Justice? Which Rationality?* is itself part of an unreflective liberalism that has been handed down across the generations.

The defense of custom and tradition is generally regarded as one of the hallmarks of Burkean conservatism, and Edmund Burke, although a reformist liberal for much of his life, was willing to defend abusive customs (such as the wealth and power of the degenerate French monarchy and aristocracy) if the alternative were a root-and-branch revolution. Tradition, Burke realized, was the painful accretion of wisdom across the centuries, while revolutions were almost always entirely destructive. "Rage and frenzy," he observed of the French Revolution, "will pull down more in half an hour than prudence, deliberation, and foresight can build up in a hundred years."[14] The conservative resistance to innovation was summed up by Viscount Falkland in the memorable aphorism: "When it is not necessary to change, it is necessary *not* to change." Falkland was no reactionary, but a supporter of parliamentary privilege against Charles I. When he saw reform turning into a revolution, he reluctantly joined the royalists.

Burkean traditionalism was a mechanism by which liberalism was able to self-correct before plunging into the abysses of hedonist individualism and Marxist collectivism. It could not, however, by itself serve as the basis of an illiberal political philosophy or movement.[15] Traditions

14. Edmund Burke, *Reflections on the French Revolution,* 456.
15. See Thomas Fleming, "Tories Back Wrong Philosopher," *Spectator,* August 24, 1996.

can, after all, go wrong. The mistakes of the French monarchy, as Burke failed to understand, were continued in worse form by the Jacobins and Napoleon, and some societies slip into such unlovely traditions as rape, incest, child sacrifice, and cannibalism. Confronted with a direct challenge to a bad or imperfect tradition, the traditionalists' answer (as Stephen R. L. Clark pointed out in his response to MacIntyre) is to give hemlock to Socrates and to crucify Jesus Christ.[16]

In confessing that some or many traditions have gone sour, we should be unwilling to concede the entire game. All good things, for the very reason that they are good, can be misused. If we eat too much food, we are gluttons, but gluttony does not make all food and all eating bad by definition. We must eat if we are to live, and if we are to live within a human social order, we must respect its customs and traditions, which represent, as Chesterton put it, "the democracy of the dead."[17] In one short lifetime, no individual can learn very much without relying on the accumulated insights and wisdom of his predecessors.

In the liberal tradition, we are always being called upon to "think outside the box," but the result is merely to change one box for another (often smaller and shabbier) box. After two thousand years the Christian religion, especially in its more traditional forms, is a vast treasury of philosophical and theological thought, poetry and art, ritual and custom. Even if there were no God and Christ were no greater than Mohammed, Christianity would offer the possibility of a rich and passionate life undreamed of by the village atheists who join objectivist circles and sue schoolteachers who tell Bible stories in class. The experience of religious faith educates the believer who lives with its scriptures and ceremonies and comes to understand the religion as no objective outsider can.

Matters of faith lie beyond reason and scholarship, and the only objectivity possible is that of the nonbeliever—who cannot be objective at all, because he rejects the phenomena under consideration. Hundreds of books have been written by atheist scientists challenging the possibility of the miracles attributed to Christ, as if a miracle were not by definition something that takes place outside the course of the everyday laws of nature. This does not mean that the scholar or journalist

16. Stephen R. L. Clark, "Morals, Moore, and MacIntyre."
17. Chesterton, *Orthodoxy*, 85.

cannot aim at the truth, and not only in matters of fact. But for a Western Christian to discover something of the truth about the Crusades, he must be willing to enter into the minds of the other side—the Orthodox Byzantines and the Muslim Arabs, Saracens, and Turks. He must be willing, in his imagination at least, to dwell in the tents of the infidels, to sing their songs and hear their poems, to find out the story they tell of themselves.

The Great Eastern Question

Like a fair-minded traveler who goes native, for a time, in foreign lands and comes back with an appreciation for the strange things he has witnessed and experienced, the historian or journalist can temporarily suspend his judgment on the aliens and enemies to whom he owes a fair and honest accounting. He must play Homer to Hector. This was the approach used by Rebecca West in depicting the three parties in Bosnia—the Serbs, the Croats, and the Muslims—on the eve of the Yugoslav bloodbath of World War II.[18]

Fifty years later, journalists who donned the mantel of impartiality expressed their opinions on the breakup of Yugoslavia, the Bosnian civil war, the Kosovo conflict, and the secession crisis in Montenegro in terms that frequently echoed the official statements issued by the U.S. State Department, yet each one would have denied having "a dog in this fight." Each would have claimed to be an enemy to the sort of nationalisms that disfigured all the parties in the conflict, and any apparent bias against the Serbs was explained as a rational response to Serbian ultranationalism. The sticking point in this argument is that the Bosnian civil war was, in fact, a conflict of nationalisms, and professions of antinationalist "impartiality" were inevitably biased in favor of any party that claimed to be advocating antinationalist multiculturalism.[19]

A remarkable example of fair-minded and generous partiality was provided by Ivo Andrić, a Bosnian writer of mixed Serbian and Croatian parentage who opted for a Serbian identity. Andrić, who was born

18. Rebecca West, *Black Lamb and Grey Falcon.*
19. Painful examples are provided by Roy Gutman's *A Witness to Genocide: The First Inside Account of the Horrors of "Ethnic Cleansing" in Bosnia;* Noel Malcolm's travesty of historical method, *Bosnia: A Short History;* and Tim Judah's *The Serbs: History, Myth, and the Destruction of Yugoslavia.* ·

in Travnik in 1892 and spent much of his childhood in Višegrad, grew up with reminders of Ottoman oppression all around him. Serbs have long memories, and their folk poems record the long struggle against Turkish occupation. Nevertheless, in what may be his greatest book, *The Bridge on the Drina,* Andrić offered a fair, even affectionate portrait of the Turks and half-Turks (Muslim Serbs) who had ruled his native land for five centuries. The bridge was built in the sixteenth century by a remarkable Turkish grand vizier, Muhammad Sokollu, whom the Serbs call Mehmed Sokolović. Sokolović had been born into a Serbian Orthodox clan (the Sokolovici) that lived around the mountain from Višegrad, but in his childhood he was stolen by the Turks as part of the blood tribute imposed on Christians. Brought up as a Muslim (his beautiful mosque still stands in Constantinople), he never forgot his people. He rose through the ranks of the Turkish bureaucracy to the supreme height of grand vizier, where he found himself in a position to help the Serbs. He restored the independence of the Serbian Church, making his brother the patriarch, and he built the bridge for which he has been remembered.

William H. McNeill, in praising Andrić's novel for its accurate portrait of Ottoman civilization, says that "no historian has entered so effectively into the minds of the persons with whom he has sought to deal."[20] And yet this generous and brilliant novel, which gained its author the Nobel Prize in 1961, has been banned (along with Serbian folk poems) by the American-dominated UN occupying force in Bosnia on the grounds that it reminds people of what they ought to forget, namely their history and their identity. The United States dragged the United Nations into the Bosnian conflict to protect a multiethnic state dominated by an Islamic fundamentalist leadership that allied itself with Osama bin Laden (who was given Bosnian citizenship) and other terrorists. It is, perhaps, the first international experiment explicitly aimed at eliminating a personal and ethnic point of view and replacing it with the political incarnation of Smith's impartial spectator.

Some Americans, naturally, were less impartial. Some were influenced by Israel's pro-Muslim stand (designed, as more than one Israeli polit-

---

20. William H. McNeill, introduction to *The Bridge on the Drina.* This edition was published in Belgrade in 2000 by DERETA, with assistance—ironically— from the Ministry of Culture of the Republika Srpska.

ical analyst has explained to me, to defuse Muslim hostility in the Middle East); others decided to back the party that seemed most anti-Western and anti-Christian (that is, the Muslims); and still others—Muslims (from anywhere), Serbs, and Croats—backed their own people. Ignorant of such complications (at least one hopes it was ignorance), the Clinton administration sent a Croat-American to be ambassador to Bosnia.

Reviewing the reporting on the Balkans (and on many other conflicts around the world), it is hard not to reach the conclusion that objectivity and impartiality have come to mean being "on the side of the angels." It is no paradox to say that the pose of impartiality no longer requires a scrupulous reporting of the facts, when it comes to any group or individual unlucky enough to be seen as nationalist, parochial, or retrograde. Whether the problem of the moment concerns Islamic fundamentalists in Algeria, Serb nationalists in Kosovo, or intransigent Orthodox Jews in Israel, those who reject the pose of objectivity cannot expect fair treatment. It is a variation on the argument once used to deprive leftists of their civil liberties: If communists ever got into power, it was argued, they would destroy the freedoms we enjoy under the First and Fifth Amendments; therefore, they may not enjoy those civil liberties they would deny to the rest of us. It should be obvious that such an argument is self-refuting. If it is forbidden to dissent, whether from the communist left or from the nationalist right, from the tenets of democratic liberalism, then the liberal claim of impartiality and objectivity is like the dictatorship of the proletariat or the destiny of the German nation—an ideological weapon used to eliminate opposition.

Rising above Ourselves

In everyday life, we are not always able to comprehend our situation, appreciate our friends, or evaluate our actions. We are too involved in our own affairs, so much a participant that we cannot assume, even momentarily, the role of a referee or an objective critic. Sometimes, whether by design or by accident, we may gain a better perspective by physically removing ourselves from the normal scene. Businessmen returning from a trip may find themselves wondering if they have been paying proper attention to their families and if spending three nights out during the week is the best use of their scarce free time. I have sometimes returned from Europe to detect a new freshness and charm in the dull Midwestern city where I live, an almost alien quality that I can appreciate only after being away. In his autobiography, G. K. Chesterton tells the fable of a sailor who lost his way and landed upon a strange island only to discover, after some weeks, that the strange island was England.

The habit of travel, which creates the opportunity for comparison, is not always so benign. The traveler can become alienated from his own people and their customs, which he grows to despise. Sinclair Lewis's Dodsworths, like so many of their nonfictional contemporaries, could scarcely endure America after they had spent a year abroad. "How ya gonna keep 'em down on the farm after they've seen Paree?" asked an American song at the end of the Great War, and an entire generation of American writers and intellectuals learned to despise where they came from and who they were. In moral terms, there might be said to be a difference between a vacation from the point of view of everyday life and a more or less permanent alienation from normal attachments to home and country.

Many human beings need, it would seem, a given point of view determined by a place, family ties, and inherited prejudices. Kaleidoscopes are an amusing children's toy, distorting our perception with shifting patterns of shape and color, but when our mind becomes a kaleidoscope of alien perceptions and other points of view, the result may be disorientation rather than entertainment. There is no worse fate than to be alienated from home, as the story of Oedipus, wandering blind and (apart from his daughter) friendless through an alien world, attests.

Epic literature is full of heroes who are forced to leave hearth and home and go off on an adventure. The most touching of these stories is the quest of Odysseus to return home to an aging wife on the rocky and worthless island of Ithaca. Even once he returns home, he cannot stay, because he is cursed to go off into the wilderness carrying an oar until he finds a man so primitive as to ask him what the oar is. That is what comes of taking a twenty-year absence from normal life.

If taking a vacation from one's self is a useful moral exercise, it is also a little like Adam Smith's initial description of the impartial spectator, the objective friend, the fresh perspective to be gained from stepping outside the first person. In the course of Smith's book, however, the impartial spectator evolves into a kind of unwanted immigrant who usurps the hearth and home of our native point of view. When he first makes his appearance, the impartial spectator is something like an acquaintance who takes an interest in our well-being and gives us good advice, but he ends up not only more abstract but also more remote. It is a small step to go from a third-person perspective to one that is so distant that it can regard ordinary human relationships with indifference. And although it is self-evident that we have a bias in favor of our own first-person perspective, no matter how broadly we conceive of our obligation to other human beings, the unremitting tendency of modern ethics has been to force us to rise above ourselves and view the whole world as if we were gods or angels: "[T]he soundest criterion of virtue is to put ourselves in the place of an impartial spectator, of an angelic nature, suppose, beholding us from an elevated station, and uninfluenced by our prejudices, conceiving what would be his estimate of the intrinsic circumstances of our neighbor, and acting accordingly."[21]

William Godwin's blunt and straightforward liberalism made *An Enquiry concerning Political Justice* one of the most influential books in the history of moral philosophy. Godwin did not hesitate to accept the logical consequences of his angelic point of view, even if it meant sacrificing those who should have been dearest to him. Suppose, he asked, a house catches on fire and you have to choose between saving the life of Bishop Fénelon or Fénelon's valet? The intellectual man must choose Fénelon because of his literary and intellectual merits. But what are you to do if the valet is your brother, your father, or your benefactor? "This would not alter the truth of the proposition. The life of Fénelon would still be more valuable than that of the valet; and justice, pure unadulterated justice, would still have preferred that which was most valuable. . . . What magic is there in the pronoun 'my,' that should justify us in overturning the decisions of impartial truth."[22]

Godwin lived out at least one-half of his creed: He married Mary Woolstonecraft only when she became pregnant, took negligent care of his daughter Mary, and for years extorted money from her seducer, the poet Shelley, who had begun by revering the nobility of the philosopher and ended up despising the greed of the pandering father-in-law. Adam Smith encountered an earlier form of this grim and abstract concept of duty among Christian writers who had argued, as he said, that "all

21. Godwin, *Political Justice*, 170–74.
22. Ibid.

affections for particular objects ought to be extinguished in our breast, and one great affection take the place of all others, the love of the deity." The obligations of gratitude and patriotism and humanity ought all, on this scheme, to be reduced to our duty to the divine: "The sole principle and motive of our conduct in the performance of all those different duties, ought to be a sense that God has commanded us to perform them."[23]

Smith asked these Christian philosophers if a benefactor was really rewarded by a man whose gratitude was confined to a sense of duty. If obedience to rules is the whole duty of man, what can one say of those bigoted Catholics who failed in their duty to persecute Protestants? The divine perspective is a property of God, and only angels can look at humanity through the eyes of angels. When mere mortals attempt to storm Olympus to get a better view of justice and humanity, they can expect to suffer the fate of Otus and Ephialtes, the monsters who piled Ossa upon Pelion and were destroyed for their presumption.

Godwin, it goes without saying, did not believe in angels, and recent philosophers are more apt to draw their analogies from science fiction than from scripture. According to Thomas Nagel, there are two points of view: the ordinary, commonsense view of the individual within his station and the extraterrestrial perspective from which "*everyone's* life matters as much as his does, and his matters no more than anyone's."[24] Viewed in this light, the personal perspective is at best a fact of life like the sense of pain that discourages us from doing things that would destroy us. From the impersonal point of view, one should spend one's life alleviating the circumstances of unhappy strangers. What used to be called prudence, then, would be the art of navigating between the two perspectives: preserving a satisfactory minimum of personal interest while maximizing the comfort of those who stand in greatest need.

If we take the impersonal point of view, our first priorities must inevitably include the alleviation of poverty and powerlessness and the elevation of our fellow human beings to a decent standard of existence. Therefore, the first requirement of any social or political arrangement

23. Smith, *Moral Sentiments*, 283.
24. Thomas Nagel, *Equality and Partiality*, 13–14. See Jacques Maritain's criticisms of Descartes' "angelism" in *Three Reformers: Luther, Descartes, Rousseau*, 53–89.

would be its likelihood of contributing to these goals. That is the clear impersonal judgment as to what matters most—the judgment one would make if one were observing the world from the outside as "a powerful and benevolent outsider, dispensing benefits to the inhabitants of the world."[25]

Taking the angelic perspective, William Godwin decided that his father meant less to him than a philosophe who is now scarcely more highly regarded than Godwin's father. Viewing himself from the wrong end of the telescope, a more recent philosopher has decided that neither "I" nor my close personal connections matter very much, when compared with the needs of humanity. My children can even come out ahead, he concludes, if I devote more of my resources to other people's children (that is, so long as other people follow suit). Such an argument is persuasive only if we ignore the plain facts of common sense: that I do care about myself and my own children in ways that I do not and probably cannot care for other people, and that anything left up to common benevolence is likely to suffer the fate of the collective farm.

In rejecting common sense, this philosopher is forced to invoke mysticism. Believing in the significance of his own identity, he says: "[M]y life seemed like a glass tunnel through which I was moving faster every year, and at the end of which there was darkness. When I changed my view, the walls of my glass tunnel disappeared. I now live in the open air. There is still a difference between my life and the lives of other people. But the difference is less."[26] It is obviously impossible to argue against a mystical insight that requires a suspension of reason, but the philosopher might ask himself if the very valuation he places upon his own contentment does not refute his basic claim to have transcended the egoism of commonsense morality. In fact, the assumption of indifference towards one's self and one's friends is more likely to end in a generalized indifference to other people. We are not and cannot be benevolent outsiders looking down upon ourselves and our situations. Even to imagine that we might be borders on something more dangerous than megalomania. When finite and mortal creatures lay claim to the perspective of divinity, the real effect is to diminish the importance of all the other

---

25. Nagel, *Equality and Partiality*, 14.
26. Parfit, *Reasons and Persons*, 281. Cf. Descartes, preface to *Principles of Philosophy*.

"first persons" in the universe. The desire to be "as gods, knowing good and evil" has been from the beginning of our race a fatal temptation, and it is important to see such claims for what they are: the assumption of superiority over lesser beings.

Observing the world from the outside obliterates all distinctions between I and thou, mine and not-mine, the near and dear, and the far and foreign. At least since Marx it has been argued that in the modern world, the significance of geographical separation has been eliminated by air travel and electronic media. However, the global village can be a dangerous metaphor. If everyone in the world is as dear to me as my next-door neighbor, I might be tempted to treat my neighbor as a complete stranger. Adolf Hitler also believed that technology had shrunk the world, and in *Mein Kampf* he used the global-village argument to justify the creation of a new European order.

One World, One Target

Hitler and modern philosophers (Godwin, Nagel, Singer, Parfit) notwithstanding, distance does matter in affairs of love as well as of hate. It is easier to drop bombs or launch rockets upon an enemy than it is to fight him face to face. Saturation bombing of civilian targets is endurable so long as we do not see the victims. But few of us could bring ourselves to murder women and children one by one, no matter what the circumstances.

An RAF crew member who watched, from twenty thousand feet, the effects of the firebombing of Hamburg described his feelings as "fascinated but aghast, satisfied yet horrified." Lt. Col. Dave Grossman comments:

> Seventy thousand died at Hamburg. Eighty thousand or so died in 1945 during a similar firebombing in Dresden. Two hundred and twenty-five thousand died in firestorms over Tokyo as a result of only two firebomb raids. When the atomic bomb was dropped over Hiroshima, seventy thousand died. Throughout World War II bomber crews on both sides killed millions of women, children, and elderly people, no different from their own wives, children, and parents. The pilots, navigators, bombardiers, and gunners in these aircraft were able to bring themselves to kill these civilians primarily through application of the mental leverage provided to them by the distance factor.... From a distance, I can deny your humanity; and from a distance, I cannot hear your screams.

Grossman, a former Army ranger who spent years of research on the combat experience, failed to turn up "one single instance of individuals who have refused to kill the enemy" from a long range nor a single instance of "psychiatric trauma associated with this type of killing." This generalization includes the flight crews of the planes that dropped the atomic bombs on Hiroshima and Nagasaki.[27] As if to prove the point, the pilot of the *Enola Gay* published a book in 1998 and went on a promotional tour, celebrating his accomplishments, under the sponsorship of *Soldier of Fortune* magazine.

Soldiers are expected to do their duty in wartime, and moral reflection is not part of the "outfit" taken into combat. One American pilot, Admiral James Stockdale, is also a philosopher who has written eloquently on the moral dilemmas that face prisoners of war, but he has, for the most part, avoided public discussion of American treatment of civilians in the Vietnam War, which included incessant raids on population centers and the use of napalm against civilians. I bring up this gap not to disparage Stockdale, an authentic American hero who has explicitly denounced the Gulf of Tonkin incident as a fraud, but to reinforce the point that long-range destruction is rarely viewed in moral terms. The exception that proves the rule is the poet James Dickey, who flew combat missions in World War II and wrote a powerful poem, not precisely autobiographical, in which a suburban American recalls his firebombing missions:

> Reflections of houses catch;
> Fire shuttles from pond to pond
> In every direction, till hundreds flash with one death.
> With this in the dark of the mind,
> Death will not be what it should;
> Will not, even now, even when
> My exhaled face in the mirror
> Of bars, dilates in a cloud-like Japan.
> The death of children is ponds
> Shutter-flashing; responding mirrors; it climbs
> The terraces of hills
> Smaller and smaller, a mote of red dust
> At a hundred feet; at a hundred and ten it goes out.

27. Lt. Col. Dave Grossman, *On Killing: The Psychological Cost of Learning to Kill in War and Society,* 101–8.

This is what should have got in
To my eye.

"Should have" but did not. Years later the pilot is still unable to come to grips with the reality, "still unable to get down there or see what really happened."[28] Commenting on his own poem, Dickey deplored the facile assumption of responsibility that characterized Sylvia Plath's "feeling guilty over the Jews." Guilt is personal, the poet insists, something that has to be earned, "but sometimes when you earn it, you don't feel the guilt you ought to have. And that's what 'The Firebombing' is about."[29]

Distance hardens us and numbs our conscience; it reduces the objects of our attention to abstractions. Take a child murderer like Harry Lime (in Graham Greene's *The Third Man*) onto a Ferris wheel and ask him about his victims.

Harry took a look at the toy landscape below and came away from the door.... "Victims?" he asked. "Don't be melodramatic.... Look down there," he went on, pointing through the window at the people moving like black flies at the base of the Wheel. "Would you really feel any pity if one of those dots stopped moving—for ever? If I said you can have twenty thousand pounds for every dot that stops, would you really, old man, tell me to keep my money—without hesitation? Or would you calculate how many dots you could afford to spare?"

At a sufficient distance, love thins out to indifference, and viewed from a sufficient height the whole Earth becomes no more than the stage for our ambitions. Tempters will take advantage of a high place and the perspective it gives upon the world: "Again, the devil taketh him up into an exceeding high mountain, and sheweth him all the kingdoms of the world, and the glory of them; And saith unto him, All these things will I give thee, if thou wilt fall down and worship me" (Matt. 4:8–9). Even God, when He took on the flesh and blood of frail humanity, rejected the temptation to look down from a high place and view the world as an abstract game board where He could manipulate the pieces.

High places were always a temptation for the children of Israel, and the prophets condemned Jews who separated themselves from their

28. James Dickey, "The Firebombing," in *The Whole Motion: Collected Poems, 1945–1992*, 193–200.
29. James Dickey, *Self-Interviews*, 137–39.

sacramental community and went up into the hills to practice unortho-
dox rituals and idolatry: "They sacrifice upon the tops of the mountains,
and burn incense upon the hills" (Hosea 4:13). The prophets associated
these rituals with sexual excesses and with every transgression of the
moral law. Morality, for them, was not a personal code worked out in
isolation from a community of faith and practice. Nonetheless, when
Jesus took several disciples into the mountains and they saw that he
was transfigured and visited by Moses and Elijah, they could not resist
the temptation to idolatry: "Peter said unto Jesus, Master, it is good for
us to be here: and let us make three tabernacles; one for thee, and one
for Moses, and one for Elias; not knowing what he said" (Luke 9:33).

In the week before he took them into the mountains, Jesus had given
them instructions on their ministry, "and he said to them all, If any
man will come after me, let him deny himself, and take up his cross
daily and follow me" (Luke 9:23). This might have served as a hint to
Peter, the most woodenheaded of disciples, that withdrawal and tran-
scendence of the human were not in the message preached by his master.
Taking up the cross, living day by day in the misery and sweat of ordinary human existence—this is a far cry from Peter's reflexive idolatry.

For mystics, Christian and non-Christian alike, there is a constant
temptation to withdraw to a mountain or take refuge on a pillar. Looking down upon an alien world, it is easy to believe that everything is
"just fantastic," which is the most eloquent comment that any astronaut
has managed to make on his experience in space. In the fourteenth century, the poet Petrarch took it into his head to climb Mount Ventoux in
the south of France. In many ways the first nearly modern man, Petrarch
had a thirst for distinction and an itch to transform European society.
Impossibly in love with a girl he barely knew, he says (in "Solo e pensoso
i più deserti campi," written about the time of his mountain-climbing
adventure) that he deliberately avoided the haunts of men. Upon reach-
ing the summit of Mount Ventoux, the poet took out the copy of Augustine's *Confessions* he always kept with him and read: "And we go about
wondering at mountain heights and the mighty waves of the sea and
wide flowing streams and the ocean amid the wheeling of the stars: and
to themselves they give no heed." Looking boldly toward the future, to
the Renaissance and beyond, Petrarch was still anchored to a medieval
world that warned him against the presumption of looking down upon
men and the world.

Although some Renaissance men, such as Pico della Mirandola, viewed medieval Christianity as the major obstacle to unlimited human progress, others, like Petrarch, were just as likely to have inherited their sense of measure and restraint from the pre-Christian classical tradition. One of the wisest of pagan poets, Horace, had said something similar, telling the tourists of his day that it is not magnificent views that calm the troubled mind but reason and good sense. "Those who change their sky, but not their mind, who run across the sea" are engaging in nothing better than exhausting idleness: "We travel by ship and chariot, seeking to live well, but what you seek is here, in a desolate village [Ulubrae] synonymous with rustic boredom, if only you will keep an open and impartial mind" (*Epist.* 1.11.27 ff). The melancholic Robert Louis Stevenson expressed a similar thought: "Change Glenlivet for Bourbon and it is still whisky, only not so good." Horace might say that the man who leaves his native land (as Stevenson did, traveling in Europe and America before settling in Polynesia), so far from acquiring objectivity, loses the impartiality that would enable him to appreciate the village he came from.

It is easy to "love all people everywhere" or to serve no "lesser loyalty than the welfare of mankind" if our concept of love and service is very thin. When a mother loves her child, she devotes countless hours of patient and long-suffering attention to a creature that often pays her back with disappointment and failure. It is hard enough to divide such love among several children; who but a saint could lavish it on more than a dozen? When a character in Dickens's *Bleak House* euphemistically describes an orphan as a "child of the universe," the young lady's guardian retorts: "The universe makes rather an indifferent parent, I am afraid." The broader our sense of responsibility, the thinner it is, and the children of the universe grow up stunted on the thin gruel of universal philanthropy.

Moral distance and the objective point of view are relevant approaches to mathematical puzzles and scientific theories; they are useful tools in the pursuit of fairness and self-knowledge; they serve to keep us in balance and prevent us from going off the deep end in pursuit of our own desires; they tend to check self-love before it turns to egomania and patriotism before it grows into chauvinism. But perspective and objectivity are essentially negative virtues, setting boundaries to our passions and imposing rules on our love. It is love that is the positive virtue, the power that enables us to do good in the world, and while love unchecked may turn to destructive ends, it is the essential foundation of our moral life. Any attempt to supplant love with a rational system of objective values will inevitably turn us into monsters who kill strangers, from a safe distance, for the sake of a higher cause.[30]

30. Salvatore Quasimodo, who survived the Allied bombing of Milan, turns the tables: "You were in the cockpit, / ... I saw you: it was you, / with your exact science bent on extermination, / without love, without Christ."

THE MYTH OF INDIVIDUALISM

6

In order to turn the individual into a function of the State, his dependence on anything beside the State must be taken from him.

—C. J. Jung, *The Undiscovered Self*

For more than five hundred years, the individual has been at the center stage of Western thought. In one age, the model individual may be a rational philosopher; in the next, a romantic poet who cuts himself free from moral and social restraints; and in the next, a revolutionary hero who may sacrifice his own life for the good of an enslaved nation or an oppressed social class, or even a villain who puts his own desires above the welfare of the oppressed.

During this period, philosophers from Montaigne and Descartes to Marx and Mill were at work, honing abstractions into weapons to cut the cords that weave men and women into the social fabric: the concept of absolute national sovereignty, which sucked away the vitality of communities, families, and the Church; the concept of equality, which obliterated all the little differences and polarities that converge into a commonwealth; and the concept of the free autonomous individual, which accomplished, from the bottom, the social and political revolution that the sovereign state was enforcing from the top.

By the twentieth century, no political discussion could be conducted if it was not expressed in the polar terms of the individual and the state. Libertarians and leftists, who might disagree on virtually everything else, concurred on the terms of a debate that reduces political theory and practice to the allocation of power between atomized individuals and the molecular state that may or may not express their "general will." These twin concepts, sown by Hobbes and Locke and Rousseau, are the dragon's teeth that have grown into men who kill each other over theories of national destiny, class conflict, and human rights.

Heroic Individualism

It is from this background that the heroic individualist emerges, the demigod who transcends the obligations of everyday life and vindicates the rights of oppressed strangers. In the case of all too many champions of human rights, neither charity nor even justice begins at home, and we have already touched upon the familiar theme of humanitarian hypocrisy that reserves its moral energies for vast undertakings and foreign affairs and refuses to waste them on spouses or friends or neighbors. That those who would save the world turn out to be hardly good enough to live in it is hardly a paradox.

All this attention paid to the individual distracts us from the obvious fact that man, as Aristotle said, is a *zoon politikon*, a creature framed to live in society, and if he thinks he can transcend the ordinary civilities of family, neighborhood, and nation, he may turn out to be that "'tribeless, lawless, heartless man' denounced by Homer" (*Iliad* 9.63), who resembles an isolated checker on the game board (*Politics* 1253a).

Heroic individualism, even of the moral variety, has its risks, even for the best and bravest of men. The heroes of myths and legends had to give up all the pleasures of ordinary living if they wished to win fame and glory. Achilles faced what would be, for most of us, a simple choice: long life or glory and an early grave. Achilles' dilemma is more complicated than it appears: His is the choice Hercules had to make between two ways of life—the one hedonistic, the other heroic—but it is also a choice between a long (not necessarily useless or hedonistic) but inglorious life and a brief heroic career in which he would gain public glory by serving his friends.

Even harder was the lot of the Serbian Prince Lazar, who received a letter from the Mother of God instructing him to choose between military victory over the Turks, which would bring glory to himself and freedom to his people, or the spiritual victory for himself and his people that only defeat could bring. If he chose the Kingdom of Heaven, she told him, he must

> weave a church on Kosovo,
> build its foundation not with marble stones,
> build it with pure silk and with crimson cloth,
> take the Sacrament, marshal the men,
> they shall all die,
> and you shall die among them as they die.[1]

Moral and spiritual heroism in Prince Lazar's case required the sacrifice not just of his own personal interest and that of his people, but also of his honor as a soldier. After six hundred years, the Serbs still celebrate the defeat at Kosovo on Vidovdan (St. Vitus' Day) as their greatest national holiday, because, according to the story, they chose in the person of their prince to renounce all individual and national glory for the sake of making themselves a Christian nation.

In carrying out the will of gods, human beings may be required to strip away everything that connects them to this world. In the case of saints who take vows of celibacy and poverty, such spiritual heroism visits little hardship upon friends and family. (Indeed, Catholic parents are expected to forbid sons and daughters from entering religious life if it would have a serious economic impact on the family.) Those who assume or inherit responsibilities are in a different position. In ancient India, Siddhartha was a wealthy prince with a wife and son whom he abandoned to pursue his quest for perfection, and some followers of the Buddha still reject this world of illusion, with all its complicating ties. The greatest of the Greek heroes, Hercules, went mad and killed his wife and children, but after a lifetime of suffering he was accepted into the company of the gods.

---

1. Anne Pennington and Peter Levi, trans., *Marko the Prince: Serbo-Croat Heroic Songs,* 17–18. For the spiritual significance of the Lazar story, see Bishop Nikolai Velimirovich and Archimandrite Justin Popovich, *The Mystery and Meaning of the Battle of Kosovo.*

There is usually something more than a little wrong with the greatest national heroes. They are illegitimate or born under strange circumstances (like Moses, Sargon of Akkad, Romulus, Siegfried, and Hercules); they display sexual appetites that border on the pathological (Gilgamesh, Hercules, Priam); they violate conventions and taboos, such violations apparently constituting a precondition for the fulfillment of their heroic quest; and they may even commit crimes (Hercules, Pelops, Siegfried, Oedipus). All these dubious qualities are shared by another category of men, the tyrants of legend and history. To be truly heroic, it seems, one may have also to be a monster.[2]

The hero's dilemma is portrayed starkly in the case of Agamemnon, Homer's "lord of men," who could not launch his divinely sanctioned expedition against Troy until he had first sacrificed his daughter. It is possible to treat Agamemnon, as Euripides did, as a cynical politician; however, in the great play of Aeschylus that bears his name, Agamemnon is a genuinely tragic figure, torn between the will of heaven and love for his daughter:

> Heavy is the fate if I disobey,
> heavy if I slaughter my child,
> the glory of my house. . . . Which is without evil?
>   (Aesch. *Ag.* 206–8)

But Agamemnon is far from an innocent victim. A man who, for whatever reason, can bring himself to kill his own child is well on his way to becoming the monster who will destroy an entire people and profane their temples: "And when he put himself beneath the yoke of necessity, shifting the wind of his mind to an irreverent, unhallowed, unholy direction, his mind changed and he was capable of anything" (218–21).

Agamemnon and Siddhartha may have made the least bad choices given the circumstances in which they found themselves, but if we can engage in a little creative vandalism and rip their stories out of their historical and cultural contexts, we might arrive at another conclusion. Does a man—let us not say "hero" or "sage"—have the right, much

---

2. Carmine Catenacci, *Il tiranno e l'eroe: Per un'archeologia del potere nella Grecia antica,* points out that many admired modern political leaders display the same qualities as ancient heroes and tyrants.

less the obligation, to neglect or abuse friends and family in order to carry out some higher duty or fulfill some higher law?

In the twentieth century, heroic individualism found philosophical expression in the writings of the existentialists. Quite apart from their metaphysics, developed out of phenomenology, which emphasized the individual's stream of consciousness as the basis for knowing reality, existentialist writers developed an heroic myth of the individual detached from all traditional ties. The most convincing expression of this point of view is Albert Camus' great novel *L'Étranger*.

Camus' stranger (or alien) is a French inhabitant of Algeria. Detached from France, Meursault treats his mother's death with the same indifference with which he views girlfriends, coworkers, and friends. Far from being bored or lonely, he has a passionate sense of life in the bright North African sun, but, finding himself entangled with a friend who lives on the fringes of the underworld, he deliberately exposes himself to revenge-seeking Algerians and puts himself in a position where he feels justified in killing one of them. The prosecutor, dwelling upon Meursault's indifference to Christ, secures a conviction and death penalty, and the hero faces an eternity of nothingness with heroic calm, condemned (as Camus explains in an introduction) because he will not lie. Camus was an honest man who broke with Sartre rather than overlook Stalin's crimes, and in holding up the ideal (so attractive in so many ways) of the detached individual, he unintentionally provided a warning to those who might embrace the ideal without fully appreciating the price that must be paid.

The Vanishing Individual

To put the question in a broader context, we might ask if individuals have rights that transcend the claims made by people they are attached to or by the ordinary duties of life. We hear of rights to privacy, to self-fulfillment, to self-expression, and to self-determination that supersede, for example, a mother's duty to her children, a husband's obligations to his wife, and a citizen's commitment to the broader community of which he is a member. "I need to be myself (or find myself)," says the middle-aged husband running off with a younger woman. "I need to have my own space," declares the mother abandoning her children. These rights are, for the most part, grounded in a general theory of individual (or human) rights, and, while the theory may be useful or true, it is, after all, just one theory among many.

Socialists have sometimes seemed to treat the individual as an unimportant and expendable cog in the vast machine of society. It is truer to say that Marx (for example, in the *German Ideology*) viewed the bourgeois ideal of the individualist as an ideological construction used to keep the masses in chains. The only real individuals will exist when a communist society has been established. Since this has never happened, however, it is not unfair to treat Marxists as enemies of the individual. Buddhists have gone further, describing the individual ego as part of the world of illusion *(samsara)* to be overcome.

The commonsense answer to such speculation is to say that I know I am an individual because my body is discrete, separate from all other individuals, and I perceive myself as an independent creature making its own decisions. But against these claims, an equally commonsensical argument can be made that the human individual is merely epiphenomenal, a developmental stage between one's parents and one's children.

We may feel that we are separate and morally independent creatures, but we are not always the best judges of ourselves. So many of our opinions have been engrafted onto us by friends, teachers, and propagandists before we were able to think for ourselves that it is hard to distinguish our own contribution to our personal mindset from the generic implants that dictate what party to belong to and what football team to root for. Free will is among the oldest and most perplexing of philosophical problems. Imbedded as each of us is in a matrix of causations, it is not easy, or even possible, to point to anything that we do that is wholly our own, wholly individual.

This is most obviously the case within that universally human institution, the family. There are, it is true, a variety of family forms and structures, but part of being human is to be born within a family and to create our own families. The species depends upon it, and what the species depends upon cannot be left up to legislation or reason or enlightenment. The mechanisms that lead us, or even compel us, to seek out mates, to propagate and to rear children, are only dimly understood, but the human animal is not unique.

The natural object of any individual (whether insect, bird, or stock-broker) is not so much survival in the here and now as it is the immor-tality that can be conferred only by having children that have children that have children. The body dies, but the genes live on in ever-new combinations. The unconscious quest for reproductive success is at the root of all social organization.

Samuel Butler once suggested that a chicken is only an egg's device for producing more eggs. In more modern terms, the individual can be seen as a mechanism by which genetic material is able to propagate it-self. This way of looking at the world, often called sociobiology, puts kinship in a new light. Since we share genetic material with our relatives, our degree of interest in other human beings depends, in general, on the extent of our relationship. Members of an intact nuclear family have the closest relationship, since parents and children, brothers and sisters each share 50 percent of the same genetic material. In this sense, my four children are, as a group, worth twice to me what I am worth my-self. Put simply, I am worth two children, two siblings, four grandchil-dren or nephews, eight cousins, and so on.

Obviously, neither wolves nor men actually calculate these ratios: Society would perish if its survival depended on reason. But, to carry out their intergenerational plots, our genes have conspired to program our nervous systems and endocrine glands to direct us in the proper path. It is simply not an accident or the result of cultural conditioning that mothers become powerfully attached to their children from the moment of birth, if not before, or that boys who grow up without a father are more prone to become delinquents.

Success or failure, in other words, does not depend entirely on an in-dividual's own exertions, and every human being born of a woman and raised in a family inherits a family curse (as well as family blessings): the ancestral physical, mental, and temperamental assets and defects that were inherited by his parents and emphasized within the household.[3]

Perhaps the individual is one more ambiguous figure that, viewed with one eye, can be discerned, but disappears when both eyes are opened (or vice versa). To get a firmer grasp on this question, we might turn to

3. For overviews of sociobiology, see E. O. Wilson, *Sociobiology: The New Syn-thesis,* and Thomas Fleming, *The Politics of Human Nature.*

a similar question that has been debated on a much smaller scale. The concept of the individual or person in early Greece has been for several decades the subject of a lively discussion, which (because of the fundamental significance of Greek philosophy and culture) is particularly relevant to the wider question. If the Greeks, who are supposed to have a word for everything, had trouble conceiving of the individual, then it might not be safe to assume that individualism (or even the individual) is a universal human norm.

Some classical scholars, most prominently Bruno Snell, have argued that, since there is no word in Homeric Greek for "person" or "individual," the concept of the person as a conscious agent was an historical discovery. In Homer, as Snell points out, the human character, rather than being represented as a spiritual totality, is divided into quasi-organic functions, for example, the heart, the diaphragm, and the *thymos* (a somewhat imaginary organ that reacts to events and serves as the locus for thought and feeling).[4] Others have questioned Snell's premise (shared by Owen Barfield in *Poetic Diction: A Study in Meaning*) that for a concept to exist, there must be a word to bear the meaning. If this theory were entirely correct, then the early Greeks were more primitive in their concept of the person than any people studied by anthropologists. Even Lucien Lévy-Bruhl, the anthropological theorist who sharply distinguished between the civilized and primitive mentality, did not go so far as to deny the concept of the person in primitive thought, and in his last work he described the two mentalities as coexistent.[5] Are we able to perceive shades of meaning and distinction without quite having the words to express them effectively? Perhaps this is why English has borrowed so many socially and psychologically descriptive words from French, such as *louche, naive* (and *faux naïf*), *patois*, and *ingenue*.

Even if they lack a theory or term for the individual, people of every culture make everyday practical decisions as if they were individuals possessed of free will and could distinguish between subject and object, image and reality. The mere fact that a people believe in magic or voodoo does not necessarily mean that they are incapable of realizing the differ-

4. Bruno Snell, *The Discovery of the Mind: The Greek Origins of European Thought,* and "Phrenes-phronesis." See also E. L. Harrison, "Notes on Homeric Psychology," and D. J. Furley, "The Early History of the Concept of the Soul."
5. Lucien Lévy-Bruhl, *How Natives Think.* See also E. E. Evans-Pritchard, *Theories of Primitive Religion.*

ence between a human being and a wax doll, between reality and dreams. At the same time, the deliberate confusion of a person and his image suggests that in some cultures, the individual is not completely detached from his context. Quite apart from beliefs in magic, premodern and non-Western peoples (and many people in modern Western societies) have trouble distinguishing the individual from his family: Inherited curses, collective responsibility for crime, even the Christian view of the married couple as "one flesh" seriously undermine the abstract concept of the individual.[6]

If we turn away from Western cultures, we can find civilized and modern societies in which the modern American sense of the individual is much less pronounced. Japanese psychiatrist Takeo Doi has attempted to distinguish the mental attitudes of his people by using the concept of *amae,* which is basically the feeling of helpless dependency that the child experiences at the mother's breast.[7] Whereas in most Western cultures this sense of dependency withers or vanishes in time, it is retained as an essential item in the Japanese mental outfit. Although Doi is well aware of the potential for pathology when Japanese dependency is carried to an extreme, he has no illusions about Americans' vaunted love of individualism and equality, which so quickly turns into the rigid conformism described by Tocqueville, when "individualism and conformism become two sides of the same coin . . . because self-determination in all things is in fact impossible, and without a tradition or some authority to rely on, the individual ultimately has no choice but to go along with everyone else."[8]

This is not to deny the existence (perhaps universal) of some concept of the individual person in the premodern cultures of North America and the ancient Mediterranean. Homer's heroes perform acts of individual bravery and speak of winning renown, and Achilles became, for later Greeks, the supreme example of a man who chose his own destiny with no regard for social pressures. On the other hand: "In Homer's time the individual did not yet know of the will as an ethical factor, nor did he distinguish between what was inside and outside himself as we do.

6. See Marcel Mauss, "Une catégorie de l'esprit humain: la notion de personne celle de moi."

7. Takeo Doi, *The Anatomy of Dependence,* 7–8 and 40 ff.

8. Takeo Doi, *The Anatomy of Self: The Individual versus Society,* 51.

When referring to themselves, the early Greeks, like other Indo-European peoples, did not primarily consider themselves to be independent individuals but rather members of a group."[9]

Achilles is the hero, in every sense of the word, of the *Iliad.* In one sense, he is a perfect example of extreme individualism: He defies the commander of the expedition over a matter of honor, and he is prepared to defy the gods if they get in the way of his revenge against Hector. Yet, when Homer tries to portray him making up his mind, he describes his "heart" as divided and brings in the goddess Athena to pull his hair. Achilles the individual is really a shadowy borderland between the various organic functions of his temperament and the divine interventions that can overwhelm him, and his rebellion against the army's authority is an unmitigated disaster.

This is an overstatement of the case. Obviously, even Homeric Greeks had names to distinguish their individuality, and there were ways of metaphorically referring to an individual as "the head of so-and-so." This usage persists in the Greek poetry of later centuries. In the first line of Sophocles' *Antigone,* the heroine calls upon her sister, Ismene, saying literally, "Oh common self-sister head of Ismene," which Sir Hugh Lloyd-Jones in his recent Loeb edition Englishes as "My own sister Ismene, linked to myself." Although *head* is used to indicate the person of Ismene, the two sisters are verbally linked to a degree that would be difficult in English, and, throughout this great tragedy, Sophocles lays great stress on the common identity of the two sisters with their two brothers and with their entire family and lineage. This work, which clearly illustrates the ambiguous Greek view of individuality, is frequently misinterpreted by critics and scholars who import modern views into the text.

The plot of the play is simple enough. King Oedipus of Thebes, who inadvertently killed his father and married his mother, has left behind four children: two daughters, Ismene and Antigone, and two sons, Eteocles and Polynices, who quarrel over power and precedence. Expelled from Thebes, a disgruntled Polynices has recruited an army of champions (the so-called Seven Against Thebes) and attacked his native city in a vain attempt to recover his power. The brothers kill each other in battle,

---

9. Jan Bremmer, *The Early Greek Concept of the Soul,* 67.

and their maternal uncle Creon, who has taken up the reins of power, decrees that the body of Polynices be left unburied and unmourned on pain of death. Antigone, after her sister refuses to help her, performs a ceremonial burial by sprinkling dust on the body, and, when guards undo her work, she is caught in the act of performing the ritual a second time. Brought to Creon, she confesses her "crime" and is condemned to be buried alive in a cave. When her fiancé, who happens also to be Creon's son Haemon, attempts to intercede for her, he is rebuffed and goes off to join Antigone in death.

Few ancient masterpieces have been revived and discussed more often than the *Antigone,* and few have been more distorted in the process. The play has been viewed as a contest between religion and the state, women and men, the individual and society. During World War II, Jean Anouilh composed a French version in which Antigone obviously represents France in resistance, while Creon is meant to be the Nazi tyrant. But most such interpretations, valid as they are up to a point, overlook certain facts of life (both ancient and modern) that are essential to any comprehensive understanding of the play—and of the individual.

The crucial problem for Antigone is the burial of Polynices: It is the family's religious duty to bury a dead member, whatever he might have done. An enemy of the state remains a member of the family, and, unless the social order is actually threatened, it can never be a good thing for a child to treat a parent with disrespect or to inform the authorities of his brother's bad habits.

Antigone justifies her defiance of authority—and public opinion— on the good Greek grounds that "There is no shame in showing regard for those of one's own stock." However, Creon, thinking as a statesman, insists: "An enemy is never a friend, even when he is dead." This sounds convincing on the surface, until Antigone goes to the heart of the question, which is the duty of blood: "I was born not to share in hatred but in love" (*Ant.* 523)—that is, it is part of the human condition to care for those we are related to.

Antigone's case is hard. Her brother, admittedly, became an enemy of the people, and he could not have been an easy man to "love." But this young woman's love is not a merely emotional attachment: it is an unseen umbilical cord that ties her to all her family, dead as well as living. Since all the male heirs of Oedipus are dead, it is up to the elder daughter to discharge the family's functions in life and death. Such *epikleroi* (often translated as "heiresses") in Athens were typically married off to uncles or cousins to preserve the lineage and property. (In this sense, it is perfectly natural that she is engaged to Haemon, whatever the two might think of each other.)[10]

Although Antigone is very brave—her actions would be heroic in any man—her defiance of the ruler is not an expression of her individual will but of her commitment to her family. Paradoxically, it is the strength of that commitment that impels her to an act of individual heroism that is not entirely approved of by the chorus. Far from being an heroic feminist or prototypical martyr, Antigone is merely an unusually strong young woman trying to carry out her duty to family and the gods.[11]

The play stands as an ancient warning against human presumption and the arrogance that derives from individualism and scientific progress. Man, sings the chorus, has invented devices with which he has tamed the beasts, and, in inventing society, has proved himself to be "all-resourceful": It is only death's kingdom that he approaches without resources. The point is driven home: "Skillful beyond hope is the contrivance of his art, and he advances sometimes to evil, at other times to good. When he applies the laws of the earth and the justice the gods have sworn to uphold he is high in the city; outcast from the city is he with whom the ignoble consorts for the sake of gain"—that is, his individual advancement (*Ant.* 332–75). So long as man continues to see himself in the context of his community, he prospers, but if he tries to set himself above the traditional prejudices and superstitious reverence of his people, he will, like Creon, destroy everything.

This play is obviously not a philosophical discourse "about" individualism; what is striking is not so much what Sophocles says about self-will and community as the social and moral attitudes that are taken for granted both in the *Antigone* and in such other plays as the *Oedipus*, where a clever intellectual destroys himself by defying religion and popular opinion, or in Euripides' *Hercules*, whose hero realizes that, while he

---

10. For a recent literary interpretation of Antigone's status as an *epikleros*, see Kirk Ormand, *Exchange and the Maiden: Marriage in Sophoclean Tragedy.*

11. For Antigone as a normal Greek woman, see Mary R. Lefkowitz, "Influential Women."

has gone around the world killing monsters, he has not taken proper care of his wife and children and father, who are his peculiar responsibility.

The conflicts between loyalties—loyalty to kin, loyalty to community, loyalty to the gods—are the constant theme of Greek literature in its "golden age." The strain of attachments was a reflection of Greek social life in places where the city-community, or *polis,* was growing at the expense of clans and kindreds.[12] Greek religion during the same period was subject to great stress from rationalizing philosophers like Pericles' friend Anaxagoras, who taught that the sun was a hot metallic ball and explained away prodigies on a naturalistic basis.

In Homer's day, human motivations were inextricably entwined with the divine, and it was not possible to conceive of man except, in some sense, as a projection or plaything of the gods. By the time of Aeschylus and Sophocles, human nature was in the forefront, but it was not to be understood except in relation to the divine—and woe unto the mortal like Creon, who defied the power of Hades, or Hippolytus, who despised the charms of Aphrodite, or Pentheus, who tried to suppress the rites of Dionysus.

It would be a long story to trace the development of individualism in the Greek world, but even in fifth-century Athens individual citizens were closely entangled in the bonds of kinship, friendship, and citizenship to an extent that is not easy for modern and postmodern men and women to grasp. Not even the will was unambiguously represented as inhabiting one side of the line that divides freedom from necessity. Among the Greeks, will was conceived of in more ambiguous terms, as "decision without choice, responsibility independent of intentions."[13] Agamemnon, in the scene we have discussed, is said to put his neck under the yoke of necessity—an elegant metaphor to describe the complex interrelationship of free will and necessity.

In their religion, too, Greeks acted more as corporate members of society than as individuals practicing a faith or seeking salvation: "The individual established his connection with the divine through his participation in a community."[14] Perhaps the closest analogies to our own

---

12. See Sally Humphreys, *The Family, Women, and Death: Comparative Studies,* 22–32.

13. J.-P. Vernant and P. Vidal-Naquet, "Ebauches de la volonté," 48.

14. J.-P. Vernant, "Aspects de la personne dans la réligion grecque," 24.

time are the Hellenistic cities, founded by Greeks (and which included non-Greeks) from different places and bound together more by legal and political ties than by common traditions.

The Romans, whose early cultural history is far more difficult to follow, must have gone through a somewhat parallel course of development, although in their case this development was affected by alien influences—Etruscan as well as Greek—from an early date. By the age of the Antonine emperors (roughly the second century A.D.), however, the empire gave as much legal and cultural recognition to the individual as the world had seen or would see until modern times.

Under the empire, broadly speaking, the most popular philosophical schools (Stoics, Neoplatonists, and Epicureans) and religious cults (Christianity, Mithraism) emphasized personal salvation more than corporate justice, and even family relations were hemmed in with restrictions that would have astonished the elder Cato. With the introduction of Christianity, a new voice was heard, stressing the divinely approved worth of every human person, Jew and gentile, free and slave, adult and child. As Marcel Mauss, a leftist social theorist (and no Christian) wrote: "It is the Christians who turned the moral person into a metaphysical entity, after having felt the religious force."[15]

The collapse of Roman authority in the West and the barbarization of Europe resulted in a retribalization that, to a great extent, submerged the individual back into the community, though the Church continued to teach barbarian and Roman alike the unique value of every human soul. The European cultural renascences of both the twelfth and the fifteenth centuries were periods of renewed individualism.[16] Romantic love, individual portraiture, and confessional autobiography, while their roots may go much deeper into historical soil, grew and flowered in the twelfth century, revealing a distinctive sense of the personal self that was partly indebted to classical literary models (which were also being rediscovered in both renascences) and partly a response to changing social and cultural circumstances.

But nothing in Greek drama, Roman law, or medieval poetry completely prepares us for the arrival of the modern individual (much less the individualist). The word *individual* is itself a medieval creation. The

15. Mauss, "Une catégorie," 357.
16. See Colin Morris, *The Discovery of the Individual, 1050–1200.*

individuum is, literally, that which is undivided, and the adjective is applied to the unity of the godhead, which is expressed in the Trinity of three Persons. In the eleventh century, there arose a school of philosophy that emphasized the individual (*this* horse, *that* man) at the expense of the genus (horses or men). This so-called nominalism can be seen as a justifiable reaction to ultra-Platonic realism, which ascribed reality to the concept or class at the expense of the real things of this world. Carried to an extreme in human terms, however, it has the effect of isolating individuals and rendering them meaningless and rootless.

The nominalists may have intended less harm than their critics (for example, Richard M. Weaver) have attributed to them. However, the most extreme and crude nominalist, Roscelin, not only described universal categories as nothing more than words, a mere *flatus vocis,* but also went on to apply his method to the concept of the Trinity, concluding that the three Persons were actually separate, individual gods— a heresy that was later condemned.

In orthodox Christian terms, it is the Trinity that is a unity, while man cannot be truly an individual because he is a compound of matter and spirit. Angels, on the other hand, are all spirit, created directly by God, and therefore (as St. Thomas concluded) each angel is a genus unto himself. If there is a fundamental problem with the term *individual,* it may derive from the misapplication of a divine and spiritual concept to man, a creature whose organic nature is perhaps more self-evident than his spiritual side. And, in emphasizing man's undivided nature, we ultimately run the risk of denying the less obvious component of that nature, namely, the spirit.

"Ideas," as the title of Weaver's attack on nominalism states, "have consequences," and if the sins of early medieval nominalism have been exaggerated, the tradition either survived or was reinvented by later European thinkers who radically shifted the argument away from universal concepts (such as human nature and human race)[17] and toward the notion of human beings as mere individuals without a common nature. Hobbesian man, Lockean man, and Marxian man are quite different creations with different political outlooks; each of them, however, is liberated from the burden of history and human nature.

17. On the political implications of the concept of human nature, see Fleming, "The Part and the Whole," chap. 1 in *Politics of Human Nature.*

Political Individualism

The beliefs and customs of a nation obviously condition its conception of the individual: The traveler who goes from London to Moscow soon realizes the not-so-subtle differences in the valuation put upon the individual by two different political cultures. If there is any truth in what the social psychologists say when they speak of the "social construction of the personality," the individual is not a hard-edged absolute, like the atoms of Democritus; it is more like a constellation of subatomic particles, behaving as if they comprised a unity but impossible to define in any absolute sense, especially when the observer is taken into account. Indeed, in trying to determine another man's individuality, I inevitably intrude my own into the analysis.

We are in danger of falling into familiar clichés, such as John Donne's "No man is an island." The unity of the human race or of a nation is perhaps too broad a concept to be very useful. It would be like analyzing the elusive electron by reference to galaxies and solar systems—a helpful metaphor but not entirely relevant. If human individuals are a social construction, then the building must be done by other individuals with whom they are in contact. Josiah Royce understood this:

> Nobody amongst us men comes to self-consciousness, so far as I know, except under the persistent influence of his social fellows. A child in the earlier stages of his social development...shows you, as you observe him, a process of the development of self-consciousness in which, at every stage, the Self of the child grows and forms itself through Imitation, and through functions that cluster about the Imitation of others.... In consequence, the child is in general conscious of what expresses the life of somebody else, before he is conscious of himself.[18]

On the other hand, the mere fact that most of us insist upon the solidity of our personhood should make us beware of denying, categorically, either the reality or the significance of the individual.

Individual liberty, as a moral (rather than political) aspiration, implies a degree of independence that, paradoxically, it may be impossible to acquire since our comfort—our mere existence—as much as our happiness depends upon other people. The mere logic of self-seeking hedonism leads to a dilemma that is perceived by many leftists:

18. Josiah Royce, *The World and the Individual*, 2:259–60.

> Suppose that I love my family and friends. On all the theories about self-interest, my love for these people affects what is in my interests. Much of my happiness comes from knowing about, and helping to cause, the happiness of those I love. . . . What will be best for me may . . . largely overlap with what will be best for those I love. But, in some cases, what will be better for me will be worse for those I love. I am self-interested if, in all these cases, I do what will be better for me.[19]

Thus, in choosing my own self-interest over the happiness of my friends, I end up making myself unhappy.

If the end of life is happiness (however defined), then that happiness has a social as well as an individual dimension. Aristotle thought happiness was an ultimate good because we would give up other things—for example, wealth and power—if they stood in the way of happiness, and because happiness is "self-sufficient"—that is, complete in itself, not requiring anything beyond it. But he recognized that self-sufficiency (or autarky) was not possible for individuals: "By self-sufficient we do not mean that which is sufficient for a man by himself, for one who lives a solitary life, but also for his parents, wife, children, and more generally for his friends and fellow citizens, since man is a naturally social creature" (*Eth. Nic.* 1097b8–11). Aristotle concedes that some limit has to be put to avoid an infinite regression toward that abstraction we now call "society" or even "humanity," and, for the sake of analysis, he agrees to isolate the quality of happiness as that which makes life happy and complete. But it was still difficult for a Greek, even in the fourth century, to isolate individual happiness from its social context.

Aristotle is often lumped together with Plato, because they both upheld the philosophical ideal of contemplation as the highest form of happiness, but Aristotle was more alive to the importance of friendship and kinship as conditions for a happy life. Anthony Kenny, who has made a controversial argument for the *Eudemian Ethics* as Aristotle's final answer, makes an essential point that Aristotle wants to prove that "the good man needs friends by showing that the good involved in perceiving and knowing is essentially a shared good."[20]

Perhaps Aristotle, in his quest for self-sufficiency, was merely riding his usual hobbyhorse—namely, teleology, the pursuit of the ultimate

19. Parfit, *Reasons and Persons,* 5–6.
20. Anthony Kenny, *Aristotle on the Perfect Life,* 50.

ends of things. But it is an observable fact that human beings are not born in isolation and that, for the most part, their happiness is bound up with the fate of those they love. Not everyone would go as far as Aristotle in wondering if the fortunes of the living affect the dead (*Eth. Nic.* 1101a22–b8), although that was a common Greek sentiment. Nonetheless, even modern Christians speak of "the communion of saints," the belief that, in receiving the bread and wine, all believers—regardless of time and space, life and death—are in mystical communion with Christ's body and blood and with each other. One might speculate that the concept of purgatory was a device enabling Christians to participate in a community that included friends and relatives who had died without achieving blessedness.

The contrast between individualist and communitarian views of happiness is brought out by the Greek historian Herodotus, who set up an imaginary dialogue between Croesus, the fabulously wealthy king of Lydia, and Solon, an Athenian statesman proverbial for his wisdom. When Croesus asks Solon whom he regards as the happiest man in the world, he is disappointed with the Athenian's first and second choices: a man who led a good life and died fighting for his city while his family flourished; and two strong sons who died after harnessing themselves to a carriage in order to take their mother to a festival of Hera. This strange answer prompts Croesus to point to his own great wealth and power, to which Solon responds that no man can be considered happy until he has died. The usual interpretation is that Solon is merely reflecting on the uncertainty of human life, but his two examples show that the happiness of a human individual cannot be divorced from the happiness of family and fellow citizens. (Croesus's subsequent misfortunes involve not only the loss of his kingdom but the accidental death of his son and heir.)

For religious people—Christians and Jews, in particular, but also Platonists—there can be no true happiness that is not connected somehow with the divine, and the godly man might be supposed to find solitary happiness in the contemplation of his creator, although even in this case, happiness depends upon another, albeit divine, person.

If Christians set aside this *perfecta beatudo* and consider only everyday happiness in this present life, however, they discover, according to St. Thomas, that it is based on "charity, which goes out to God and our neighbor. Therefore the society of friends is required for happiness."

We cannot, St. Thomas continues, exercise our natural obligations to charity without the companionship of others: "The happy man needs friends, not so much for their usefulness, since he is sufficient unto himself, nor on account of pleasure . . . but that he may do good to them and take pleasure in the sight of their good works and that he may take pleasure in being helped by them toward doing good."[21]

On a lower level, human interdependency is a fact of everyday life, as Hume realized: "Man, born in a family, is compelled to maintain society, from necessity, from natural inclination, and from habit."[22] Acknowledging the social context of the individual does not necessarily entail a denigration of the very real individualism of modern Europe and the United States. The philosophical assumptions and theories of liberal individualism are to some extent merely a reflection of the way people think they live. Ours, like every society, construes its own social reality, and if it seems strange to us that a Greek might worry about the happiness of his descendants, our own self-absorption would be viewed as cold and egotistical in many cultures. The dangers of excessive social conformity seem obvious to us, but over the past century social theorists have devoted far more attention to the alienation of the individual.

Up to a point, Western individualism is a worthy moral ideal; carried to extremes, however, it entails risks, including the risk of self-destruction. Individualism, after all, was not invented by deracinated individualists. Seventeenth- and eighteenth-century England and Scotland—where Hobbes, Locke, and Smith lived and wrote—were dominated by corporate and communal institutions: the church parish, the college, the shire and the borough, the House of Commons and the convocation. The seventeenth century in particular was an age of group petitions, remonstrances, and confessions. Above all, it was a period (like most historical ages) of estate building, the founding of family fortunes, of politics centered in the ambitions of families. In such a social context, an emphasis on the individual was merely a question of accent or embellishment.

Even though individualism is one of the main themes of political thought since the Renaissance (especially in Britain and North America), it is more often taken for granted than demonstrated. Hobbes, for

21. St. Thomas Aquinas, *Summa Theologiae*, 2.1, 4.8.
22. David Hume, "Of the Origin of Government," in *Essays Moral, Political, and Literary,* 37.

example, seems to have assumed that, by describing the human individual as self-seeking, he had laid the foundations for an account of human social life. The object of his scientific method was to "resolve existing society into its simplest elements and then to recompose those elements into a logical whole."[23] He seems never to have questioned his assumption that such simple elements actually existed independently, much less considered that his analysis might disturb the framework of society. Salt, to make an analogy, is an essential nutrient of the human nervous system, but it can be broken down into the antagonistic elements of sodium and chlorine, both of them poisonous to human life.

Locke, without sharing Hobbes's pessimism, shared his psychological egoism. For him, personal identity is defined by our consciousness of self, extending back and forth in time. Locke's atomistic treatment of consciousness and the self is the foundation for his political philosophy grounded in individual rights. It also leads, with or without rights, to a very skeptical treatment of the community as a merely fictitious body. Margaret Thatcher put it directly: "The community does not exist." This tendency of thought inevitably polarizes the world into individual and society (or the state), and the relationship between the two becomes a question of "the nature and limits of the power which can be legitimately exercised by society over the individual," as John Stuart Mill put it in the first sentence of *On Liberty*.

Mill did, however, acknowledge that his autonomous individual was less a universal reality than an ideal for which one had to strive:

> If it were felt that the free development of individuality is one of the leading essentials of well-being; that it is not only a co-ordinate element with all that is designated by the terms civilization, instruction, education, culture, but is itself a necessary part and condition of all those things; there would be no danger that liberty should be undervalued, and the adjustment of the boundaries between it and social control would present no extraordinary difficulty. But the evil is, that individual spontaneity is hardly recognized by the common modes of thinking as having any intrinsic worth, or deserving any regard on its own account.

Mill here puts himself into a sort of bind. Individual liberty, it seems, is part of a certain kind of civilization, though it is not appreciated even

---

23. C. B. MacPherson, *The Political Theory of Possessive Individualism: Hobbes to Locke*, 30.

by members of that civilization. Beyond the obvious paradox, Mill seems to have contradicted his own utilitarian principle. If pleasure is indeed the object of human life, and if most men do not regard individual fulfillment as "having any intrinsic worth," then the pursuit of individual development must be a question more of religious than philosophical argument.[24]

What is striking is not so much what philosophers have occasionally said in defining the individual as what they omit. Hobbes, for example, in arguing for natural liberty, simply leaves out all the social attachments that might have been included by earlier writers. Since men are naturally competitive, the exercise of natural liberty results—or, rather, would result if it were possible—in the war of all against all. Contrast this abstract and absolute certainty with Aristotle's hesitancy on the subject of natural justice, which he compares to right-handedness, a tendency that is quasi-universal but does not exclude the possibility of ambidexterity (*Eth. Nic.* 1134b18 ff.). Natural justice, of course, is the universal component of the virtue of justice, which Aristotle defines in social terms as "complete virtue in relationship to the other." From this perspective, a man cannot be "just to himself" (*Eth. Nic.* 1129b24–25).

The rejection of social identity is not unrelated to the development of political and economic individualism that finds extreme expression in Mill's defense (in *On Liberty*) of the free individual against all forms of coercion, including both democratic politics and the power of public opinion. For Mill, mere social disapproval of a lifestyle is an intolerable invasion of personal liberty.

The apotheosized individual will be a rare bird in any civilization, and the aristocratic insistence upon individual liberty invites the revenge of society, but individualism also changes the concept of society itself. For Aristotle and Richard Hooker, community is neither an external set of forces nor a mere aggregate of individuals: it is an organic completeness bound together by natural bonds of kinship, affection, and common experience. Once human society has been reconceived as a collection of individuals, then social order will have to be imposed.

---

24. Mill, *On Liberty*, 54. John Gray, *Mill on Liberty: A Defense*, has attempted to resolve the apparent contradictions, and the result, while an admirable defense of individualism, is more Gray than Mill. G. E. Moore's criticisms in *Principia Ethica*, 64–81, still seem telling.

From the socialist perspective, the problem becomes one of class conflict and the construction of a state that fulfills the needs of the working classes; for the nationalist, the object is the creation of a nation-state expressing the national will and the national identity; in democracies, the social identity is based on majority rule, and so on. The point is that virtually everyone, both fascists and communists, accepts the liberal premise of individualism. Humpty Dumpty has fallen and smashed to smithereens; the debate is over whether and how "all the king's horses and all the king's men" shall set him up again.

The individual, then, is inextricable from the affections and ties that bind him with those other individuals who comprise society. This is true whether or not we regard personal development as a moral obligation. If this sounds paradoxical or absurd, it may be because the word *individual* is itself a kind of abstraction meant to define the human person as an object of inquiry, a material that is divorced from a spirit he may or may not be supposed to possess. Man is a subject, after all, and not an object, and to treat him as an object is to dissolve the integration of spirit and matter that constitute human beings as persons.[25]

The word *person,* then, refers to the organic totality of the human being, viewed subjectively, with the right of its own first-person perspective. The individual, on the other hand, is a despiritualized abstraction viewed objectively and (contradicting the root meaning of *individual*) divisible into parts. Over the years, sciences have grown up to explain or justify each category of human activity, and the result is a series of partial snapshots of the human personality taken from different angles with equipment of varying quality.

One set of liberals has given us a view of economic man, as if it were profitable or even possible to imagine single human beings who make rational choices in isolation from all the things and people that give savor to their lives. Other liberals have sketched out a juridical man, endowed with rights to life, liberty, property, and so forth, and argue that it is the defense of these rights that justifies the existence of government. Schools of psychology have given us sexual man, aggressive man, and so on.

Some good, no doubt, derives from such particular studies, but only if we are willing to take these various bits of evidence for what they

25. See Pier Luigi Zampetti, *La Sfida del Duemila: L'uomo può salvare il mondo dalla catastrofe?* 21.

are—mere gropings in the dark, like the blind men who tried to describe the elephant. The beast itself eludes our definition.

If "I" (by which I mean someone speaking in his own right) were to attempt to give an account of the human individual, I should begin with my consciousness of "myself." At the age of thirty-five or sixty, I must have changed a great deal from the boy of eight or student of eighteen I once was, and yet I am the same person. By luck and with some effort, I have got beyond some of the follies of youth. I no longer think myself the most brilliant of men and can only regard my pranks and infatuations with the indulgent resignation an old man reserves for wayward nephews and grandchildren.

On the other hand, a responsible religious convert, if questioned about the sins and vices of his youth, the hopeless love and desperate abandon, would have to say: "I am still the man who did those things. I was a reckless libertine then or a fool, and although I am, thank God, now a sober member of the Church and a pillar of my community, I am still the man I always was." In converting to a religious faith or in gaining wisdom, we do not have our slates wiped clean; we are only given more space in which to write new chapters.

I have never liked to hear the confessions of converted sinners. They always seem either to be reveling in what they once did or, far worse, attempting to distance themselves from their earlier selves. Augustine struggled, albeit unsuccessfully, to free himself from the memory of his mistress and child, and even as a bishop he brooded over the sin of stealing an apple. When he ultimately decided that a man who abandons his concubine to marry another woman is guilty of adultery, he seemed to be acknowledging that he was the same man he always had been.

There are reformed abortionists who go about the country condemning their former colleagues. Whatever they do now, however, they are still in their own eyes men who murdered babies, and no amount of enlightenment can wash the blood off their hands. One might be better convinced of their sincerity if the good doctors would give all they have to the poor, including the Mercedes in which they ride to their next inspirational lecture. If their money is so tainted, they should get rid of it.

Shame is the recognition that we can never escape the consequences of our sins or the self that committed them, and converted sinners who regale audiences and congregations with their former depravities are without shame. Am I saying there is no forgiveness for those who repent? Not at all, but denial is not the sign of repentance, and any man who says, "I am not the man I was" is lying, if only to himself. "I am a part of all that I have met," says Tennyson's Ulysses, and if repentance means only that we think we have escaped from what we were, then it is better not to repent; it is better to remain an embittered sinner who has laid his neck beneath the yoke of necessity. In other words, it may be morally better to be a courageous pagan than a cowardly Christian.

Clearly demarcated periods of infancy, adolescence, and adulthood have their place in enabling us to speak generally about stages of development, but too much emphasis on stages of development and states of consciousness can obscure the more fundamental fact of continuity. Radical disjunctions in any theory are fatal to our appreciation of the greater picture, whether we are positing a cultural break between the days of Pericles and the time of Alexander or a chasm between the fall of Rome and the barbarians' world of early medieval Italy or an unbridgeable gap between chimpanzees and man.

When we place too much stress on being reborn, regenerated, we are apt to minimize the permanence of human character. The reformed alcoholic still has an "addictive personality," except that he is now addicted to AA meetings. The apostle Paul was intemperately zealous in opposing the first Christians and held the cloaks of the men who stoned the first martyr. Upon seeing the light—quite literally—Paul did not acquire humility and an easygoing disposition. On the contrary: While he boasted of being the worst of sinners, he defied the Jewish establishment and successfully challenged St. Peter on the question of circumcision for converted gentiles.

Our first requirement as individual human beings who wish to be fully human is to declare, like Popeye the Sailor, "I am what I am and that's all what I am." In other words, the first requirement of real human life is authenticity or integrity, a life that is solid rather than diffuse, integrated rather than compartmentalized. Horace articulated the common ideal of the ancients: *Integer vitae scelerisque purus*—that is, "whole in life and free from the taint of crime."

The bigamist and the serial monogamist lead lives of fraud and inconsequence. In separating their marital lives into discrete blocks of time or space, they are dividing their own personalities against themselves. There are other modes of self-division: dishonest businessmen and crooked politicians who pose, in their own households, as pillars of virtue. Better the crime lord who makes his money in a war against rivals and enemies and enlists the support of his family in the enterprise than a patriotic statesman who cheats on his wife.

The Individualist Virus

The individual, almost by definition, is the self divided against itself. This habit of seeing ourselves as discrete entities, cut off from the social context, encourages us to discover multiple personalities within ourselves, distinguishing the "bad old me" who chased girls and preached communism from the "good new me" who takes care of his family and teaches Sunday school. Occasionally, when some gray-haired sixties revolutionary or octogenarian communist spy is dragged out of hiding, she attracts sympathy from people who cannot accept the fact of continuity between the soccer mom and the terrorist she once was. These tragically divided selves are only one small instance of the wider problem, diagnosed since the beginning of the nineteenth century, of the individualist virus that eats up all the little communities, like a computer-game monster devouring everything in its path.

After the French Revolution, intellectuals on both the left and right were convinced that French society was in crisis, and they looked for ways of putting Humpty together again, whether through some form of socialism or by way of a new "science of society." For Emile Durkheim, suicide was a symptom of social dissolution. Excessive individualism was the disease; social solidarity was the cure. As the late Robert Nisbet put it:

> [Durkheim] knew that no stable order could be built *directly* on the intellectual pillars of modernism; that until the values of science and liberal democracy were rooted in *social* contexts as secure and binding as the contexts in which religion and kinship had once been rooted, and endowed with *moral* authority, the *sacredness*, that these more ancient institutions had once known, European society would continue in the state of crisis that would subvert each and every political remedy that the reformers put forward.[26]

26. Robert Nisbet, *The Sociological Tradition*, 304.

One by one, according to Durkheim and his predecessors, human social contexts had been destroyed, either through violent revolution or as a result of natural decay. The clan, the Church, the village existed only as withered relics of the powerful social organisms that once had flourished, and even the nuclear family—the last redoubt of solidarity—has given way in the twentieth century.

In the great classic ages of art and civilization, a balance is struck between the human and the divine, between the abstract mathematical ideal and the imperfect human reality, between the individual and the little communities that shape his identity. That balance is the essence of classicism, and, once it is lost, religion retreats into the realms of fables and philosophy and artists learn to be content with flesh alone (until they flee reality into the realm of pure abstraction). The tension in the Greek mind was restored only when we recovered the sense of the divine by learning to accept the man Who is God.

And so it went for a thousand years and more, as the Western mind recovered its virility, the primitive vigor of archaic Greece, in that richly creative millennium we used to call the Dark Ages. Another set of classic moments was reached in the Renaissance, as one by one the cities and peoples of Europe rediscovered the individual without, at least at first, losing their faith in the divine. But this time around, the descent was more precipitous. Instead of sinking into the glorious mediocrity of Hellenistic civilization—which lasted, after all, for a thousand years—we slid violently into the abyss. While philosophers and political leaders dreamed of being Napoleonic heroes and Nietzschean strongmen, in reality they were only becoming individualists, producers and consumers whose highest conception of love and community was mutual exploitation. Their true philosopher was neither Mill nor Nietzsche but the Marquis de Sade, a man born two hundred years before his time. In the name of individual liberty, Sade opposed capital punishment but championed abortion and women's rights. (In more playful moments, he also defended the value of theft, rape, infanticide, and murder.)

If the "divine Marquis" (note the transvaluation of values, if you please) could walk up and down upon the earth today, he would give his blessing to the films and television programs that encourage us to think of children not as extensions of a family but as individual objects for sexual exploitation, of a global political economic system that, in the name of "individual human rights," has assumed more power over the world than Creon ever dreamed of exercising in tiny Thebes and that, like him, is bent on eradicating "the justice the gods have sworn to uphold." Indeed, the "gods" themselves are made the enemy of the state, as if America were the Thebes of Pentheus and Creon.

GOODBYE, OLD RIGHTS OF MAN

7

Speak of a social contract and the revolution is made.

—Metternich, *Political Confession of Faith*

As ordinary men and women in Belgrade and Novi Sad were digging out from the rubble and attending funerals, Vaclav Havel issued a statement praising the NATO bombardment of hospitals, buses, bridges, television stations, Albanian refugee columns, and other civilian targets in Serbia as the "first war in history fought for human rights." It was tempting, at the time, to think that Havel was simply indulging in the comedic absurdity that won him a reputation as a playwright, but the Czech leader and hero of the Velvet Revolution was speaking in dead earnest. At the end of the second millennium, the death of actual people, innocent people, counts for less in the scheme of things than the hypothetical advancement of intangible rights.

Such absurd contradictions are an everyday occurrence in Europe and North America: To promote what amounts to an advertising slogan—an abstract and hypothetical "quality of life"—we kill real unborn children; to advance the ideals of democracy, we impose our will on small nations; and to provide equality of opportunity, we make everyone equally miserable. We live and die by clichés that have no discernible reference to reality: We fight wars to end all wars and liberate women by sending them to work; we give children the right to be sexually exploited by adults;[1] and we empower the poor by making them depend more and more on government. War Is Peace; Freedom Is Slavery; Work Makes Free.

It is not simply that we live by illusions but that our illusions have a nasty way of destroying things that are really valuable: Nationalists, to build a great nation, destroy their own real people and real cultures; Marxists, who claimed to be fighting on behalf of the workers, made their existence a living hell; parents who say they want the best for their families end up working so many hours that they have no time to notice that their children are growing up wrong. We are back to the dilemma of the Greek king Agamemnon, who sacrificed his own child in order to fulfill the will of Zeus, or to satisfy his career ambition, or to punish the innocent subjects of the guilty king of Troy.

In addressing this dilemma, many philosophers would analyze the choice of Agamemnon as a conflict of individual rights and/or duties. If a child has a right to live, a right that is universal, then no one, not even a father, is justified in killing her. When asked who is to protect that right, the philosopher's stock response would be society or government, but when pressed on who will protect Agamemnon's family from the government, he might speak of the rights of parents, and so on, in an infinite regression whose effect is always the empowerment of another set of guardians. In Agamemnon's case, the problem is even more acute, since he, as the king, *is* the government, and he was neither the first nor the last political official to misuse his authority over children.

Although talk of rights seems to come naturally to Americans, it is more political theology than philosophy. We like to think of ourselves as living in an enlightened age that has escaped from superstition, but earlier ages were not so dark as we like to think, and the brightness of human reason in the past two centuries has been clouded by smugness, imperialism, war, and genocide. We like to think that we moderns have created the only really rational civilization, but even premodern philosophical systems were, after all, subject to objective judgment and skeptical inquiry, and even in this most rational of worlds, reason is

---

1. That is the significance of the European and American political movements that aim to lower the age of consent to fourteen or even twelve.

suspended, *on principle,* in the case of natural rights: "We hold these truths to be self-evident, that all men are created equal, that they are endowed by their Creator with certain unalienable Rights, that among these are Life, Liberty and the pursuit of Happiness."

Jefferson's platitudes have often been ascribed to the direct influence of John Locke, but this language of rights was in the very air that was breathed throughout the eighteenth century. The dispute over Locke's influence on the American Revolution and the Declaration of Independence is endless, with Louis Hartz and Carl Becker taking the affirmative and Bernard Bailyn, Gary Wills, and J. G. A. Pocock taking the negative position. At this point, only one thing can be safely concluded—namely, that Locke's influence cannot be held to be self-evident. Jefferson himself, in replying to Richard Henry Lee's accusation that he had borrowed from a pamphlet of James Otis and Locke's treatise, said in a letter to Madison (August 30, 1823): "Otis' pamphlet I never saw, and whether I had gathered my ideas from reading or reflection I do not know. I know only I turned to neither book nor pamphlet while writing it. I did not consider it as any part of my charge to invent new ideas altogether."

One sign that we are dealing with a superstition is the unwillingness of the believer to question basic assumptions. Ask a fundamentalist why he believes what he believes, and he will explain that the Bible is not only inspired by God but inerrant, even in its mathematics and science. If you ask how he knows it to be inerrant, he will quote ambiguous lines from the Old Testament—lines set down long before the Gospels were written—as self-evident proof. Tradition and authority are of no account, he will say, misapplying the Protestant phrase *sola scriptura* (a criterion aimed at scholars and not a license for casual Bible readers to make up their own interpretations), but he will never answer the question of how the various books of the Bible came to be included. Why does he not regard Tobit or Susanna as authentic but place great weight on Revelation, a book that raised doubts in the early centuries of the Church? If he is very learned, he might quote the Calvinist opinion that the authenticity of his particular selection of scriptures is so obvious as to be beyond doubt, but he will refuse to discuss the proposition that the Church itself, through its traditions and councils, made the Bible, not vice versa. He believes because he believes because he believes.

Believers in the theory of rights take exactly the same point of view. Asked where rights come from, they will either refer to a mythical story (such as the wondrous tale of the social contract), or, following Calvin, they will dismiss all criticism by saying that everybody knows what rights are. If the believer in rights is Catholic, he will quickly proceed to confound the liberal theory of rights with the rather different teachings of St. Thomas on natural law, or he will refer loftily to a divine origin for rights, though there is nothing in scripture and very little in the traditions of the Church to justify such a notion.[2]

A nonbeliever—a libertarian, for example, who cannot have recourse to any supernatural arguments—will attempt to deduce his theory of "rights" from other unprovable principles he happens to believe in, such as the principle of nonaggression.[3] This tactic resembles that of some neo-Darwinists who, confronted with the apparent impossibility of life spontaneously originating on earth, take refuge in the extraterrestrial theory that life arrived on earth in the form of spores, as in the film *Invasion of the Body Snatchers*. If there is a convincing proof of the existence or origin of rights, I have never read it in a book or article and never, in discussions with true-believing philosophers, heard anything persuasive, much less convincing. Rights, one has to conclude, are to be taken on faith—but only by those who profess to have no religion.

Paine versus Jefferson

Though many of the men who took the lead in the American secession from Britain professed belief in natural rights, the more conservative leaders were increasingly wary of such language, especially when they were able to view the impact of such opinions on France. Even among the believers in natural rights, a distinction can be made between a comparatively radical republican like Thomas Jefferson and the ultimate spokesman for the rights of man, Thomas Paine. Though the two Toms shared a common political language and collaborated

---

2. Fr. Fagothey says: "We need not prove there are such things as rights, for no one denies it" (*Right and Reason*, 244).

3. The argument concerns only natural or human rights. Civil or legal rights, granted by a constitution or prescribed by tradition, are an entirely different matter.

during the Revolution, they were poles apart in temperament, experience, and in the vision they had for the American future. Jefferson was a landed aristocrat attached to Virginia and to his kin, as rooted as a man can be. Paine was a wanderer who came to America a little more than a year before the Revolution, which he regarded not so much as a defense of specifically American liberties as one act in a universal struggle for the rights of man. When the Revolution was over, he ended up in France, joined the Girondin wing of the Jacobins, and accepted French citizenship. He owned nothing and belonged to nothing. Like Anacharsis Klootz, Paine's German colleague in the French National Assembly, Paine could have proclaimed himself a "citizen of the world."

The propertyless Paine wrote Jefferson that he believed that property rights were only secondary civil rights as opposed to the rights of man, such as the right of propagandists to speak and write freely without fear of consequences. In his pamphlet "Agrarian Justice," Paine recommended that the French levy a stiff tax on real estate and use the revenue to pay the poor, who had lost their "right" to land. From the perspective of Paine (and of other advocates of human rights), the title to property depends on government, which may, in the short run, confiscate some of it in the form of taxation and may ultimately take it all away for the public good.

Jefferson, in contrast, belonged to the landed gentry, and, despite the theories he toyed with, was very much attached to land and property. He did oppose primogeniture and entailment laws that enabled men of property to pass along their estates intact through the generations, maintaining frequently that "the land belongs to the living." But although he lacked direct male heirs, he took an active interest in the success of his nephews and dispersed younger kinsmen, and (like Washington and Adams) prided himself as much on his farming as on his statesmanship.

In questions of religion, Paine and Jefferson were both deists, but while Jefferson merely wanted to purify Christianity of what he thought were later accretions and put together his own "Bible" to show that Jesus taught a purely rational morality, Paine was a mocker, as he showed in *The Age of Reason,* a book that scandalized his former friends in America. Hypocrite that he was, Paine defended himself by arguing in Jeffersonian terms that he was promoting the cause of true religion, but in *The Age of Reason* Paine had described Christianity as the worst of religions.

Nearly two thousand years of Christian experience meant nothing to Paine, who regarded all arguments drawn from history and antiquity as useless. The only historical precedent of any importance was the example set by the hypothetical first man on earth and the rights he is supposed to have possessed. Paine based his account of primitive man on his entirely erroneous notion of how native Americans lived—a subject on which he knew less than any educated Parisian. Rejecting the only other available account, in Genesis (which, however, he was hypocritical enough to cite), the retired tax-collector was free to make up everything as he went along and to dismiss with a wave of his hand all the evidence of history and civilization.

Jefferson, while accepting the theory of natural rights, preferred to trace American liberties back through the constitutional struggles between king and parliament to the Magna Carta and ultimately to the Anglo-Saxons, who lived in freedom before the Norman Conquest of 1066. He even learned the Anglo-Saxon language and proposed putting Hengist and Horsa (the Anglo-Saxon chiefs who led the invasion of Britain) on the Great Seal of the United States. Jefferson could cite many precedents from ancient history, but since Paine knew neither Latin nor Greek—much less Anglo-Saxon—and very little history, he was free to invent imaginary societies as he pleased. The first man *must* have possessed all his human rights, which have been passed down to us, subject to certain restrictions imposed by good governments (where they can be established) for our own good. That is all Paine knew of man's political experience; it is all he wanted to know.

Paine was a dogmatic and uneducated liberal, but he saw more clearly than Jefferson that the theory of human rights was inconsistent with Christianity, which was to be supplanted by this new religion. The stories of Genesis, with their emphasis on man's dependency on God, his disobedience, and his presumption in building the Tower of Babel, stood in the way of a world order based on the rights of man and the myth of the social contract.

Political theology is not necessarily a bad thing. Holding truths to be self-evident can be a convenient shorthand for preserving a set of fundamental rules that are not open to dispute, and so long as the sloppy language and fuzzy logic of natural-rights theories are not taken as the starting point for policies that empower the masters of rights—judges, politicians, social workers, the police—little mischief will be done, probably. Jefferson's theory of rights, unfortunately, proved to be a problem even during his lifetime.

Missouri and Kansas

When Northern congressmen agitated for an antislavery article as a prerequisite for Missouri's admission to statehood, Thomas Jefferson understood immediately what the debate portended and set down his fears in a famous letter that has been frequently misrepresented as an attack on slavery. Writing to John Holmes, a Massachusetts congressman who opposed northern sectionalism, Jefferson said:

> This momentous question, like a firebell in the night, awakened and filled me with terror. I considered it at once as the knell of the Union. It is hushed, indeed, for the moment. But this is a reprieve only, not a final sentence. A geographical line, coinciding with a marked principle, moral and political, once conceived and held up to the angry passions of men, will never be obliterated; and every new irritation will mark it deeper and deeper. I can say, with conscious truth, that there is not a man on earth who would sacrifice more than I would to relieve us from this heavy reproach, in any practicable way.

The slave-owning Jefferson said he was happy to sacrifice his own property interests by freeing all his slaves if "a general emancipation and expatriation could be effected." But, he insisted, "we have the wolf by the ears, and we can neither hold him, nor safely let him go."[4]

As a liberal proponent of natural rights who owned slaves, Jefferson exposed himself, even in his own lifetime, to the charge of hypocrisy. Hypocrisy aside, Jefferson never denied the evils of slavery, though he did suggest that those evils were magnified by northerners who had never visited a plantation. The problem over Missouri, he was convinced, was partly due to fanaticism whipped up by his old enemies in the defeated Federalist Party, which hoped to return to power—if not in the entire United States, then at least in New England.[5]

4. Thomas Jefferson to John Holmes, April 22, 1820.
5. For a discussion of Jefferson's complex views and the historical context, see Dumas Malone, *The Sage of Monticello*, 328–44.

The hard-won constitutional liberties offered by the American union were precious to the former president. If northerners abstained from a spiteful political act designed to punish their southern rivals, Jefferson wrote Holmes, he believed they "would remove the jealousy excited by the undertaking of Congress to regulate the condition of the different descriptions of men composing a state. This certainly is the exclusive right of every state, which nothing in the Constitution has taken from them and given to the general government."

The speciousness of his argument (do abusive institutions really disappear more quickly if no one criticizes them?) was a symptom of his desperation, and later, when pressed on the question by Lafayette, he did not defend his position. The situation, however, was serious. Hardly anyone in America was more serious about ending slavery, and much of the antislavery rhetoric was derived from the language Jefferson had used in the Declaration of Independence, but the question for Jefferson was not *if* slavery should be ended but how and when and at what cost. At the very time the Sage of Monticello was championing Missouri's constitutional right to enter the union on the same terms as other states, he was arguing that the Missouri controversy made it imperative for Virginia to take steps toward emancipation. Jefferson concluded his letter to Holmes with a melancholy resignation to the inevitable: "I regret that I am now to die in the belief that the useless sacrifice of themselves by the generation of 1776, to acquire self-government and happiness to their country is to be thrown away by the unwise and unworthy passions of their sons."

Extremism in Defense of Liberty

The former president signed this depressing missive, truthfully, "as the faithful advocate of the Union." Moderate statesmen from the North and the border states (such as Henry Clay, Daniel Webster, and, later, Stephen Douglas), who also appreciated the urgency of the situation, were willing to make whatever compromises might hold the union together. Southerners did not help their cause by turning to ever-more-radical arguments: the threat of secession and the defense of slavery, not as an evil to be ameliorated and eventually eliminated, but as a positive good. In the end, the hotheads (on both sides) had their way, and, although slavery had been ended in Britain and would be ended peacefully in Brazil, the United States, apparently, could solve its problem only by engaging in a destructive civil war.

Such was not the opinion of many northern Democrats in 1860. Herman Melville was both a northerner and a unionist. He disapproved of slavery and had scant affection for the South. Yet, like his friend Nathaniel Hawthorne, Melville regarded the war as a tragedy. In his poem "Ball's Bluff: A Reverie," Melville says he "saw a sight—saddest that eyes can see— / Young soldiers marching lustily / Unto the wars," and, in his poem on Shiloh, he brings to mind the uneasy spectacle of "dying foemen mingled there— / Foemen at morn, but friends at eve."[6]

In his youth, Melville had tended to see issues as black-and-white confrontations between freedom-loving young savages and the corrupt representatives of despotic authority, and he had twice, as a sailor, rebelled against what he regarded as the despotism of ship captains. The young Melville had even fulfilled the romantic fantasy of going to live on a South Sea isle with primitive Polynesians. But, made sadder and wiser by his experience of the destruction unleashed by the Civil War, Melville produced his most complex and mature exploration of the human condition, *Billy Budd.*

The young sailor Billy Budd is impressed into the British Navy from the merchant ship *The Rights of Man.* Taking one last look at his old ship, the simple, Christ-like sailor declares, without intending any irony, "And good-bye to you, old *Rights-of-Man.*" Billy truly gets off on the wrong foot on the HMS *Indomitable,* which has little in common with any society imagined by Rousseau or Paine, though it is reminiscent of Halifax's comparison of humanity with "a great galley where the officers must be whipping with little intermission, if they will do their duty."

Teased and tormented by John Claggart, the sadistic master-at-arms, Billy finally strikes out and commits the murder for which he is executed. Melville saw in Claggart an example of "natural depravity" and regarded the master-at-arms as a refutation of any simplistic philosophy based on the legal rights espoused by Coke and Blackstone. Melville had himself been a mutineer who rebelled against sadistic officers, and

---

6. Both poems are in Melville's *Battle-Pieces and Aspects of the War.* For more on Melville's view of the war, see Stanton Garner, *The Civil War World of Herman Melville.*

yet he refused to treat the case as a struggle between good and evil. The well-intentioned but weak Captain Vere, who passes sentence on Billy, may represent the British Navy's failure (and, perhaps, the failure of all social authorities) to provide justice, but Vere is also doing his duty, however reluctantly.

At the very least, the seafaring novelist offers us a moral casuistry less like that of Locke and more (as he says explicitly) like that of the Hebrew prophets. Setting aside (as postmodern critics are entitled to do) Melville's intentions in writing the story, one might read *Billy Budd* as a healthy antidote to America's infatuation with an Enlightenment political philosophy whose emphasis on the rights of man was to lead straight to the most deadly war of the nineteenth century. Well over half a million American men, North and South, lay dead, and yet, despite the self-congratulatory rhetoric about minority progress heard from white philanthropists, it would be another hundred years before African Americans were to make real political and economic progress. "With mankind," as Captain Vere observes, "forms, measured forms are everything."

The radicals would have nothing to do with "measured forms." The Constitution itself, they declared, was a pact with a devil. If slavery was an evil that denied one segment of humanity its human rights, then one could not object to any means used to eliminate the institution. Old John Brown himself would have heartily endorsed Barry Goldwater's "Extremism in the defense of liberty is no vice" (though the conservative senator was hardly a spokesman for the civil-rights movement). Brown was an unsuccessful farmer, tanner, and wool merchant who was convinced that only bloodshed could wash away the stain of slavery. From Brown's own letters, it is clear that he was a disunionist who hoped to break up the union over slavery and then to conquer the South by force, using the slaves he intended to liberate.

After taking part in a set of mostly minor skirmishes in Kansas, Brown rose to prominence in May 1856 when he and his company of Free State volunteers murdered five men settled along the Pottawatomie Creek. Although the victims were southern and belonged to the proslavery Law and Order Party, they were not themselves slaveowners. At the Doyle farm, Mrs. Doyle, her daughter, and fourteen-year-old John were spared, but James Doyle and two of his sons, William and Drury, were dragged outside and hacked up with short, heavy sabers donated to Brown by well-wishers in Akron, Ohio. (What did they think when they read of the murders?) The gang then moved on to Allen Wilkinson's place. He was "taken prisoner" amid the cries of a sick wife and two children. Two saddles and a rifle were also stolen. The third house visited that night was owned by James Harris, a farm laborer. In addition to his wife and young child, Harris had three other men sleeping there. Brown killed one of them, William Sherman, and stole weapons, a saddle, and a horse.

For his actions in Kansas and later at Harper's Ferry (where his first victim was a free black), Brown deserves the title "first terrorist in American history," and, like other terrorists and psychotic killers—Charles Manson, for example—he lived off his victims. He and his sons and followers became accomplished stock-rustlers and plunderers, though they carefully avoided clashes with armed Missourians. Brown claimed credit for defending the Osawatomie settlement from Missouri militiamen, but the real defenders always said he had nothing to do with it, and, besides, there was not much credit to claim. As the Missouri commander, General Reid, put it, "It was like driving quail through a field." But Osawatomie Brown, as he now called himself, was able to manipulate the eastern press to make even his looting seem heroic. He had, as the great liberal abolitionist Wendell Phillips put it, "letters of Marque from God."[7]

Individualism, Again

Obviously, most defenders of human rights are not psychotic killers, but more than a few war crimes and atrocities have been committed by governments that claimed to be upholding a higher law. Letters of marque from God aside, the assertion of rights sets the stage for a struggle between one set of individuals, the angels, against another, who are regarded as devils deserving of any punishment. All ordinary social bonds are destroyed. To reduce all relations between human beings to an abstract antagonism between those who possess rights and those who violate them is to deny humanity to the designated oppressor, whether he is a proslavery Missourian who has never owned slaves or a "patriar-

7. On the events and significance of John Brown's career, see the quite different accounts in biographies by Robert Penn Warren and Stephen B. Oates and in Leverett Wilson Spring, *Kansas: The Prelude to the War for the Union.*

chal" husband and father who has spent most of his life supporting and cherishing his family or a man who eats steak and his wife who wears fur. Men and women are not unidimensional figures cut out of cardboard by a philosopher's scissors. To treat them in such a way, demonizing some of them as deniers of rights in order to subjugate or kill them, is to deprive them of what religious people might describe as "the right to be human."

The greater difficulty with rights-based arguments may not lie so much with the concept of rights as with the assumption that it is always and only individuals that bear them (and government that enforces them). Of course, one does hear of group rights, but, in nearly every case, the group in question is a minority—racial, sexual, behavioral—whose past experience of deprivation and oppression justifies current favoritism toward *individual* members of the group. Because some Africans were enslaved, the argument goes, individuals of African descent now have a special claim on the whole of society (including black taxpayers who may not agree with this theory).

Notice that this claim is rarely put forward as a corporate right. Only the most militant activists (such as Louis Farrakhan and his followers in the Nation of Islam) would ask for a reservation or homeland in which African Americans could collectively pursue their own destiny. Farrakhan's policy is generally not praised as an assertion of rights but condemned as a form of racial nationalism. To impose collective guilt on the white majority is seen as praiseworthy so long as the black minority is not treated collectively as a nation. The same "logic" was evident in the Bosnian conflict: So long as Bosnian Muslims disguised their nationalist aims in the language of multiethnic multiculturalism, they were the darlings of the same Western journalists who expressed strong disapproval of similar Islamic movements in Algeria, Turkey, and Iran.

Even in ethnic conflicts, it seems, it is individual rights that matter and not group identities.[8] Individualists, however, can talk as much as they like about there being "no such thing" as society or nations, but they will never succeed in eliminating group identity, if it is only the identity of desperate Chicagoans rooting for the Cubs.

8. For a useful discussion of individual and group rights, see Richard E. Flathman, *Willful Liberalism: Voluntarism and Individuality in Political Theory and Practice*, 50.

Despite the modern conviction that only individuals have rights, that justice is always and only a question of individuals and governments, group after group has stepped up to claim peculiar rights based on its history and identity: African and Native Americans, Jews, women, homosexuals, cigarette smokers, women with silicone breast implants, gun owners, victims of gun violence, men who grow fat from eating junk food, women who want abortions, spokesmen for babies who presumably do not want to be aborted, celebrities who want to live in the limelight without seeing flashbulbs, and people who say they are allergic to peanuts or the smell of perfume.

Liberals are naturally sympathetic to every claim of victimization, but their individualist bias often puts them at a loss when they deal with the group claims they support. The history of modern liberalism might be written as a series of efforts to balance the rights of individuals against the rights of groups made up of individuals. Lani Guinier, although she stirred up considerable controversy by her advocacy of group freedoms through such mechanisms as "supermajorities," was in the mainstream of modern liberalism, and she was quite unfairly stigmatized by conservative activists as an extremist advocate of quotas. Her solutions to the problems of minorities may all turn out to be impractical, but there is nothing un-American or inherently unjust in her acknowledgment that, in some cases, people behave as members of a group rather than simply as isolated individuals.[9]

Equality versus Equity

One main argument over rights, so it seems, is between traditional or individualist liberals (in America, they call themselves "conservatives") who say that all rights, such as the rights to life, liberty, and free expression, are universal and individual, that no group qua group is possessed of particular privileges, and the newer (comparatively), more collectivist liberals who insist that some circumstances justify special treatment for individuals belonging to a group that has been the victim of persecution or discrimination. Underlying both sets of arguments,

9. Lani Guinier, *The Tyranny of the Majority: Fundamental Fairness in Representative Democracy.*

though, is the assumption that human beings are or ought to be equal in their opportunity for success or happiness. Since common sense tells us that human individuals are inherently unequal in every respect—looks, strength, intelligence, virtue—the concept of equality, in order to be swallowed, requires a thick coating sugared heavily with speculative justification.[10]

Suppose life could be compared to a race, runs one familiar argument in discussions of public policy. Obviously, fairness dictates that everyone start the race at the same point. Unfortunately, there is nothing obvious about the parallel between life and athletic competitions. Life is not a race, except in the narrow sense that men and women compete for goods and status. Success, however, as measured by income and prestige, is far from the whole of life, and it is a truism that many successful people are less happy than those who are content with mediocrity.

If, for the sake of argument, we concede the sports parallel, we have to begin by recognizing that a fair race depends upon more than a straight starting line. Is it fair to pit an undernourished child or an arthritic old man against an Olympic athlete? Not if *fair* means equal access to success. Is it fair to ask an unathletic intellectual to compete against a teenager who plays basketball four hours a day? Equality in these cases would require staggered starts and handicapping—the basketball player might have to carry a thirty-pound feed sack on his back.

Egalitarians argue that some inequalities are fair, because they are the result of hard work. The basketball player has earned his advantage by constant exercise and assiduous practice. While his schoolmates were frittering their time away on algebra and French verbs, he was preparing for his career by shooting baskets. But some, at least, of his advantage is inherited. How fair is it that Americans of African descent have been able to dominate professional basketball (until the arrival of East European players)? The same question might be asked of Jewish lawyers and scholars, French chefs, and Anglo-Celtic bassmasters.

The second line of defense is that superior skill levels are a rational advantage that everyone can understand, unlike the prejudice and discrimination that white athletes face every time they pick up a basketball or—to be more serious—that black men and women have faced

---

10. The best critiques of equality have come typically from conservative liberals, such as Fitzjames Stephen and Sir Henry Sumner Maine.

when they aspired to a professional career. But why is inherited physical strength (or intelligence) a more "rational" advantage than the lucky accident of being born to rich or competent parents? Some of the runners in our race might have the good fortune to be the children of athletes, whose aptitudes they have inherited, while others have parents who are willing to spend time training them. To devise a system of handicapping to account for all these subtle exigencies would require a computer of infinite capacity.

It would also beg the question of fairness. Even if life could be supposed to be anything at all like a race, what makes us so certain that the race is run entirely by individuals and not by groups? Perhaps it is more like an intergenerational relay event, in which the present generation of runners have taken their batons from parents who received it in unbroken succession from twenty generations of ancestors. From this perspective, fairness could be judged only in terms of kinship groups and families, and the success or failure of a given individual would be incidental. It is not individual runners who win a relay, but teams. On this understanding, group rights become intelligible, as do group responsibilities (and even inherited curses).

Solon, in his famous answer to King Croesus of Lydia, seemed to be saying that we should not call anyone happy until he has died in the knowledge that his family and friends are doing well. Of course, one could construct an affirmative-action policy on the basis of kindred rather than of individuals, though such calculations, in order to produce an equitable outcome, would have to be infinitely complicated. It might be easier simply to explain *some* current inequalities as the result of previous generations of actors whose hard work or laziness and good or bad luck has put their descendants into the affluent or impoverished circumstances in which they find themselves.

The State of Nature

As liberals, we feel instinctively that there is something wrong in allowing parental incompetence to affect a child's success, but, practically speaking, there is little that can be done about it unless we are willing to engage in massive national and international programs of child exchange.

Even Christopher Jenks, in his highly influential book promoting social and economic equality, failed to find evidence that schools could overcome the advantages that birth into a good family brings.[11] To sidestep these messy complexities of everyday life, philosophers have recourse to myths and imaginary models, which, by definition, eliminate all the historic and concrete differences between people and peoples.

Man, according to one early version of the myth, lived originally "in the manner of the beasts," gathering and hunting the spontaneous products of nature. "They could have no regard for the common good nor did they know how to make use of customs or laws; each one, trained by his own will to seek life and power, took whatever fortune put his way, and Love joined lovers' bodies in the woods." Eventually, these early men learned to make clothes and live in primitive houses, and marriage and family came into existence. They developed language and fire.

This seemingly scientific account of man's social evolution, although it sounds like something from a 1950s anthropology textbook, was actually written by Lucretius (*De rerum natura,* 925–1160), a contemporary of Julius Caesar. What is amazing is its overall resemblance to what most people are taught to believe in the twenty-first century. Lucretius was a follower of Epicurus, and the stated purpose of the Epicurean school was to free man from the supernatural terrors of religion by providing him with rational—not necessarily true—accounts of thunder and lightning, sex and death. The physical universe, the Epicureans taught, was explicable in terms of the motion and qualities of atoms, which were the hypothetical building blocks of all matter.

The Epicurean account of human evolution has exactly the same function: to dismiss any supernatural notion of a human soul, divine spark, or even reverence for life itself. In their writings on human behavior, the Epicureans offered a scientific—that is, materialistic—account of knowledge and perception. In matters of religion, they said, the wise man will be (as Descartes was to pretend to be) carefully conventional. He will love his country but avoid politics; on questions of the divine, he will be skeptical but take part in his country's rites. He will not

---

11. Christopher Jenks, *Inequality: A Reassessment of the Effect of Family and Schooling in America.*

overindulge in sex, but he will not marry. His studies will liberate him from the fear of death.

As for "justice" or "right," Epicurus himself said that "natural justice" is an expression to signify expediency, to keep men from hurting one another. Animals, because they are incapable of making agreements with one another, are outside the sphere of justice. In opposition to Plato and Aristotle, who sought a transcendent or divine basis for justice, Epicurus was purely pragmatic. One of his sayings, recorded in his *Principal Doctrines,* explicitly repudiates the notion of natural law or justice: "There was never any justice, pure and simple, only an agreement made in reciprocal dealings within particular communities for the avoidance of inflicting and suffering harm."

A universe ruled by the iron laws of atomic physics, a humanity that becomes more civilized on the basis of contracts and agreements... What is this but the Victorian liberal's view of the world? The purpose, in the case both of Epicurus and of Thomas Henry Huxley (nicknamed Darwin's Bulldog), is the destruction of a traditionally religious view of life and the substitution of a mechanical theory for which there is no better evidence.

If the biblical story of Adam and Eve is to be regarded as an ancient myth, the Epicurean myth of social evolution and social contracts deserves the same treatment. But if the story told in Genesis is one of the founding myths of Christendom, Epicurus's tale of primitive man and the social contract has become a founding myth of the modern state and, therefore, not so easy to dispel; it is embedded in a political ideology and enforced by law.

A myth is an explanatory story, but an ideology is the set of stories used to justify a regime. The myth of natural rights was used by Spanish Jesuits during the Renaissance to justify the authority of the Church, which opposed the growing power of secular rulers. However, by the end of the seventeenth century, the "state-of-nature" myth had taken on new life as a justification for the political program advanced by English Whigs, who wanted to transfer power from Church and crown to landowning aristocrats and London merchants. John Locke, a Whig propagandist, described the state of nature as "a state of equality, wherein all the power and jurisdiction is reciprocal, no one having any more than another, there being nothing more evident than that creatures of the same species and rank, promiscuously born to all the same advantages of Nature, and the use of the same faculties, should also be equal one amongst the other."[12] Locke never invoked the principle of equality as a means of overturning conventional social and economic distinctions. His object was more narrowly focused on the king himself and the Church that supported monarchical privilege.

The state of nature and the theory of rights, which were commonplaces of seventeenth-century political discussion (for example, in the writings of John Selden and Thomas Hobbes and the legal theorist Hugo Grotius), became useful brickbats for both sides in the conflicts that tore apart Stuart England. Hobbes could use man's natural depravity in the state of nature as a justification for a powerful state, while Locke could view man's natural freedom as the foundation of parliamentary rights, but the differences are not so great as they appear on the surface. Whether natural man is conceived of as comparatively happy (Locke) or miserable (Hobbes), he is driven, so the theory goes, by a natural necessity to seek companionship, economic exchange, and protection from other natural men, with whom he strikes a bargain of the type: "If you respect my rights, I shall respect yours." Hence civil society—and government—are born.

Some philosophers write as if such a state of nature had actually existed once; others, like John Rawls, prefer to use this image of natural equality (Rawls's so-called "original position") as the hypothetical basis on which human social life is constructed. It goes without saying that, of all the societies that have been adequately described, none resembles any form of the state of nature. Even among the most "primitive" peoples—if they are indeed primitive, as opposed to merely differently evolved—distinctions of status, wealth, and power are observed.

Locke developed his political philosophy in his *Two Treatises on Civil Government*. The first of them is devoted primarily to attacking Sir Robert Filmer's *Patriarcha*. Filmer, an apologist for legitimate royal authority, had traced the power of kings back to the dominion exercised by fathers, particularly by the first father, Adam. The analogy between the family and the state is as old as Aristotle, and Locke hardly laid a glove on Filmer's real arguments, preferring to set up a straw man and attributing

12. Locke, *Second Treatise on Civil Government*, "On the State of Nature," 2.5.

to Filmer the notion that the Stuarts held royal power in direct and unbroken line from Adam.[13] In fact, Filmer, by criticizing Selden's conservative version of the social contract, offered an obvious refutation of the entire theory before Locke had written a word.

Filmer directly confronted the argument that originally there was no property and all things were held in common (a notion found commonly in poems celebrating the "Golden Age") until men consented to acknowledge territory and property. But, scoffed the royalist, "How the consent of mankind could bind posterity when all things were common, is a point not so evident. Where children take nothing by gift or descent from their parents, but have an equal and common interest with them, there is no reason in such cases, that the acts of the fathers should bind the sons."[14]

Applied to Locke's later theory of the social contract (and to more recent versions), Filmer's argument is devastating. Supposing there really were a state of nature and supposing further that primitive men agreed to give up some of their liberty in exchange for a secure social order, how would such an agreement be binding upon their descendants? One could argue that authority can in fact be transmitted from father to son—but that is precisely the patriarchalist case, that all power derives from the original authority inherent in the family.

David Hume makes a similar argument in his essay "Of the Original Contract," which completely explodes the fantasy: "But besides that this supposes the consent of the fathers to bind the children, even to the most remote generations (which republican writers will never allow) besides this I say, it is not justified by history or experience in any age of the world."[15] Hume understood all too well that any theory of natural rights was a fictional philosophy to be compared with the parallel fiction that the power of kings is biblical, because, as he continues, no party in the eighteenth century could "well support itself, without a philosophical or speculative system of principle, annexed to its political or practical one." In other words, natural-rights theories constituted an *ideology* (in one of Marx's senses of the term), a system designed to

13. See Peter Laslett, introduction to *Patriarcha and Other Political Works of Sir Robert Filmer.*
14. Robert Filmer, *Patriarcha and Other Political Works of Sir Robert Filmer,* 65.
15. David Hume, "Of the Original Contract," 471.

justify the power of a ruling class. Ideologies are not purely philosophical theories whose object is to elucidate reality but myths invented for the defense of a regime or party.

Well, then, suppose we say that the state of nature (and the human rights derived from the state of nature) is a myth. The lifeblood of a society is its mythical imagination: Oppressed peoples have nourished themselves on legends of liberators from Moses to Robin Hood and tales of battles like Bunker Hill and the Alamo. Plato sometimes expressed his deepest meanings in the form of *mythoi*—stories, myths—of his own invention. So long as we choose to accept them, where is the harm in believing in Pandora's box or the ring of the Nibelungen? None whatsoever, so long as the myth is rich enough to infuse life into social relations and so long as the blood does not prove to be diseased or the wrong type.

Within a society, the most constructive myths are those that tend to reconcile differences and promote solidarity. The ancient Athenians, for example, believed they were all descended from the soil of Attica itself, and this account of their origins imbued them with a sense of unity. Other myths may emphasize the uniqueness of "our" people against outsiders, but even these racialist myths may foster a national identity that overrides internal differences.

Social and political myths that emphasize internal differences, however, may be more dangerous. In the antebellum South, some defenders of slavery—for example, some of the contributors to *DeBow's Review* in Louisiana—argued that whites and blacks had evolved separately from simian ancestors, and this doctrine of separate evolutions encouraged those who accepted it to regard blacks as less than fully human. Similarly, doctrines of equality that explain current economic and social differences as the product of oppression and exploitation aggravate existing tensions arising from differences of race and class. Many middle-class people reject such arguments and prefer to regard *themselves* as victims of exploitation and reverse discrimination. Once the apple of discord is cast into the midst of a society, an unending cycle of demands and counterdemands is sure to ensue, and it makes little difference what is written on the apple—"to the fairest" or "to the meritorious" or "to the victims of oppression."

Academic philosophers have, for the most part, given up on traditional myths, but they continue to look for models and scenarios to use as vehicles for their message. In an effort to flesh out the state of nature, Bruce Ackerman devised a number of scenarios involving spaceships landing in a new world. In one version, there are two ships, and, when the first lands, the commander proceeds to claim all the new world's resources. When the second ship lands, its party demands a share and is refused. A debate ensues. Since both parties consist of liberals, the first group must prove that their claim to exclusive citizenship (and, hence, the right to all the planet's resources) is rational. Of course, they cannot.[16]

As Ackerman probably realized, such a dialogue would never take place. If the two parties shared a community of discourse, then they would also share some common identity, as earthlings, as Europeans, or as Frenchmen. An appeal would be made to the specific traditions and principles that bind them together. Identities are, after all, expansive. A well-known American historian is fond of saying that, in the South, he is a Texan; in the North, a southerner; in England, a Yankee. In France, he is presumably an Anglo; in China, a Euro; and so on. Such was the rhetoric of the Greeks, appealing to their common identity as Hellenes while at the same time refusing to merge into one political state. As Greeks, they could have referred, in principle, to the common customs of the Greeks, just as the Romans were later to appeal to the *ius gentium,* the law that is common to all nations.[17]

Unless there is some basis of commonality, arbitration and debate are impossible. Even where such commonalities exist, one side may simply deny legitimacy to any moral principle except power, as the Athenians did when they told the people of the tiny island of Melos (who were refusing to break their historic alliance with Sparta) to submit or die. A dialogue between the two parties can resemble the exchange of notes between Adolf Hitler and the heads of state of Czechoslovakia or Poland or Yugoslavia or the debate Thucydides stages between the Athenians and the Melians. As the hawk said to the nightingale it had caught: "He is a fool who wishes to contend with the stronger: He not only loses, but he suffers shame in addition to his pain" (Hesiod *Works and Days* 210–11).

16. Bruce Ackerman, *Social Justice in the Liberal State,* 89 ff.
17. Greek commonalities provided a basis for the panhellenic cooperation that emerged in the course of the retreat of the ten thousand Greek mercenaries narrated by Xenophon in his *Anabasis.*

If Ackerman's two parties have absolutely nothing in common, they might ignore each other and coexist as lions and lichens. If both groups require the same resource, then they might fight it out like cats and dogs, thus fulfilling Gause's law of competitive exclusion (that perfect competition for an ecological niche is impossible). In any event, they would not be abstract beings applying universal arguments. Liberal societies do not exist except in the minds of philosophers, who only occasionally act on their principles. When a school for minority children was going to be set up in an affluent neighborhood of a northeastern university town, prominent liberals in the neighborhood did not hesitate to petition against it. The debate was quite a different affair from the dialogue between Ackerman's spaceships.

The liberal ideal of universal fairness is an interesting and valuable artifact of the civilization that has grown up in Europe since the renascence of classical languages in the fifteenth century. It has many thing to tell us about human dignity and responsible government, but its language of rights and justice is not spoken by peoples that are relatively untouched by the West. Suppose the first spaceship were captained not by a liberal philosopher but by a Comanche warrior or an Homeric prince. In this scenario, the combat would be conducted not with words but with weapons. "But that's unfair," the liberal captain of the second ship would exclaim. "Why should the irrational accident of your superior strength and firepower determine the outcome of a controversy?"

If the Comanche were disposed to argue for a moment, he might ask why superior mental strength, legal acumen, or verbal agility should prevail in a contest to determine access to food. In his bargaining, he would bear in mind the Comanche ethic that "the ultimate power [i]s the resort to force."[18] Even nonphilosophers have to eat. Besides, he might say, everyone knows that in a liberal society the rich and powerful are able to hire the best mouthpieces and cheat the poor of their due. At least in a trial by combat, it is a man's own strength, skill, and courage that prevails. It is mere ethnocentrism to insist that the values of the modern West are superior to all others.

The Comanche, like the medieval knight, would commit the issue to the god of battles; the liberal, to the god of reason. An Eskimo might demand a song-duel, while an archaic Greek might rest his case on a

18. E. A. Hoebel, "Law Ways of the Comanche Indians," 193.

disputed passage of the *Iliad*. Man's nature is artifice, and he carries all his artifice with him into the wilderness of new worlds. Philoctetes, on his desert island, built himself a hut and nursed his resentful memories of the Greek army that had marooned him. Even as an outcast, he defined himself as a member of society. The English Philoctetes, Robinson Crusoe, did not find his desert island at all charming; he passionately bewailed the fate that had made him a solitary exile.

Splendid Isolation

The creator of Captain Ahab and Billy Budd had himself, as a mutineer, escaped from all civil authority and gone to live on Nuku Hiva in the Marquesas. A year later, he took part in a second mutiny and escaped to Tahiti. The literary results of his adventures, *Typee, Omoo,* and *Mardi,* are revealing. Far from finding peace and happiness in a condition of natural liberty, Melville was frequently afflicted with a nameless melancholy. In *Typee,* the discovery that his gentle companions are headhunting cannibals disabuses the young romantic of some of his notions. Society among the cannibals, though sexual mores might be looser, is no less formal than in a drawing room or on a sailing ship. The cliché is worth repeating: Art is man's nature, whether the art takes the form of Pheidias's Athena or an Easter Island megalith.

If there were any truth to the state-of-nature hypothesis, one might expect men on desert islands or the colonists of new worlds (on or off this planet) to exult in their liberty or at least to devise new social arrangements that were more consistent with principles of fairness and justice. But the opposite is typically the case. Spanish, French, and English colonists treated the land and peoples of the Americas as spoils to be taken and exploited, and they almost immediately sought to replicate Old World conditions. The American doctrine of exceptionalism—that, in leaving Europe, the colonists left patriarchy, authoritarianism, and the ties of clan and kindred behind and that whatever residual patriarchy remained vanished as Americans moved westward—is simply a myth. New England villages, as much as southern plantations, were settled by several generations of kinfolk, and the frontier was settled by families and clans, not individuals, moving west in search of better farmland.

Fictional accounts of desert islands strike the same note. In *Treasure Island,* poor Ben Gunn hoards his money and lies awake craving cheese; the choirboys in *Lord of the Flies* do not become bestial so much as human in forming their gang and murdering the opposition. Instead of developing a romantic appreciation for nature in the raw, Robinson Crusoe (like his real-life prototype, Alexander Selkirk) immediately undertakes the task of constructing a palisade to set himself apart from nature, and, so long as the shipwreck is accessible, spends his days salvaging fragments of civilization, much of it junk he might instead learn to live without. But Crusoe regards bread and boiled meat as essentials, and, instead of adapting his diet to the island, wastes years of hard labor on the cultivation of the grain that allows him to eat like a Christian. Even if he was content to go native, though, Crusoe would still devote a large part of his waking hours to just two activities: providing himself with food and constructing defenses against potential attacks.

Crusoe has to do everything for himself, because he is alone. With the arrival of Friday on the scene, society is born, but it is no liberal state of equality. The civilized man saves the savage from cannibals, and, by the laws of nature, the savage becomes his slave. Later, Crusoe saves a white man, who turns out to be Spanish, and the new problem of ethnic rivalry arises. Crusoe's solution is to make the Spaniard swear fealty to him. He does the same with an English ship captain whose crew has mutinied. From the right of conquest to the bargain of feudal loyalty, Crusoe retraces the history of European political life. Prior possession, superior force, and sworn fealty make Crusoe the king of his island.

This is merely a story, but it is a familiar story for anyone acquainted with the history of colonial ventures. When the Greeks planted colonies in Sicily and Magna Graecia, they took pains to reproduce all the features of their original cities. The native Italians from whom they took the land were not considered worthy of citizenship, and those natives who did inhabit the colony were most likely to be slaves. Greek colonization did, however, produce at least one social innovation: a heightened sense of Hellenic social cohesion. The colonists, while they might be drawn from different cities, were nonetheless members of a joint venture, and, in the early days at least, all the citizens owned sufficient property to maintain independence. Colonization of a strange land engendered both a stronger sense of citizenship in the group and a feeling of self-importance in the individual: "Therefore, the colonist exchanged his old dependency for a bond with the entire new colonial community, a bond that included land tenure."[19]

Colonies can be established for any number of reasons, but we are looking only at the implications for "the state of nature." Among the most rugged and instructive tales are those that concern the settlement of Iceland. The Norwegians who settled Iceland were fleeing, so their descendants claim, the oppressive new order imposed by the king of Norway, and they brought the language and customs of the Vikings with them and preserved them more faithfully than their kinsmen in Scandinavia. Today, the language of Iceland is largely unchanged since the Viking age.

The settlers also brought with them their social structures, and their chieftains brought their authority, along with their dependents (including their women), with them. "The earliest landsnamsmenn [land-takers], often ship owners who arrived as the heads of families with dependents and slaves, took huge portions of land."[20] Viking women, although more liberated than other European women, lived in subjection to husbands and fathers. While Crusoe had to content himself with the companionship of a cannibal, the Icelanders had wives and mistresses, who bore them children. In this way, the second great necessity of life (survival being the first) occupied the colonists' attention and made their settlements into something more than raiding outposts. (Crusoe himself, later in life, returns to his island and imports women as helpmeets for the marooned mutineers and Spanish refugees he had settled on it.)

With wives and children the future's horizon expands, and a man is concerned with more than his daily comforts; he must work to ensure the success of his offspring, that their access to wealth and power will be greater than that of their fellows. Since there is no state of nature, there can be no social contract except the bonds that connect a man with his family and with his friends.

The Icelandic society that emerged is often described as egalitarian and democratic, and, compared with medieval Europe, it may have been, but it was a democracy of chieftains who competed for followers to support them in their feuds and their struggles for power in the *Things*

19. Frank J. Frost, "Aspects of Early Athenian Citizenship," 47.
20. Jesse L. Byock, *Medieval Iceland: Society, Sagas, and Power*, 55.

(parliaments). Eventually, this competition corrupted and destroyed Iceland's decentralized social structure and invited the intrusion of Norwegian and Danish rulers who exploited and abused Iceland as a not-very-valuable resource.

For a brief period of two or three centuries, the quarrelsome chieftains and farmers of Iceland created the most brilliant Nordic civilization that has been known, and their literary accomplishments make up a significant part of the Nordic and Germanic cultural inheritance. So long as they were isolated from outside interference, and so long as farmers were able to find sufficient land to feed their families, they could survive their feuds and petty wars. Once power was centralized and they were integrated into Europe, the Icelanders sank into obscurity.

The parallel with the English colonies in America is striking, although the cultural accomplishments of the Americans were comparatively less impressive and the period of unfettered liberty briefer. Like the Icelanders, Americans settled a frontier where land was available; both peoples lapsed into something like household patriarchy and grew highly resentful of any government intrusion into local affairs; both were comparatively egalitarian in the sense that free men who owned their own land refused to bow and scrape before their "betters"; and both lost their local liberties after a period of civil war, national centralization, and involvement with European affairs.

Some of the differences between America and Iceland are also instructive. The Norwegians, in going to Iceland, were rejecting the authority of their king. Their colonies were not "planted" by government or corporations; they were seized by powerful families. The American experience was, for the most part, quite different. If the settlement of Iceland was like a folk migration, the American colonies were established by charter and by law, and, far from throwing off the yoke of the old country, the Americans—down to the eve of the Revolution—claimed only the rights of Englishmen.

In American pamphlets of the 1770s, one can find any number of arguments against Parliament's right to establish an arbitrary authority over North America, but the most influential writers—John Adams, John Dickinson, and Thomas Jefferson—all insisted upon both the traditional rights of Englishmen, infringed upon by Parliament, and the independence of the colonial legislatures, not from the crown but from Parliament. Once they had made up their minds to assert themselves, some Virginians claimed that the act of migration made them as independent of England as their Anglo-Saxon ancestors, in going to Britain, were from the authority of continental Saxon rulers. The myth of Saxon independence, borrowed from the English Whigs, proved far more persuasive to the American leadership than all of Tom Paine's fine pronouncements on the rights of man.[21]

The colonist in the wilderness may have severed his immediate connections with the land of his birth, but he retains his social identity. As a father, he has authority over his children; as his cousin's poor retainer, he is dependent; and, even if he has freed himself from the authority of his king, he brings an entire culture with him in his mind and in his habits. His cultural baggage may include a theory of the rights of Englishmen, but—and here, at last, is the central point of this digression on islands and colonies—such rights are the gift of his society and its history; they are not given by some god or implanted into human nature through the genetic code.

Arguments for the divine or literally natural origin of natural rights would not be accepted by modern theorists of human rights, who explicitly repudiate human nature (to say nothing of God) as a politically relevant concept. For them, rights are mathematical abstractions (like the Pythagorean theorem), which exist apart from us and need to be discovered. In fact, the opposite is true: It makes absolutely no sense to speak of human rights or duties that do not derive from the human condition, and rights—far from being abstract and ahistorical—are simply an expression of a particular cultural history. Like family portraits, the English concept of the rule of law, or the European use of knives and forks, our political outlook is a family heirloom we take with us wherever we may go. If we fled to another planet, the same sorts of stories would be told of us.

"Why can't you just understand that we are all, as human beings, traveling together on Spaceship Earth?" That question was once put to me by a prominent liberal philosopher when I pointed out that there was no rational (much less scientific) evidence for his theory of natural rights and equality. I answered him that I was perfectly willing to entertain his metaphor of Spaceship Earth. But my spaceship has separate

21. See H. Trevor Colbourn, *The Lamp of Experience: Whig History and the Intellectual Origins of the American Revolution*, and Gray, *Liberalism*.

rooms and compartments, different classes and sections reflecting the complexity of human history and social life. "On yours," I concluded, "everyone travels steerage."

The doctrines of natural equality and individualism are political myths that have contributed something to the development of Western character and political institutions, but they are useless and destructive myths to the extent they blind us to the reality of human life. For the most part, it is not as individuals that we possess rights or exercise duties but as parents and neighbors and citizens.

For the most part. If we do have individual rights, however, the clearest example would be rights to do something that does not involve other human beings, for example, hunting for food or committing suicide. Postponing a final decision on the state of nature and the social contract, we might stop to ask ourselves, before going on to consider the broader obligations that derive from men and women living together in society, if we owe ourselves anything as individuals and if, as individuals, we incur any obligations that do not involve other persons or society as a whole.

Right versus Rights

The term *rights* is shifty, since it may imply either that which is right or correct (as in "You got that right") or a claim on someone else (as in "You have no right to . . ."). It is in the first sense that ancient and medieval philosophers usually speak of "natural right" or "natural justice," by which they mean that which is right or just in nature. St. Thomas, for example, says that, since justice is the virtue that is directed to what is right or just in relationship to other people, the object of this virtue is called just *(iustum)*; and this just thing, in fact, is what right *(ius)* is. It is perfectly possible to declare, as does Thomas, that something is naturally right, such as taking proper care of one's children, without concluding that the object of right behavior (one's children in this case) has a claim—that is, a right in the second sense—to be treated justly.[22]

Where would such a distinction get us? To the place where we can say that there may well be "rights" in nature (that is, actions or duties

22. St. Thomas Aquinas, *Summa Theologiae,* 2.2, 57.1.

that are naturally right to do) without accepting the very dubious notion that human individuals, in the absence of some ulterior and metaphysical justification, have natural claims upon each other or upon some third party such as a government, or even upon themselves. If such claims were intuitively obvious or easily deducible, it is extraordinary that philosophers speaking the language of rights should so frequently have recourse to myths, fables, and religious justifications.

Even if there are such things as rights (apart from legal rights guaranteed by, for example, the U.S. Constitution), how should we "know" that individuals have any rights? Many ordinary people would say that, of course, we have a right to life, even though it might not extend to certain categories, such as condemned criminals, unborn children, enemy soldiers, and civilians unfortunate enough to live under a regime that has antagonized a great power. Most modern religious traditions defend the dignity of life, but Catholics and Muslims—to take just two cases—have rather different views of suicide, war, and "terrorism." So long as a believer grounds his right to life in a specific tradition, there is no problem. But, setting aside the problem of nonbelievers, what do Catholics and Muslims do when they have to come to a joint decision about, for example, the right to life of someone caught preaching the Gospel in an Islamic state or a Muslim practicing his religion in sixteenth-century Spain?

If individuals have a right to life, do they also have a right to give up their own life? It can be argued, of course, that, since survival is an individual's right, it is also his obligation to do what he can to stay alive. On the other hand, there are libertarians who affirm the right to commit suicide, and this individualistic argument is sometimes heard from the mouths of otherwise conventional liberals.

One common argument for the existence of individual rights takes the form of the Golden Rule or Kant's categorical imperative. As a rational being who insists upon preserving his own life, liberty, and property, an individual must also accord to others what he demands for himself—even before he has contracted an alliance with them. If he does not wish to be killed or robbed or cheated, he ought not to kill, rob, or cheat others.[23]

23. See Immanuel Kant, *Lectures on Ethics*, 116–29.

Supposing, for the sake of argument, that we agree to the principle of *pacta servanda*—that is, agreements must be kept (though why they should be—apart from practical, religious, or traditional grounds—is not at all obvious). On that assumption, once the individual has entered into contractual relations with his fellows, he is also bound by the terms of his agreements, and while contractual language may not be the best way of describing human social life, it will do for the moment. The fact that someone is willing to accept the benefits of living within a social order—the police, the streets, the army, unemployment insurance—obliges him to obey all the rules, even those he may dislike, though there may be exceptional cases that might justify conscientious refusal or civil disobedience. It is the argument Socrates (in Plato's *Crito*) puts in the mouth of his city's laws: He had been born, reared, educated, and defended by the city's laws and customs; he ought to be willing to die by them.

Socrates' argument for civil duties, however, works only within a civil order. The more general argument, unless it is backed up by the sanctions of religion and tradition, has little to be said for it. That human beings have a powerful urge to preserve their own existence cannot be denied. But without introducing some external source of authority, such as the "life force" or a creator God, we are hardly justified in converting "want" to "ought." Most human beings have sexual urges, but few would argue that either celibacy or chastity is unlawful.

If by duty or obligation we mean some principle of justice, such as "render everyone his due," then we might translate *due* (as regards ourselves) as all those natural necessities on which existence depends. Aristotle, however, did not think an individual could do himself an injustice, because no one can rob himself of what he is unwilling to lose. Of course, once we are commanded to preserve our lives, we are bound to do so—so long as we recognize the authority of the superior being who is commanding us.

Even if we are not under a natural obligation to provide for our necessities and to defend ourselves against assaults, most human creatures will make every effort to preserve their existence. We live as if we had a duty to preserve and reproduce ourselves, and a clever person might construct an ontological argument for self-preservation, on analogy with Anselm's proof of the existence of God. We might, for example, argue: Our ability to make an argument depends on our being alive, and if we must conceive of a right in order to enforce it and preserve our lives, then it is pointless to deny a principle on which our existence (and our argument) depends.

Rational arguments like this one or others might persuade a happy man to stay alive and have children, but it would have little effect on someone who, like the ancient neoplatonist Porphyry, has become convinced that human life is evil and not worth either preserving or perpetuating. To dissuade someone overcome by failure and disappointment, it is necessary to point to other, less abstract obligations: his parents and friends, the people who depend upon him, a religious prohibition on celibacy or suicide, or some other external consideration. Hamlet longed for death, but he feared the punishment that lay beyond the grave and he was unwilling to betray the obligation to avenge his father. Suicide, with good reason, is commonly regarded as an act of selfish betrayal: An individualist might think he lives for himself; a husband and father knows he does not.

Theories of rights are expressed as lofty ideals, but they have done little to deter those who believe in them from killing themselves or other people. If the twentieth century was the age of human rights, it was also the age of mass killings that were almost always justified by a theory, whether national socialist, international socialist, or global democratic. When apologists for democracy claim that democratic states have always sought peace and freedom, the people of Melos, savaged by democratic Athens; Dresden, terror-bombed by the democratic British; and Hiroshima, annihilated by an atomic bomb dropped by the Democratic president of the democratic United States, must be laughing from their graves. There is no remedy, neither in political theories nor in political systems, for human nature.

As members of a society, human beings are inevitably bound to live according to the norms of that society, and whether we choose to describe some of the social rules as "rights" may be simply a matter of taste. In the eighteenth century, such language was almost inevitable, and it was sometimes difficult for an alternate point of view to receive a fair hearing. Today, now that the concept of rights has been invoked to justify everything from abortion to apartheid to total war, we have a right (how hard it is to avoid this way of thinking) to be more skeptical.

Neither Crusoe nor Philoctetes could escape their backgrounds: Both longed for the company of their fellows, both tried to construct—as all colonists will—a replica of their former social lives. Given the opportunity for libertarian individualism, they rejected it with horror. Returned to a state of nature, they did their best to reinvent society, and if they had secured wives they would have succeeded. Their longings are evidence both of the social origins of the individual identity and of the inevitability of natural impulses. Poor old Ben Gunn, who hadn't "spoke with a Christian these three years," admitted only to longing for cheese, but he was speaking to a young boy in the pages of a Victorian novel. Biology may not quite be destiny, but it writes a script within which we, as actors, have limited opportunity for improvisation.

It is an idle fiction to declare that an individual, as a natural being, can have any claims that are not derived from his own nature. (I am, for the sake of argument, excluding the possibility of divine commandment and of any other metaphysical foundation for justice.) If there are things that are naturally "right," they are observable tendencies of human behavior that allow for survival and propagation. To feed oneself is natural and, in this limited sense, right; to copulate and reproduce is natural, necessary, and right; and, after copulation, it is also natural and right to take proper care of the fruits of copulation—which is, after all, the natural point of the process: the replication of genetic identity across the generations. To convert these right forms of behavior into natural claims on someone else seems, on the face of it, absurd or, at the very least, in need of a better justification than can be devised through historical fantasies or a priori reasoning. This much, however, can be conceded: that men and women who refuse to eat or procreate or rear their offspring will quickly eliminate themselves (and their descendants) from the argument.

There is, therefore, some basis in the hard core of reality for the older theories of rights: The rights to life, liberty, and property (however hard to justify in principle) do correspond to what ordinary people regard as natural. But theories of rights long ago escaped the everyday basis of practical necessity. By the twentieth century, individuals had a right to a free education, women had the right to be treated as men, children had the right to be brought up by enlightened and nonauthoritarian parents, mothers had the right to abort their unborn children. Even animals were said to have rights, which, given the rationalist basis of rights, is a contradiction in terms, and I have heard environmental philosophers (at an academic conference held in a state university I have no wish to deride) debate the question of whether stone cliffs have "intentionality" and, thus, the right not to be altered by human beings. One philosopher, partly in jest, even raised the question of intentionality in connection with subatomic particles.

Chesterton saw it all long ago. In the introduction to his novel *The Napoleon of Notting Hill,* he extrapolated from the vegetarian craze (already in full swing by the beginning of the twentieth century) that someone would be sure to oppose the shedding of "the green blood of the silent animals," and he predicted that men in a better age would live on nothing but minerals. "And then came the pamphlet from Oregon . . . called, 'Why should Salt suffer?'"

These newly discovered rights (and many older ones) cannot be exercised, practically speaking, by one individual against another. Children are in no position to claim any of the rights given to them by international declarations of children's rights. In fact, it is only governments that possess the means to enforce these rights, and, for all practical purposes, then, rights can be treated as blank checks for governments. Since there is a finite amount of moral and social authority in any society, with every new right, the power of government grows at the expense of people.

One small example: Socialists (including socialist liberals) assume that society, by which they really mean government, is responsible for something like equal access to education and economic opportunity. Once it was determined that some groups (women, ethnic minorities) had been denied such equal access, various quota systems, minority set-asides, and "affirmative action" programs were designed to redress the historical inequities. So-called conservatives (that is, free-market liberals who believe in competition as the basis of fairness) complained that such programs distorted markets and unfairly punished those who were guilty of no discrimination, either because they were too young or because they were children of immigrants who had themselves suffered discrimination. As an alternative, the conservatives (or liberal individualists) usually proposed plans that either ensured equal opportunity or offered milder forms of affirmative action. But the doctrine of "equal opportunity" begs the obvious question: How can poor and underprivileged victims of discrimination possibly have equality of access, if special provisions are not made for them? Equal opportunity must always imply some form of affirmative action.

In moral terms, most of us know this. Every special case requires special treatment. A teacher inevitably spends more time on a slow student; charitable people are more likely to give money to the undeserving poor than to the deserving rich; we make allowances for the hobbyhorses and vices of our friends. For people who have grown up poor, through no fault of their own, it is not enough, if we wish to give them equal opportunity to thrive and succeed, to level the playing field once they have reached the age of eighteen. The social choice that modern societies have to make is not between the alternatives of "affirmative action" and "equality of opportunity" but among three historical scenarios: Christian charity, ruthless liberal individualism, and Marxian egalitarianism. Conservatives, as liberals, have been forced into choosing the last.

As traditional liberals, American conservatives cannot get over their commitment to equality and individualism, and they are therefore unable to offer a coherent challenge to what they instinctively feel is unfair. However, there is a serious moral problem with affirmative-action programs that is not touched on by any argument that depends on the theory of equal rights for individuals. A representative of earlier moral traditions, whether peasant or philosopher, would respond with a quite different argument, saying something like this: "These programs are asking me, as a citizen and taxpayer, to transfer wealth and career opportunities from my children to someone else's children, based on a decision-rule that favors non-Europeans and will always work against my children. It is not that I have a 'right' to oppose affirmative action, but that, as a parent, I have a duty (subject to certain qualifications) to favor my children over your children."

This peasant/philosopher is not making an argument against social assistance (which he may well approve of) per se or even against special programs designed to remedy injustice (so long as the injustice is commonly acknowledged); acts of repentance and restitution are not unknown. The problem is not economic or political, but moral: "Ask me to contribute freely of my abundance to help my fellow citizens, and I shall cheerfully give. Ask me to pay taxes in support of special programs for minorities, and I will make a decision based on my political perspective and the merits of the proposal. But if you require me to deprive my own children in order to help strangers, not because they are my fellow citizens but because they are different from me, then I must regard myself as a slave and you as a tyrant." In this example, the pursuit of equal rights does not so much represent an invasion of individual liberty as a threat to the autonomy of families and communities, and the same conclusion could be drawn from an analysis of tax policies, which transfer money and power not from the rich to the poor, but from working families to the government.

We Are the World

Most theories of right have been limited to one civil society or state, and, although international law has frequently been invoked in settling disputes between nations, the eighteenth-century Enlightenment's dream of an international order based on human rights remained only a dream until the twentieth century. It is important, however, to distinguish between the concept of a league of sovereign states committed to avoiding war and the mystical concept of the brotherhood of man, which goes back to the Stoic concept of world citizenship (Cosmopolitanism) and to Christian teachings on the Kingdom of Heaven. The United Nations, most people have believed, was established as a league of sovereign states that wanted to take practical measures to prevent war. It has evolved, however, into a transnational government that claims the authority to enforce an international rule of rights. This development was hardly unanticipated by the founders of the United Nations; indeed, the assertion of international human rights was part of the organization's original mission.

Many practical objections have been raised against the implementation of an international order of human rights, particularly against the deliberations of special tribunals (such as those convoked at Nuremberg and the Hague), which have been plausibly accused of serving the interests of the stronger or victorious nations. A more serious question arises, however, if we try to imagine an international order in which human rights could be guaranteed. If rights are claims to be enforced by government, then what are "international human rights" if not the theoretical justification for world government?

Many, probably most, advocates for human rights would concede the point: To enforce human rights around the globe would require not only a global legislature to make the laws and a global court to pass judgment but also a global police force to enforce the judgments of the court and a global network of intelligence and espionage agents to ferret out evildoers. The United Nations, the International Court of Justice, and NATO, imperfect as they are, represent a significant step in the direction of an international regime whose legitimacy is rooted in human rights and in which historic differences between nations, religions, and cultures will be subordinated to a political theory developed in Europe during the past few centuries.

It would be tedious to enter into the details of the various covenants and agreements guaranteeing the rights, for example, of women or of children. Although the guarantees made in these documents to provide universal access to contraception and sex education have not gone unchallenged by Muslim and Catholic religious leaders who claim to speak for a large part of the world's population, they do represent the official moral doctrine of the emerging global order, which continues to expand its power with ease, encountering less resistance than European states met with when, in their infancy, they subdued unruly provinces and small states on their borders. Even the European Union has the power to dictate what can be called beer in Bavaria, to ruin the cider business in Britain and damage northern Italian vegetable farming, to interfere in elections in Italy and Austria, and to challenge religious instruction in Ireland as well as that country's reluctance to accept unlimited numbers of Third World "refugees" (that is, immigrants). All this is done in the name of human rights, often with explicit reference to the United Nations' Universal Declaration of Human Rights.

"Well, what is the harm in any of this?" a human-rights advocate might ask. "Cider and beer are small potatoes compared with the brotherhood of man invoked by the Declaration." The brotherhood of man is a noble moral and spiritual ideal, derived from Christians and ancient Stoics, but it has little if any practical bearing on international relations. The Declaration, however, is more than a statement of moral ideals; it is a purely political instrument that is supposed to transform the way ordinary people live. Consider Article 2:

> Everyone is entitled to all the rights and freedoms set forth in this Declaration, without distinction of any kind, such as race, color, sex, language, religion, political or other opinion, national or social origin, property, birth or other status. Furthermore, no distinction shall be made on the basis of the political, jurisdictional or international status of the country or territory to which a person belongs, whether it be independent, trust, non-self-governing or under any other limitation of sovereignty.

This is familiar language, but the comforting banality of the bureaucratic jingo should not lull us into unwariness. All previous human societies on this planet and most societies at this time do make distinctions based on sex, religion, nationality, and culture. Israel, for example, is virtually an ethnic and confessional state, a tiny and beleaguered Judaic island in an Islamic sea. If the Declaration were to be enforced against Israel, she would cease to exist. Strict Muslims, on the other hand, could not possibly accept the equal rights of women or of non-Muslims, and so on.

It gets worse. The concluding clauses of the article more than imply that residents of provinces, protectorates, tribal reservations, and so on, have the right to appeal over the heads of their government if they feel themselves deprived of their human rights. Although NATO and the United Nations have in the past displayed some reluctance about intervening in the internal disputes of sovereign nations, the NATO attack on Yugoslavia was undertaken precisely to guarantee the rights of ethnic Albanians in Kosovo, which was legally and politically a province of Serbia and not even a federal republic (such as Bosnia, Croatia, and Slovenia had been), and the United States–led invasion of Iraq in 2003, though its immediate goal was the elimination of weapons of mass destruction, was also justified as a war to liberate Kurds and Shia Muslims from political and religious repression.

In Iraq, the vast stockpiles of nuclear, chemical, and biological weapons of whose existence and location U.S. authorities said they were certain have never been located. In Yugoslavia, once the shooting stopped and international reporters and monitors were able to gather evidence, it became clear that the crimes of the (admittedly ugly) Milosevic regime had been exaggerated and that the real effect of the war had been to give Albanian militants a license to destroy over two hundred churches, some of them ancient, and to murder and persecute all non-Albanians—Serbs, of course, but also Catholics, Gypsies, and even non-Albanian Muslims.[24] The best that can be said of that operation is that it did not improve the situation, and a good deal worse can and has been said by journalists and experts who witnessed events firsthand.[25]

To enforce the theory of international human rights, the United States and its allies bombed real people—commuters on the way to work in Novi Sad, employees of television stations, Albanian refugees—and unleashed a fury upon Christians in Kosovo, which quickly spilled across the border into Macedonia. But there is no sign, either in the U.S. State Department or at NATO headquarters or at the Hague Tribunal, that anyone has repented or even been willing to admit the facts. Why should they? If the war for Kosovo demonstrated nothing else, it proved that the proponents of human rights and world government were willing to apply force in exactly the same way that every previous empire had done.

Let us recall that Zeno's dream of world citizenship (and, hence, a world in which all peoples enjoy the same civil rights) was inspired by Alexander the Great's conquest of the Persian Empire. It was Rome, eventually, that actually succeeded in establishing something like a global civilization, one that stretched from the Scottish border to Persia, to the Sudan, and west to Spain. The collapse of the Western half of that empire near the end of the fifth century left a gaping hole in the political mentality of Europe, and a series of political leaders—Charlemagne, Hapsburg emperors, Russian czars, Napoleon Bonaparte, Hitler, and Mussolini—all dreamed of resurrecting "the grandeur that was Rome." Some based their power on political fictions, such as the pope's right to designate a Frank or Swabian king as Western emperor or the theory that Moscow was the Third Rome; others relied simply on the power of the sword. Hitler believed that the German army was carving out a "new European order," a term that seems unpleasantly prophetic.

24. See Aleksandar Rakovic, "Letter from Serbia," *Chronicles*, March 2003, 37–38.
25. Criticism of the reporting on the NATO war against Yugoslavia spans the political spectrum, from English conservative John Laughland to German leftists Peter Händke and Jurgen Elsässer and British-born American leftist Alexander Cockburn.

No would-be neo-Roman emperor ever fought a war of naked aggression; there was always a noble (and not always invalid) justification. Charlemagne was crusading against the pope's enemies (the Lombards) and pagan Saxons; Napoleon was bringing the fruits of the French Revolution (liberty, equality, and the principle of self-determination) to all of Europe; the Führer claimed to be saving Aryan civilization from its inferiors: Jews, Slavs, and mongrel Americans. Today, the dream of global empire rests upon a theory of rights that is used one-sidedly to eliminate all rivals to the hegemony of the United States and its allies.

There is never a dearth of speculative reasons to justify violence. The terrorists who flew their hijacked planes into the World Trade Center and the Pentagon were advancing the cause of Islam; Timothy McVeigh was avenging the slaughter of the innocents in Waco; John Brown was working to free the slaves. All the do-gooding busybodies who slaughter the unjust and the violent are working for universal peace and justice. "They make a desert," said Tacitus of the rulers of the Roman World Order, "and they call it peace."

Coda

Rational, universal, objective ethics, culminating in the doctrine of international rights, represents a more profound threat to the human future even than the environmental havoc (nuclear waste, industrial pollution, devastated farmlands and wilderness) that is also the residue of Western liberalism. Serious resistance, supposing there is to be resistance to the global regime, will begin only when intelligent people have understood the theoretical justifications of this Fourth Rome and rejected them.

"We murder to dissect" was Wordsworth's reaction to the rationalism of the Enlightenment, before whose withering gaze all traditions and customs, even nature itself, were reduced to historical footnotes. Romanticism, despite its eccentricities and perversions, was a healthy reaction to destructive liberalism. There have been many such reactions, each (it sometimes seems) more perverse than the last, but always in defense of something real against the deadly abstractions. Utopian socialism, aestheticism, the agrarian movements in Europe and the United States, the various conservative parties that sprang up after World

War II, and even the environmentalist movement—they all aspired to a human goodness that was not determined by the getting and spending of rational individuals. None, unfortunately, could accomplish anything significant, because they were all permeated with the same principles of objectivity, universalism, rationalism, and human rights that are the underpinnings of the liberal tradition. In rejecting those principles root and branch, postmodern men and women can turn to the philosophy and the literature of ancient Greeks, Romans, and Jews; to the Christian traditions of the Middle Ages; and to the humane wisdom, deeper than Descartes or Locke, to be found in our greatest poets and novelists and even in popular literature. There is more humanity in Sophocles than in Plato, a profounder morality in Trollope than in Adam Smith.

Real people and the problems of everyday life are withered under the vision of objective reason in pursuit of universal peace. Only a planetary empire can eliminate war, and only a global despotism, more total than the despotisms of Hitler and Stalin, could eradicate evil. Evil is a part of earthly experience, and it is not only unreasonable but unhealthy to think that it might be eradicated. In Georges Bernanos's novel *Journal d'un curé de campagne,* a hearty older priest warns the narrator against being too spiritual and tells him of a nun who wore herself out, tirelessly cleaning the church. In one sense she died a martyr, he concedes, but, in another, she made the mistake of not just fighting against dirt but of wanting to annihilate it.

Everyday life does not admit of abstract perfection, and the procrustean solutions offered by modern moral and political philosophers wreak havoc and destruction on the poor frail creatures we are. Ancient Greek sculptures had "canons" of mathematical and geometrical proportions to represent the ideal human form, but no Greek physician attempted to cut and trim the bodies of real human beings to fit the canon of Polyclitus or Lysippus. "Human, all too human," Nietzsche found even the best of us. His mistake lay in thinking (like Bernanos's dirt-haunted sister) that we could be anything else. Nietzsche, a typical pastor's son, blamed Christianity for holding up an impossible ideal of saintliness, but the Christian story is not of men who calculated and worked their way to perfection but of a God Who found men and women so worthy of salvation that He took on their weakness and became one of them. It is the purpose of ethical philosophy to provide guidelines and signposts to assist us on the way toward justice and truth. The mistake is to confuse those guidelines, whether they are couched in terms of human rights or social justice or perfect rationality, with the road itself, which must take many a twist and turn before the all-too-human pilgrims reach their destination.

BIBLIOGRAPHY

Ackerman, Bruce. *Social Justice in the Liberal State.* New Haven: Yale University Press, 1980.

Acton, John E. D. "Nationality." In *Essays in the History of Liberty,* 3 vols., 1:409–33. Indianapolis: Liberty Fund, 1985.

Adelson, Joseph, and Bernard Green. "Growth of the Idea of Law in Adolescence." *Developmental Psychology* 14 (1969): 327–32.

Adelson, Joseph, and Robert P. O'Neil. "Growth of Political Ideas in Adolescence." *Journal of Personality and Social Psychology* 4:3 (1966): 295–306.

Adeney, Miriam. *God's Foreign Policy.* Grand Rapids, Mich.: William B. Eerdmans, 1984.

Adkins, M. R. *Merit and Responsibility: A Study in Greek Values.* Oxford: Oxford University Press, 1962.

Aeschylus. *The Oresteia.* Trans. Douglas Young. Norman: University of Oklahoma Press, 1974.

Aiken, William, and Hugh La Follette, eds. *World Hunger and Moral Obligation.* Englewood Cliffs, N.J.: Prentice-Hall, 1977.

Ainsworth, Mary D. Salter, Mary C. Blehar, Everett Waters, and Sally Wall. *Patterns of Attachment: A Psychological Study of the Strange Situation.* Hillsdale, N.J.: Lawrence Erlbaum Associates, 1978.

Alphonsus Maria de Liguori, Saint. *Practica del Confessore*. Frigento, Italy: Casa Mariana, 1987.

————. *Theologia Moralis*. 4 vols. Rome: Ex Typographia Vaticana, 1935.

————. *The True Spouse of Jesus Christ*. Fillmore, N.Y.: Most Holy Family Monastery, n.d.

Althusius [Johannes Althaus]. *Politica Methodice Digesta of Johannes Althusius*. Ed. C. J. Friedrich. Cambridge: Harvard University Press, 1932.

Arblaster, Anthony. *The Rise and Decline of Western Liberalism*. Oxford: Basil Blackwell, 1987.

Arnove, Robert F., ed. *Philanthropy and Cultural Imperialism: The Foundations at Home and Abroad*. Boston: G. K. Hall, 1980.

Ayres, Robert. *Banking on the Poor: The World Bank and World Poverty*. Cambridge: MIT Press, 1983.

Baier, Annette C. *Moral Prejudices: Essays on Ethics*. Cambridge: Harvard University Press, 1994.

Baldry, H. C. "Zeno's Ideal State." *Journal of Hellenic Studies* 79 (1959): 3–15.

Banfield, Edward C. *The Moral Basis of a Backward Society*. New York: Free Press, 1958.

Bauer, P. T. *Equality, the Third World, and Economic Delusion*. Cambridge: Harvard University Press, 1982.

Beitz, Charles R. *Political Theory and International Relations*. Princeton, N.J.: Princeton University Press, 1979.

Bennet, Jon. *The Hunger Machine: The Politics of Food*. Introduction and conclusion by Susan George. Oxford: Blackwell, 1987.

Bentham, Jeremy. "Anarchical Fallacies." In *The Works of Jeremy Bentham*, 22 vols., 2:489–534. Edinburgh: William Tait, 1843.

————. *An Introduction to the Principles of Morals and Legislation*. 1823. Reprint, Oxford: Oxford University Press, 1907.

Berman, Edward H. *The Ideology of Philanthropy: The Influence of the Carnegie, Ford, and Rockefeller Foundations on American Foreign Policy*. Albany: SUNY Press, 1983.

Besterman, Theodore. *Voltaire*. Chicago: University of Chicago Press, 1976.

Billington, James H. *Fire in the Minds of Men: Origins of the Revolutionary Faith*. New York: Basic Books, 1980.

Blum, Lawrence A. "Gilligan and Kohlberg: Implications for Moral Theory." *Ethics* 98 (1988): 472–91.

Borgin, Karl, and Kathleen Corbett. *The Destruction of a Continent: Africa and International Aid.* New York: Harcourt Brace, 1982.

Boswell, James. *Boswell's Life of Johnson.* 6 vols. Ed. George B. Hill, rev. L. F. Powell. Oxford: Oxford University Press, 1934.

Bowlby, John. *Attachment and Loss.* 3 vols. New York: Basic Books, 1969–1980.

Bradley, F. H. *Ethical Studies.* 2nd ed. Oxford: Clarendon Press, 1927.

Brandt, Willy, ed. *North-South: A Programme for Survival.* Cambridge: MIT Press, 1980.

Bredvold, Louis I. *The Natural History of Sensibility.* Detroit: Wayne State University Press, 1962.

Bremmer, Jan. *The Early Greek Concept of the Soul.* Princeton, N.J.: Princeton University Press, 1983.

Brown, Roger, and Richard Herrnstein, *Psychology.* New York: Little, Brown, 1975.

Burckhardt, Jakob. *Reflections on History.* Indianapolis: Liberty Classics, 1979.

Burke, Edmund. *Reflections on the French Revolution.* Vol. 3, *The Works of the Right Honorable Edmund Burke.* Boston: Little, Brown, 1904.

Burkert, Walter. *Creation of the Sacred: Tracks of Biology in Early Religions.* Cambridge: Harvard University Press, 1996.

———. *Homo Necans: The Anthropology of Ancient Greek Sacrificial Ritual and Myth.* Berkeley and Los Angeles: University of California Press, 1983.

Burnyeat, Miles. "Aristotle on Learning to be Good." In *Essays on Aristotle's Ethics,* ed. A. O. Rorty, 69–92. Berkeley and Los Angeles: University of California Press, 1981.

Byock, Jesse L. *Medieval Iceland: Society, Sagas, and Power.* Berkeley and Los Angeles: University of California Press, 1988.

Camps, Miriam. *Collective Management: The Reform of Global Economic Organizations,* with the collaboration of Catherine Gwin. New York: McGraw-Hill, 1981.

Carter, L. B. *The Quiet Athenian.* Oxford: Clarendon Press, 1986.

Casson, Lionel. *Ancient Trade and Society.* Detroit: Wayne State University Press, 1984.

Catenacci, Carmine. *Il tiranno e l'eroe: Per un'archeologia del potere nella Grecia antica.* Milan: Mondadori, 1996.

Chai, Ch'u, and Winberg Chai, ed. and trans. *The Sacred Books of Confucius and Other Confucian Classics.* Hyde Park, N.Y.: University Books/Bantam, 1965.

Cheney, Dorothy, Robert Seyfarth, and Barbara Smuts. "Social Relationships and Social Cognition in Nonhuman Primates." *Science* 234 (1986): 1361–66.

Chesterton, G. K. *Orthodoxy.* 1908. Reprint, New York: Dodd, Mead, 1955.

Clark, Stephen R. L. "How to Reason about Value Judgments." In *Key Themes in Philosophy,* ed. A. Phillips-Griffiths. Cambridge: Cambridge University Press, 1989.

———. "Morals, Moore, and MacIntyre." *Inquiry* 26 (1984): 425–45.

Cohen, David. *Law, Sexuality, and Society: The Enforcement of Morals in Classical Athens.* Cambridge: Cambridge University Press, 1991.

Colbourn, H. Trevor. *The Lamp of Experience: Whig History and the Intellectual Origins of the American Revolution.* 1965. Reprint, Indianapolis: Liberty Fund, 1998.

Colby, Anne, and Lawrence Kohlberg. "Invariant Sequence and Internal Consistency in Moral Judgment Stages." In *Morality, Moral Behavior, and Moral Development,* ed. William M. Kurtines and Jacob L. Gewirtz, 41–51. New York: John Wiley & Sons, 1984.

Coleridge, Samuel Taylor. *Specimens of the Table Talk of the Late Samuel Taylor Coleridge.* 1835. Reprint, London: J. M. Dent, Everyman's Library, 1934.

Coles, Robert. *The Moral Life of Children.* Boston: Atlantic Monthly Press, 1986.

Cooper, John. "Aristotle on Friendship." In *Essays on Aristotle's Ethics,* ed. A. O. Rorty, 301–40. Berkeley and Los Angeles: University of California Press, 1981.

Curti, Merle. *American Philanthropy Abroad.* 1963. Reprint, New Brunswick, N.J.: Transaction Publishers, 1988.

Cutlip, Scott M. *Fund Raising in the United States: Its Role in Philanthropy.* New Brunswick, N.J.: Transaction Publishers, 1990.

Danchin, Antoine. "Stabilisation fonctionelle et epigenèse: Une approche biologique de la genèse de l'identité individuelle." In *L'Identité,* ed. Claude Lévi-Strauss. Paris: Bernard Grasset, 1977.

Denselow, Robin. *When the Music's Over: The Story of Political Pop.* London: Faber & Faber, 1989.

Descartes, René. *Des passions de l'ame.* Vol. 11, *Oeuvres de Descartes,* ed. Charles Adam and Paul Tannery. Paris: Libraire Philosophique J. Vrin, 1967.

————. *The Philosophical Works of Descartes.* 2 vols. Trans. E. S. Haldane and G. R. T. Ross. Cambridge: Cambridge University Press, 1931.

Dickey, James. *Self-Interviews.* Ed. Barbara Reiss and James Reiss. 1970. Reprint, Baton Rouge: Louisiana State University Press, 1984.

————. *The Whole Motion: Collected Poems, 1945–1992.* Hanover, N.H.: Wesleyan University/New England University Press, 1992.

Dickinson, J. C. *The Later Middle Ages from the Norman Conquest to the Eve of the Reformation.* London: Black, 1975.

Doi, Takeo. *The Anatomy of Dependence.* Tokyo: Kodansha International, 1973.

————. *The Anatomy of Self: The Individual versus Society.* Tokyo: Kodansha International, 1985.

Dover, K. J. *Greek Popular Morality in the Time of Plato and Aristotle.* Berkeley and Los Angeles: University of California Press, 1974.

Dunn, Judy. "The Beginnings of Moral Understanding: Development in the Second Year." In *The Emergence of Morality in Young Children,* ed. Jerome Kagan and Sharon Lamb, 90–112. Chicago: University of Chicago Press, 1987.

Durkheim, Emile. *Moral Education: A Study in the Theory and Application of the Sociology of Education.* New York: Free Press, 1961.

Edwards, Carolyn P. "Culture and the Construction of Moral Values." In *The Emergence of Morality in Young Children,* ed. Jerome Kagan and Sharon Lamb, 122–51. Chicago: University of Chicago Press, 1987.

————. "Moral Development in Comparative Cultural Perspective." In *Cultural Perspectives on Child Development,* ed. Daniel A. Wagner and Harold Stevenson, 248–303. San Francisco: W. H. Freeman, 1982.

————. "Societal Complexity and Moral Development." *Ethos* 3 (1975): 505–27.

Engelhardt, H. Tristram. "Individuals and Communities, Present and Future: Toward a Morality in a Time of Famine." In *Lifeboat Ethics: The Moral Dilemmas of World Hunger,* ed. George R.

Lucas, Jr., and Thomas W. Ogletree, 70–83. New York: Harper & Row, 1976.

Erikson, Erik H. *Identity: Youth and Crisis.* 1968. Reprint, New York: W. W. Norton, 1994.

Evans-Pritchard, E. E. *Theories of Primitive Religion.* Oxford: Oxford University Press, 1965.

Evola, Julius. *Men among the Ruins: Post-War Reflections of a Radical Traditionalist.* Trans. Guido Stucco, ed. Michael Moynihan. Rochester, Vt.: Inner Traditions, 2002.

Fagothey, Fr. Austin, S.J. *Right and Reason: Ethics in Theory and Practice.* 2nd ed. Rockford, Ill.: TAN Books, 2000.

Fishkin, James. *Justice, Equal Opportunity, and the Family.* New Haven: Yale University Press, 1983.

Flanagan, Owen, and Kathryn Jackson. "Justice, Care, and Gender: The Kohlberg-Gilligan Debate Revisited." *Ethics* 97 (1987): 622–37.

Flathman, Richard E. *Willful Liberalism: Voluntarism and Individuality in Political Theory and Practice.* Ithaca, N.Y.: Cornell University Press, 1992.

Fleming, Thomas. "The Federal Principle." *Telos* 100 (Summer 1994): 17–36.

———. *Montenegro: The Divided Land.* Rockford, Ill.: Chronicles Press, 2002.

———. *The Politics of Human Nature.* New Brunswick, N.J.: Transaction Publishers, 1988.

———. "Three Faces of Democracy." *Telos* 104 (Summer 1995): 51–67.

Foot, Philippa. "Morality, Action, and Outcome." In *Morality and Objectivity: A Tribute to J. L. Mackie,* ed. Ted Honderich, 23–38. London: Routledge & Kegan Paul, 1985.

———. *Theories of Ethics.* Oxford: Oxford University Press, 1967.

Forster, E. M. *Two Cheers for Democracy.* New York: Harcourt Brace, 1951.

Fosdick, Raymond B. *The Story of the Rockefeller Foundation.* 1952. Reprint, New Brunswick, N.J.: Transaction Publishers, 1987.

Freeman, Edward A. "Race and Language." In *Historical Essays,* 3rd ser., 173–226. London: Macmillan, 1879.

Frost, Frank J. "Aspects of Early Athenian Citizenship." In *Athenian Identity and Civic Ideology,* ed. A. L. Boeghold and A. C. Scafuro. Baltimore: Johns Hopkins University Press, 1994.

Furet, François. *Penser la Révolution française.* Paris: Gallimard, 1978.

Furley, D. J. "The Early History of the Concept of the Soul." *Bulletin of the Institute for Classical Studies* 3 (1956): 1–18.

Gallois, Pierre M. *Le Sang du Petrole, Bosnie.* Lausanne: L'Age d'Homme, 1996.

Gardner, Howard. *The Mind's New Science: A History of the Cognitive Revolution.* New York: Basic Books, 1985.

Garner, Stanton. *The Civil War World of Herman Melville.* Lawrence: University of Kansas Press, 2000.

Gedicks, Al. *Resource Rebels: Native Challenges to Mining and Oil Corporations.* Cambridge, Mass.: South End Press, 2001.

Ghiselin, Michael. "The Assimilation of Darwinism in Developmental Psychology." *Human Development* 29 (1986): 12–21.

Gibbs, John C. "Kohlberg's Moral Stage Theory: A Piagetian Revision." *Human Development* 22 (1979): 89–112.

Gilligan, Carol. *In a Different Voice: Psychological Theory and Women's Development.* Cambridge: Harvard University Press, 1982.

Gilligan, Carol, and Grant Wiggins. "The Origins of Morality in Early Childhood Relationships." In *The Emergence of Morality in Young Children,* ed. Jerome Kagan and Sharon Lamb, 277–305. Chicago: University of Chicago Press, 1987.

Gilligan, Carol, Janie Victoria Ward, and Jill McLean Taylor, with Betty Bardige, eds. *Mapping the Moral Domain: A Contribution of Women's Thinking to Psychological Theory and Education.* Cambridge: Harvard University Press, 1989.

Gino, Carol. *The Nurse's Story.* New York: Linden Press/Simon & Schuster, 1982.

Godwin, William. *Enquiry concerning Political Justice.* Ed. Isaac Kramnick. London: Penguin, 1976.

Gould, Stephen Jay. "Relationship of Individual and Group Change: Ontogeny and Phylogeny in Biology." *Human Development* 27 (1984): 233–39.

Gray, John. *Liberalism.* Minneapolis: University of Minnesota Press, 1986.

———. *Mill on Liberty: A Defense.* London: Routledge & Kegan Paul, 1983.

Greven, Philip J., Jr. *Four Generations: Population, Land, and Family in Colonial Andover.* Ithaca, N.Y.: Cornell University Press, 1975.

Grossman, Dave. *On Killing: The Psychological Cost of Learning to Kill in War and Society.* Boston: Little, Brown, 1995.

Guinier, Lani. *The Tyranny of the Majority: Fundamental Fairness in Representative Democracy.* New York: Free Press, 1994.

Hancock, Graham. *Lords of Poverty: The Power, Prestige, and Corruption of the International Aid Business.* New York: Atlantic Monthly Press, 1989.

Hardin, Garrett. "Living on a Lifeboat." *Bioscience* 20 (October 1974): 561–68.

Harrison, E. L. "Notes on Homeric Psychology." *Phoenix* 14 (1960): 63–80.

Hawke, David Freeman. *Paine.* New York: Harper & Row, 1974.

Herder, Johann Gottfried von. *Outlines of a Philosophy of the History of Mankind.* Trans. T. O. Churchill. London: J. Johnson, 1800.

Heron, Echo. *Intensive Care: The Story of a Nurse.* New York: Atheneum, 1987.

Hoebel, E. A. "Law Ways of the Comanche Indians." In *Law and Warfare: Studies in the Anthropology of Conflict,* ed. P. Bohannon. Austin: University of Texas Press, 1976.

Hume, David. "Of the Original Contract." In *Essays Moral, Political, and Literary.* Indianapolis: Liberty Press, 1986.

———. *A Treatise of Human Nature,* 2 vols. Ed. Páll S. Árdal. Glasgow: Fontana/William Collins, 1972.

Humphreys, S. C. *The Family, Women, and Death: Comparative Studies.* London: Routledge & Kegan Paul, 1983.

Hunter, Virginia. *Policing Athens: Social Control in the Attic Lawsuits, 420–320 B.C.* Princeton, N.J.: Princeton University Press, 1994.

Jenks, Christopher. *Inequality: A Reassessment of the Effect of Family and Schooling in America.* New York: Basic Books, 1972.

Johnson, Kay. "Adolescent Solutions to Dilemmas in Fables: Two Moral Orientations—Two Problem Solving Strategies." In *Mapping the Moral Domain: A Contribution of Women's Thinking to Psychological Theory and Education,* Carol Gilligan et al., eds., 49–69. Cambridge: Harvard University Press, 1989.

Johnson, Paul. *Intellectuals.* New York: Harper & Row: 1988.

Johnson, Samuel. *The Idler and the Adventurer.* Ed. W. J. Bate, J. M. Bullitt, and L. F. Powell. Vol. 2 of *Works of Samuel Johnson.* New Haven: Yale University Press, 1963.

————. "Of a Free Enquiry into the Nature and Origin of Evil." In *Reviews and Political Tracts*, 217–54. Troy, N.Y.: Pafraets Press, 1903.

————. "The Patriot." In *Political Writings*, vol. 10 of *Works of Samuel Johnson*, ed. Donald J. Greene. New Haven: Yale University Press, 1977.

————. *The Rambler*. Ed. W. J. Bate and A. B. Strauss. Vols. 3, 4, and 5 of *Works of Samuel Johnson*. New Haven: Yale University Press, 1969.

Kant, Immanuel. *Lectures on Ethics*. Trans. Louis Infield. New York: Century, 1930.

Kenny, Anthony. *Aristotle on the Perfect Life*. Oxford: Oxford University Press, 1992.

————. "The Nicomachean Conception of Happiness." In *Oxford Studies in Ancient Philosophy*, sup. vol., ed. H. Blumenthal and H. Robinson, 67–80. Oxford: Oxford University Press, 1991.

Kohlberg, Lawrence. "A Cognitive-Developmental Approach to Moral Education." *Humanist* 23 (November–December 1972): 13–16.

————. "The Future of Liberalism as the Dominant Ideology of the West." In *Moral Development and Politics*, R. W. Wilson and G. J. Schochet, eds., 55–68. New York: Praeger, 1980.

Kohlberg, Lawrence, and Daniel Candee. "The Relationship of Moral Judgment to Moral Action." In *Morality, Moral Behavior, and Moral Development*, ed. William M. Kurtines and Jacob L. Gewirtz, 52–73. New York: John Wiley & Sons, 1984.

Lagemann, E. C. *Private Power for the Public Good: A History of the Carnegie Foundation for the Advancement of Teaching*. Middletown, Conn.: Wesleyan University Press, 1983.

Laslett, Peter. *The World We Have Lost: England before the Industrial Age*. New York: Scribner's, 1965.

————, ed. *Patriarcha and Other Political Works of Sir Robert Filmer*. Oxford: Basil Blackwell, 1949.

Lee, Ming, and Norman M. Prentice. "Interrelations of Empathy, Cognition, and Moral Reasoning with Dimensions of Juvenile Delinquency." *Journal of Abnormal Child Psychology* 16:2 (1988): 127–39.

Lefkowitz, Mary R. "Influential Women." In *Images of Women in Antiquity*, ed. Averil Cameron and Amélie Kurht, 49–64. Detroit: Wayne State University Press, 1983.

Legge, James, trans. *The Texts of Taoism.* 2 vols. New York: Dover, 1962.

Leites, Edmund. *The Puritan Conscience and Modern Sexuality.* New Haven: Yale University Press, 1995.

———, ed. *Conscience and Casuistry in Early Modern Europe.* Cambridge: Cambridge University Press, 2002.

Leopold, Nathan F. *Life plus 99 Years.* Garden City, N.Y.: Doubleday, 1958.

Levin, Meyer. *Compulsion.* New York: Simon & Schuster, 1956.

Lévy-Bruhl, Lucien. *How Natives Think.* 1910. Trans. Lillian A. Clare. Reprint, Princeton, N.J.: Princeton University Press, 1985.

Livingston, Donald. *Philosophical Melancholy and Delirium: Hume's Pathology of Philosophy.* Chicago: University of Chicago Press, 1998.

Lloyd-Jones, Hugh. *The Justice of Zeus.* Berkeley and Los Angeles: University of California Press, 1971.

———, trans. *Antigone.* In *Sophocles,* vol. 2. Loeb Classical Library 20–21. Cambridge: Harvard University Press, 1994.

Locke, John. *An Essay concerning Human Understanding.* Ed. Alexander C. Fraser, New York: Dover, 1959.

———. *Some Thoughts concerning Education.* Ed. John W. Yolton and Jean S. Yolton. Oxford: Oxford University Press, 1999.

Lorimer, James. *The Institutes of the Law of Nations: A Treatise of the Jural Relations of Separate Political Communities.* Edinburgh and London: William Blackwood & Sons, 1884.

Macaulay, Lord T. B. [Thomas Babington], J. M. MacLeod, G. W. Anderson, and F. Millett, "Notes [on the Indian Penal Code by the Indian Law Commissioners." In *Miscellaneous Works of Lord Macaulay edited by his sister Lady Trevelyan,* 5 vols., 4:199–409. Philadelphia: University Library Association, n.d.

Macdonald, Dwight. *The Ford Foundation: The Men and Their Millions.* 1956. Reprint, New Brunswick, N.J.: Transaction, 1989.

MacDowell, Douglas M. *Athenian Homicide Law in the Age of the Orators.* Manchester, U.K.: Manchester University Press, 1963.

———. *The Law in Classical Athens.* Ithaca, N.Y.: Cornell University Press, 1976.

MacIntyre, Alasdair. *Three Rival Versions of Moral Enquiry: Encyclopedia, Genealogy, and Tradition.* South Bend, Ind.: University of Notre Dame Press, 1990.

————. *Whose Justice? Which Rationality?* Notre Dame, Ind.: University of Notre Dame Press, 1988.

Mack, Eric. "Bad Samaritanism and the Causation of Harm." *Philosophy and Public Affairs* 9 (1980): 230–59.

MacPherson, C. B. *The Political Theory of Possessive Individualism: Hobbes to Locke.* Oxford: Oxford University Press, 1962.

Malone, Dumas. *The Sage of Monticello.* Vol. 6 of *Jefferson and His Time.* Boston: Little, Brown, 1981.

Marcel, Gabriel. *Man against Mass Society.* Trans. G. S. Fraser. Chicago: Regnery, 1952.

Maritain, Jacques. *Three Reformers: Luther, Descartes, Rousseau.* New York: Scribners, 1950.

Marx, Karl, and Friedrich Engels. "The Communist Manifesto." 1848. Authorized English translation of 1888 reprinted in *Collected Works,* 6:476–519. New York: International Publishers, 1976.

Mauss, Marcel. "Une catégorie de l'esprit humain: la notion de personne celle de moi." In *Sociologie et Anthropologie,* 333–61. Paris: Presses Universitaires de France, 1968.

Mayr, Ernst. *The Growth of Biological Thought: Diversity, Evolution, and Inheritance.* Cambridge: Harvard University Press, 1982.

McIntyre, Alison. "Guilty Bystanders? On the Legitimacy of Duty to Rescue Statutes." *Philosophy and Public Affairs* 23 (1994): 157–91.

McNeill, William H. Introduction to *The Bridge on the Drina,* by Ivo Andrić, trans. Lovett Edwards. Belgrade: DERETA, 2000.

Meier, G. M., and Dudley Seers, eds. *Pioneers in Development.* New York: Oxford, 1984.

Mill, John Stuart. *On Liberty.* Ed. David Spitz. New York: Norton, 1975.

————. *Utilitarianism.* In *On Liberty and Other Essays,* ed. John Gray. Oxford: Oxford University Press, 1991.

Mises, Ludwig von. *Liberalism in the Classical Tradition.* San Francisco: FEE/Cobden Press, 1985.

Molnar, Thomas. *Politics and the State.* Quincy, Ill.: Franciscan Press, 1981.

Moore, G. E. *Principia Ethica.* Cambridge: Cambridge University Press, 1959.

Morris, Colin. *The Discovery of the Individual, 1050–1200.* New York: Harper Torchbook, 1973.

Mosca, Gaetano. *The Ruling Class (Elementi di Scienza Politica)*. Ed. Arthur Livingston, trans. Hannah D. Kahn. New York: McGraw-Hill, 1939.

Moshman, David, and Edith Neimark. "Four Aspects of Cognitive Development." In *Review of Human Development*, ed. T. M. Field, A. Huston, H. C. Quay, L. Troll, and G. E. Finley. New York: John Wiley & Sons, 1982.

Murphy, John Michael, and Carol Gilligan. "Moral Development in Late Adolescence and Adulthood: A Critique and Reconstruction of Kohlberg's Theory." *Human Development* 23 (1980): 77–104.

Nagel, Thomas. *Equality and Partiality*. New York: Oxford University Press, 1991.

Neusner, Jacob. *Rabbinic Political Theory: Religion and Politics in the Mishnah*. Chicago: University of Chicago Press, 1984.

Nichols, J. Bruce. *The Uneasy Alliance: Religion, Refugee Work, and U.S. Foreign Policy*. New York: Oxford University Press, 1988.

Nielsen, Waldemar A. *The Golden Donors: A New Anatomy of the Great Foundations*. New York: Truman Talley Books/E. P. Dutton, 1985.

Nisbet, Robert. *The Sociological Tradition*. New York: Basic Books, 1966.

Oates, Stephen B. *To Purge This Land with Blood: A Biography of John Brown*. New York: Harper & Row, 1970.

Ormand, Kirk. *Exchange and the Maiden: Marriage in Sophoclean Tragedy*. Austin: University of Texas Press, 1999.

Orwell, George. "Notes on Nationalism." In *England, Your England & Other Essays*. London: Secker & Warburg, 1953.

Parfit, Derek. *Reasons and Persons*. Oxford: Oxford University Press, 1986.

Payer, Cheryl. *Lent and Lost: Foreign Credit and Third World Development*. London: Zed Books, 1991.

———. *The World Bank: A Critical Analysis*. New York: Monthly Review Press, 1982.

Pearse, Andrew. *Seeds of Plenty, Seeds of Want: Social and Economic Implications of the Green Revolution*. Oxford: Clarendon Press, 1980.

Pellicciari, Angela. *Risorgimento da riscrivere: Liberali & massoni contro la chiesa*. Milan: Edizioni Ares, 1998.

Pembroke, Simon. "Oikeiosis." In *Problems in Stoicism*, ed. A. A. Long, 114–49. London: Athlone, 1971.

Pennington, Anne, and Peter Levi, trans. *Marko the Prince: Serbo-Croat Heroic Songs.* London: Duckworth, 1984.

Philippson, Robert. "Hierocles der Stoiker." *Rheinisches Museum,* N.F. 82 (1933): 97–114.

Piaget, Jean. "Intellectual Evolution from Adolescence to Adulthood." *Human Development* 15 (1972): 1–12.

———. *The Moral Judgment of the Child.* Trans. Marjorie Gabain. New York: Free Press, 1965.

Piozzi, Hesther Lynch. *Anecdotes of the Late Samuel Johnson, LL.D.* Ed. S. C. Roberts. Freeport, N.Y.: Books for Libraries Press, 1969.

Rachels, James. *The Elements of Moral Philosophy.* New York: Random House, 1986.

Rawls, John. *A Theory of Justice.* Cambridge: Harvard University Press, 1971.

Reed, Henry. *Collected Poems.* Oxford: Oxford University Press, 1991.

Reid, Barbara V. "An Anthropological Reinterpretation of Kohlberg's Stages of Moral Development." *Human Development* 27 (1984): 57–64.

Rest, James R., Mark L. Davison, and Steven Robbins. "Age Trends in Judging Moral Issues: A Review of Cross-Sectional, Longitudinal, and Sequential Studies of the Defining Issues Test." *Child Development* 49 (1978): 263–79.

Riesman, David, with Nathan Glazer and Reuel Denney. *The Lonely Crowd: A Study of the Changing American Character.* New Haven: Yale University Press, 1963.

Roberts, Jean. "Political Animals in the Nicomachean Ethics." *Phronesis* 34 (1989): 185–20.

Royce, Josiah. *The Philosophy of Loyalty.* New York: Macmillan, 1924.

———. *The World and the Individual,* 2 vols. London: Macmillan, 1904.

Sams, Eric. *The Real Shakespeare: Retrieving the Early Years.* New Haven: Yale University Press, 1995.

Schaeffer, Neil. *The Marquis de Sade: A Life.* New York: Knopf, 1999.

Scruton, Roger. *The Meaning of Conservatism.* 3rd ed. South Bend, Ind.: St. Augustine's Press, 2002.

Simpson, Evan. "The Development of Political Reasoning." *Human Development* 30 (1987): 268–81.

Singer, Peter. *The Expanding Circle: Ethics and Sociobiology.* New York: Farrar, Straus, 1980.

Smith, Adam. *Theory of Moral Sentiments*. 1759. Reprint, Indianapolis: Liberty Press, 1976.

Smith, Denis Mack. *Italy: A Modern History*. Ann Arbor: University of Michigan Press, 1959.

Snell, Bruno. *The Discovery of the Mind: The Greek Origins of European Thought*. Oxford: Oxford University Press, 1953.

———. "Phrenes-phronesis." *Glotta* 55 (1977): 34–64.

Spring, Leverett Wilson. *Kansas: The Prelude to the War for the Union*. Brooklyn, N.Y.: AMS Press, 1973.

Steinberg, Laurence, and Susan B. Silverberg. "The Vicissitudes of Autonomy in Early Adolescence." *Child Development* 57 (1986): 841–51.

Taine, Hippolyte. *The French Revolution*. 3 vols. Trans. John Durand. Indianapolis: Liberty Fund, 2002.

Thayer, William Roscoe. *The Dawn of Italian Independence*. Boston: Houghton Mifflin, 1892.

Titmuss, Richard M. *Essays on "The Welfare State."* Boston: Beacon Press, 1969.

Todd, Janet. *Sensibility: An Introduction*. Methuen: London, 1986.

Toulmin, Stephen. *Cosmopolis: The Hidden Agenda of Modernity*. New York: Free Press, 1990.

———. *The Place of Reason in Ethics*. 2nd ed. Chicago: University of Chicago Press, 1986.

Trevelyan, G. M. *English Social History: A Survey of Six Centuries, Chaucer to Queen Victoria*. London: Longmans, Green, 1942.

———. *Garibaldi and the Making of Italy*. London: Longmans, Green, 1909.

———. *Garibaldi and the Thousand*. London: Longmans, Green, 1909.

Van de Laar, A. J. M. *The World Bank and the World's Poor*. The Hague: Institute of Social Studies, 1976.

Van Gennep, Arnold. *The Rites of Passage*. Trans. M. B. Vizedom and G. L. Caffee. Chicago: University of Chicago Press, 1960.

Velimirovich, Bishop Nikolai, and Archimandrite Justin Popovich. *The Mystery and Meaning of the Battle of Kosovo*. Trans. Todor Mika and Stevan Scott. Gray's Lake, Ill.: Serbian Orthodox Metropolitanate of New Gracanica, 1999.

Vernant, J.-P. "Aspects de la personne dans la réligion grecque." In *Problèmes de la personne*, ed. Ignace Meyerson. Paris: Mouton, 1973.

Vernant, J.-P., and P. Vidal-Naquet. "Ebauches de la volonté." In *Mythe et tragédie en grèce ancienne.* Paris: Maspero, 1973.

Vivencio, Jose R., ed. *Mortgaging the Future: The World Bank and IMF in the Philippines.* Quezon City: Foundation for Nationalist Studies, 1982.

Wain, John. *Samuel Johnson: A Biography.* New York: Viking, 1974.

Walker, Lawrence J. "The Sequentiality of Kohlberg's Stages of Moral Development." *Child Development* 53 (1982): 1330–36.

Wall, David. *The Charity of Nations: The Political Economy of Foreign Aid.* New York: Basic Books, 1983.

Ward, Barbara. *The Rich Nations and the Poor Nations.* New York: W. W. Norton, 1962.

Warren, Robert Penn. *John Brown: The Making of a Martyr.* 1929. Reprint, Nashville, Tenn.: J. S. Sanders, 1993.

Wells, H. G. *The New World Order.* New York: Knopf, 1940.

West, Rebecca. *Black Lamb and Grey Falcon.* 1942. Reprint, London: Penguin, 1984.

Weyl, Nathaniel. *Karl Marx: Racist.* New Rochelle, N.Y.: Arlington House, 1979.

Williams, Bernard. *Ethics and the Limits of Philosophy.* Cambridge: Harvard University Press, 1985.

Wilson, E. O. *On Human Nature.* Cambridge: Harvard University Press, 1978.

———. *Sociobiology: The New Synthesis.* Cambridge: Harvard University Press, 1975.

Zampetti, Pier Luigi. *La Sfida del Duemila: L'uomo può salvare il mondo dalla catastrofe?* Milan: Rusconi, 1988.

INDEX